Discover the
Adirondack High Peaks

Discover the Adirondack High Peaks

Barbara McMartin

With Lee Brenning, Phil Gallos, Don Greene,
E.H. Ketchledge, Gary Koch, and Willard Reed

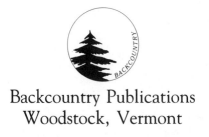

Backcountry Publications
Woodstock, Vermont

An Invitation to the Reader

Over time trails can be rerouted and signs and landmarks altered. If you find that changes have occurred on the routes described in this book, please let us know so that corrections may be made in future editions. The author and publisher also welcome other comments and suggestions. Address all correspondence to:

Editor
Discover the Adirondacks Series
Backcountry Publications
P.O. Box 175
Woodstock, Vermont 05091

Library of Congress Cataloging-in-Publication Data

McMartin, Barbara.
 Discover the Adirondack high peaks / Barbara McMartin, with Lee Brenning . . . [et al.].
  p. cm. — (Discover the Adirondacks series; 11)
 Bibliography: p.
 Includes index.
 ISBN 0-942440-47-1 : $14.95
  1. Hiking—New York (State)—Adirondack Mountains—Guide-books.
 2. Trails—New York (State)—Adirondack Mountains—Guide-books.
 3. Adirondack Mountains (N.Y.)—Description and travel—Guide-books.
 I. Brenning, Lee M., 1955-   . II. Title. III. Series.
 GV199.42.N652A34425 1989
 917.47'5—dc20   89-15035
                                                                          CIP

Printed in the United States of America by McNaughton & Gunn
Typesetting by Sant Bani Press
Series design by Leslie Fry
Layout by Barbara McMartin

Photograph credits
Georgie Brenning, 82
Lee Brenning, 67, 78
Phil Gallos, 168, 243, 250
Don Greene, 120, 142
Gary Koch, 12, 47, 48, 50
Willard Reed, 2, 94, 117, 145, 233, 272, 278, 281
Edythe Robbins, 154, 208
All other photographs by Barbara McMartin

Photographs
Cover: *Gothics from Pyramid*
Page 2: *Gothics from Saddleback*
Page 6: *By Avalanche Lake*

Acknowledgments

The number of individuals who have helped with this guide is commensurate with the region covered. Among those who wrote portions of the guide were co-authors Bill Reed, who described many of the trails in the northeast quadrant; Phil Gallos, who wrote about a number of the shorter routes in that section; Ed Ketchledge, who wrote on Alpine flora; Gary Koch, who described and photographed the slide on Santanoni; and Lee Brenning, who researched the northwest quadrant, including the Seward Range. Don Greene not only hiked and wrote up a number of the unusual bushwhacks and accompanied us on a few of them, he read and made corrections in a good portion of the guide and suggested important ways for organizing it.

Additional trail information came from many sources: Brian McDonnell, Mike Douglass (the outlet of Wallface Ponds), Jim Sansville (the slide on Nye), Pat Collier (the Northville-Placid Trail to Wanika Falls), Philip G. Terrie (Blueberry Mountain), Chuck Bennett and Edythe Robbins (Fairy Ladder Falls). Chuck shared his records of trail times to compare with the one we compiled.

Rangers Michael Frenette, Clyde Black, and Gary Hodson contributed current trail information.

The historical background is more important here than in any guide in the series. Gerold Pepper, librarian of the Adirondack Museum, was most helpful in finding obscure publications, and the museum provided a wonderful place to do research. Francis B. Rosevear contributed many historical notes, especially on the Colvin record, and he wrote about Railroad Notch. Warder Cadbury wrote part of the introduction on the naming of Colden and loaned us a file that details all the events relating to it. Mary McKenzie detailed the history of Averyville. Clarence Petty talked to us about the Cold River and the Santa Clara Lumber Company. Jim Bailey and Tony Goodwin helped us trace down the origins of many place names.

Adelbert Young helped us search the files of the DEC's Real Property Office for information on state acquisitions. Margaret Baldwin, DEC cartographer, helped us draw private land boundaries on the new metric map by interpreting many of the land surveys.

Tony Goodwin, who assisted the USGS in mapping for the metric series, corrected the trail errors he knew about—corrections he had suggested in vain to the USGS.

Companions on the trail are most important: Kris Reed was an enormous help to his father; Georgie Brenning sustained her husband, Lee; Chuck Bennett, Edythe Robbins, and the Edwards family (John, Sandy and son Scott) made two backpacking trips among the most memorable ever; and my husband, Alec Reid, hiked many miles with me and spent many hours in the dark room, printing all our pictures.

Our thanks to all of them for making this a most enjoyable cooperative effort.

Contents

Introduction

THE MOUNTAIN RANGES of the High Peaks symbolize the Adirondacks for most people, yet they comprise less than fifteen percent of the public lands within the park, and they amount to only six percent of all the lands both public and private within the blue line that defines the park. However, the network of trails that traces almost every peak and valley of the eastern High Peaks is greater in density than found anywhere else within the park.

Variations in altitude—ranging from valleys a little more than a thousand feet in elevation to mountains over a mile high—bring a more rugged scale to the horizon than is found elsewhere in the park. In the 1870s, Verplanck Colvin conceived the idea of an Adirondack Park after he surveyed the High Peak landscape on his 1870 trip to Seward. During the course of the Adirondack Survey, he put his mark on about half of the highest mountains.

For most of the nineteenth century, these peaks were the realm of dreamers and hikers, guides and painters, and mountain men and women seeking adventure, not sport, in the wilds. But even as late as the 1930s, there were relatively few climbers, and the majority of them scaled the heights only from Keene Valley or St. Huberts, resorts with a small but dedicated clientele.

Loggers came late in the nineteenth century and as late as the 1920s to some of the more remote High Peak valleys. They managed to harvest the virgin timber when the mountains were gripped in a series of droughts. Fires then swept great patches of the High Peaks, leaving them black and denuded.

When the Marshall brothers, Robert and George, and Herb Clark—the first of a new breed of dedicated mountain climbers—began to ascend the peaks, they followed old logging roads toward the scrubby spruce and balsam stands that ring the summits. They bushwhacked through these dense stands to rocky summits, from which they surveyed expanses of charred stumps, grasses, and brambles as well as vast slopes cloaked in the green of dense wilderness. Between 1921 and 1924, these men became the first to climb eight of the highest mountains and the first to climb all of the forty-six peaks over four thousand feet. Today over fifty thousand hikers a year are attracted to this small segment of the park.

While the other guides I have written for the *Discover* series have been just that, books of discovery, there is no question that the High Peaks have already been found. Indeed, parts of them have been loved and trampled for many years. The Adirondack Mountain Club Guide to the High Peaks was first published in 1935, and because it was the only existing park guide for forty years, it enticed people to focus their adventures solely in that one small area of the park.

Ermine Brook Slide on Santanoni

So, what is left to discover? What is there that will make this book a true part of the *Discover* series? More than you might at first imagine. There are still a number of little-used trails and routes, some notable bushwhacks, and some secret places. Most High Peak hikers concentrate on a few trails. This guide describes every trail in the High Peaks; but it was written for the connoisseur, who wants to savor the peaks as if they were still wilderness retreats. It is for the hiker who wants to luxuriate in the waterfalls, valleys, and the small pleasures of noble forest stands.

You will spend a much smaller proportion of your hiking time on mountaintops than you do on the trails to them; so this guide tries to make the joys of getting to the top as much a part of the High Peaks experience as realizing that final destination. In general, the less well-known trails and less followed routes are described in greater detail than those that are already popular. These less-known routes also happen to be among the easiest in the High Peaks.

This guide starts at the less-used portals along routes that will make it possible for you to avoid some of the crowds. Nevertheless, you are still advised to hike in spring and fall and during the week if you can. Remember, most of the summits are very small outcrops—even one other small group beside your own will seem like too large a gathering for a wilderness peak. And, even though there are nearly three hundred miles of trails in the region, you will rarely enjoy a major valley trail without meeting others.

How to Use This Discover Guide

This guide differs from the rest of the *Discover* series in one major way. All the others let you know which trails are suitable for hiking, snowshoeing, cross-country skiing, fishing, swimming, and so on. This guide gives this greater detail only for part of the western High Peaks. Unless otherwise described, it assumes the excursions are hiking routes. However, almost every route attracts winter users.

Even in summer, the High Peaks are known for weather extremes, and you must be prepared for them. Snow often falls before Labor Day, invariably before Columbus Day, and lasts on the highest peaks until June. Mountaintops are often shrouded in dense clouds, making it difficult to find trails above tree line. This can be a problem in both summer and winter.

Winter is exceptionally unpredictable. With experience, you can use the trails in winter, but I caution you to get lots of experience with the trails in summer first and then to spend some time learning firsthand about the rigors of winter camping and climbing from groups who teach these techniques or guides who can accompany you as you learn. Navigating is difficult enough in fog, let alone snow and blizzards. Trails marked by cairns and paint blazes can be impossible to follow or even find in winter. You can use this guide and map to navigate in winter, but you will need a lot of experience before you should try it.

TYPES OF ROUTES

Trails in the High Peaks have many origins. As in the rest of the Adirondacks, some were old logging or tote roads. Unlike the rest of the Adirondacks, many were cut expressly for hikers, quite a few by nineteenth-century guides. Their design was basically directed at the need to find the shortest route straight up; few of these zigzag across the steep slopes adequately to prevent erosion.

Most trails are currently maintained by the Department of Environmental Conservation (DEC), but the majority of recent trail work has been done by the Adirondack Mountain Club (ADK) trail crews under contract to the DEC. ADK chapters and volunteers also maintain other trails and facilities. Some crews have performed Herculean feats in the past few years. Volunteers are always needed. The Forty-sixers, an organization of those who have climbed the peaks over four thousand feet, maintain some trails, repair lean-tos, rebuild outhouses, and maintain canisters with registers on the trailless peaks. The Adirondack Trail Improvement Society (ATIS) maintains all the trails around the Ausable Lakes on Adirondack Mountain Reserve (AMR) land. ATIS continues to maintain trails to the Range and other routes that AMR has given or sold to the state.

This guide refers to a trail as any route bearing either a DEC, ADK, or ATIS marker. ADK and ATIS markers are bright red for all their trails, with disks bearing their distinctive emblems. The marking on DEC trails can be quite confusing—there is no consistent pattern to the colors and many of the routes described will follow a number of differently colored markers.

Trails have been named for their original builders, to honor someone who has left a mark on the Adirondacks, or to reflect the group responsible for their maintenance. This, too, is sometimes confusing. For instance, the Range or Great Range Trail runs over the summits of all the mountains from Keene Valley to Haystack, but the ADK Range Trail only approaches that ridge-line route from Johns Brook Valley, while the eastern summit chain is sometimes referred to as the ATIS Range.

The direction of the major faults creates another source of confusion: The faults are basically parallel, running northeast-southwest. A trail to the north of Johns Brook Valley is called Northside; a trail in the same position with regards to the Ausable Valley is called West River.

Much has been written about Adirondack mud—in fact I wonder if it is not the most-used three-letter word in this guide. The quality of trail conditions seem to break into three groups. One group contains the heavily used trails that range from the two most popular portals, Adirondak Loj and the Garden above Keene Valley. The vast majority of these trails have been hardened in the past few years and mud is kept to a minimum, but sometimes you feel as if you were walking on a city sidewalk and not on a wilderness trail. The second group is make up of the little-used trails, especially those that were well designed. They are rarely wet and usually pleasant to walk. The third group has some of the worst trail conditions you can imagine, due to poor design, with water coursing down them even in dry times. Some of these problems defy fixing, but they are super routes, so that you may want to hike anyway. This guide will let you know what to expect.

A *path* is any route with a sufficient foot tread that can be followed, but a path has no official marking. Some paths are very easy to follow, others very difficult. Be prepared with map and compass and a good knowledge of how to use them before trying any of the described paths.

The term *herd path* usually refers to a path leading to a trailless summit. It seems to denigrate those hikers whose feet have worn the paths. Herd paths are as Adirondack as the ubiquitous lean-tos.

Over the years, hikers have worn, hacked, flagged, and beaten herd paths to every one of the tallest summits. Walking to create a path is permitted as well as throwing deadfalls from a route, but every other means of marking a route is strictly illegal, unless done under DEC supervision. Unfortunately, not only are all sorts of methods illegally employed to create paths, a few of the trailless peaks have such a plethora of paths that they confuse even the best of woods navigators. It is hoped that the Unit Management Plan, called for by the Adirondack Park Agency State Land Master Plan, will recommend the marking without clearing of one well-designed route to all the major peaks with such problems.

Some paths and herd paths are as obvious as any trail; a few require real off-trail navigating. Some are very difficult to find. But with all unmarked routes, it is wise to treat them as if you could get lost following them.

A *bushwhack* is any cross-country trip where there is no trail or path to follow. It requires a knowledge of the use of a map and compass, as well as an understanding of the terrain.

Bushwhacking in the High Peaks is generally extremely difficult, not just because of the terrain and the heights and distances, but because of the impenetrable stands of balsam and fir that ring the majority of summits. Some great but challenging bushwhacks follow streams toward summits, and this guide describes a few in detail. These are still for the experienced hiker only. What makes a few of the superb bushwhacks fairly easy is that they are in the Dix Range—the friendly forests of the eastern edge of the High Peaks. The guide mentions a few other routes that experts in various areas have suggested. If you have enough skills to navigate these bushwhacks, you will need little more than the hints given to be able to plan your trips. If you have any doubts about your bushwhacking ability, test yourself with section 72 (see page 156).

Slide climbing is the most exhilarating fun. The slides are highways to the sky, parabolic routes that start gently, then curve more and more steeply until you feel they will thrust you to the heavens.

Slides are the Adirondack version of mountain avalanches. Most have occurred during heavy rains, often in late summer, though one was dislodged by an earthquake. Sometimes torrential rains from hurricanes are the cause. Sometimes thunderstorms seem to get stuck on a mountaintop, dropping up to ten inches of rain in a few hours. Soil and rock at the top of a transient watercourse become soggy and heavy, and the weight causes the mass to become loose. It starts to slide or roll, picking up trees and soil and finally gravel and boulders as it falls, sweeping away everything below. In this way, nature has built the most wonderful of trails; what is left after the cataclysm is often a smooth rock surface leading toward the summit.

Some of the slides are quite new, such as those on Nye and Santanoni mountains, while others predate man's arrival on the scene. Some are fairly easy to walk, others so vertical as to be considered technical rock climbs. This guide describes the former, but even here great caution is advised.

First, slides are usually watercourses and can be very slippery when wet. Some are wet even in dry times. All are dangerous when wet.

Second, where smooth and not too steep, walking can be quite safe and easy. However, many slides are rubble-coated—"dirty," as slide climbers say. Even the best of slides have dirty patches. These are quite dangerous—you can slip and lose your footing or, worse, dislodge a falling rock toward a companion below.

Whatever the problems, if you are adventurous, you will undoubtedly find these are the most exciting routes in the High Peaks.

DISTANCE AND TIME

Information about *times* is a valuable tool in trip planning and one method of describing distances on bushwhacks. The guide has attempted to give consistent time estimates for hikes without backpacks, except in such places as the Cold River and Panther Gorge, where packs are almost essential. Take a few hikes and compare your times with those stated. You may be consistently faster or slower, so you can determine a factor by which to compare the rest of the times in the guide. Remember that very hot weather will lengthen the stated times as much as will rain and wet conditions. Times are not intended for use in winter climbs.

Mileages are computed several ways and are given to the nearest tenth or half-tenth of a mile (or in yards for shorter distances). Most mileages are taken from the new USGS metric maps of the High Peaks, with compensation for elevation changes. This guide does not refer to the mileages given on DEC or other guide boards. They present a perplexing situation. Those near the heavily used trailheads of Adirondak Loj or the Garden above Keene Valley tend to be very accurate, though there is occasional ambiguity about the location of destinations mentioned. (For instance, the trail signs on Yard Mountain and the Klondike Trail, stating mileages to Big Slide, do not give the mileage to that summit, but to an intersection nearly 0.3 mile to the east of it.) However, the farther you go from these major trailheads, the greater the number of errors in trail signs. In parts of the High Peaks, mileages appear to have been computed from maps without regard to elevation changes, and errors in the signs exceed ten percent in places.

ELEVATION

An *altimeter* is a most valuable tool in locating yourself with respect to the trail and a map. It is an invaluable way to describe turnoffs for certain bushwhacks and the location of view spots. It is also a great way to estimate your progress on a steep climb where your sense of distance will undoubtedly fail you. However, trying to give elevations based on the new metric maps has created a serious planning problem for this guide. The majority of altimeters available in this country, even fairly sensitive ones produced overseas, are calibrated in feet. The new High Peaks metric maps are drawn in ten-meter contours. This guide gives most elevations in feet and since many elevations are pinned to specific points like cols, summits, or trail intersections with streams, you can easily read those points from the metric maps. For no reason other than the fact that it would add just too many numbers to an already busy text, metric elevations are not always included. Since a meter equals 3.28 feet, the factor 3 ¼ gives a rapid and usually adequate conversion. Even easier is reading the conversion from the scale provided on the accompanying maps.

The corrected elevations given on the new metric USGS maps vary considerably from those of previous maps. These changes significantly alter previous lists of the highest peaks, but this guide advances no new list. The Forty-sixers, however, have decided to continue with their traditional list, which was based on much older versions of the USGS maps.

TRAILHEADS

This guide is arranged in chapters that reflect the major trailheads. Trailhead *registers* exist at all the major High Peak trailheads, and you should sign in and out when hiking, both for your own safety and so the DEC can determine use levels.

A glance at the map will tell you just how many routes traverse the High Peaks. This guide breaks most routes into basic segments, so you can easily make any one of the seemingly limitless combinations and permutations of routes available. However, the order in which the segments are presented is intended to suggest long loops and day hikes from the various trailheads. This means that some trails are described in descending rather than ascending fashion to reinforce the desirability of certain loops. These routes will help you plan a number of exciting day hikes without the need to camp in the interior. In the future this will be a valuable tool, for there is no question that camping in the interior of the eastern High Peaks will be more and more restricted. The area just cannot support the pressures of camping.

Many destinations can be reached via two or more routes. This means there is some redundancy in the descriptions. To keep this to a minimum, however, not all details are repeated. So, if you plan to hike to a given destination, check the index first to see what is said about it in *all* the references.

This guide explores the origins of some land now owned by the state, the New York Forest Preserve. It mentions a few of the logging operations, the locations of some of the larger forest fires, some extraordinary natural events, and a few of the political issues that swirl around the High Peaks. Because there are so many related topics to interest the hiker, this guide can only touch on them. But, unlike the rest of the Adirondacks, those interested can often easily find information in existing literature (see References and Resources on page 280).

Protecting the Land

CAMPING

Camping does not exist near some of the trailheads—this is especially true at Tahawus, Elk Lake, and the Ausable Club (AMR), where you must walk considerable distances to reach state land. For day hikes from those trailheads, there are public accommodations in Newcomb and North Hudson and campgrounds at Harris Lake. Keene Valley also has a growing number of excellent bed and breakfast places.

Much work has been done to limit camping at the most heavily used places on public land. Suitable locations are designated, but many spots are now posted against camping. A few lean-tos have been relocated back from water. *No camping is permitted within 150 feet of water, within 150 feet of a trail, or above 4000 feet unless at a site designated for camping.* Because of these rules, many traditional campsites are no longer legal. Where no other nearby sites exist and where impact is not a problem, some camping sites have been and may be designated within these no-camping corridors. Unless a site is so designated, the regulations are enforced by Interior Rangers.

Wash yourself and all dishes away from water and trails. Bury all human wastes at least eight inches deep and more than 150 feet from water and trails. Burn combustible trash in protected fire rings. Carry out all other garbage and everything else you bring with you into the woods.

CAMPFIRES

Only dead and downed wood may be used for campfires, and it is strongly recommended that all cooking be done with portable stoves. No trees may be cut on the Forest Preserve.

PRIVATE LANDS

Many High Peaks trails cross private lands where the public has deeded access to the trails. On private lands, no straying from the trails, camping, campfires, or pets are permitted. Some trails cross private land where there is no deeded access. In all cases be very respectful of the rights of the landowners.

Safety in the Woods

HIKING ALONE

While hiking alone is never recommended, it is especially dangerous in the High Peaks, where accidents and rescues are all too commonplace. If you are a novice hiker, walk first in one of the less demanding regions outside the High Peaks, then try a few of the High Peaks' peripheral trails before hiking in the interior. Make sure someone knows where you are going and when you are expected to return.

WHAT TO WEAR AND CARRY

Your day pack should have a map, compass, written guide, water, altimeter, small first aid kit, flashlight, insect repellent, binoculars, emergency food as well as lunch, matches, whistle, rain gear, windbreaker, and a woolen sweater, even in summer. The last is especially important in the High Peaks. For camping trips or winter hiking, consult a skilled guide or organization that promotes group activities. Always wear glasses when bushwhacking! You can hike a few trails with sneakers, but for the rugged mountain climbs, and especially for the slides, sturdy boots that protect the ankles are a must.

Blackflies and mosquitos can be especially bad in the High Peaks, where they persist well into summer. Everyone has a different method of dealing with them—light-colored clothing, hats, and so on. You will just have to find out what works best for you.

WATER

Always carry enough water for your day trip. Many mountaintops are very dry, and heat exhaustion and dehydration are real problems in warm weather. Carry a filter or boil water when camping. *Giardiasis* can be a problem, but so can many other diseases transported by the improper handling of human wastes. Protect yourself by drinking only pure water and prevent the spread of diseases carried in human wastes by burying all of it properly.

MAPS

The map accompanying this guide is based on the new USGS metric maps: Ampersand Lake (1978), Elizabethtown (1978), Keene Valley (1979), Kempshall Mountain (1979), Mount Marcy (1979), Santanoni Peak (1979), Tupper Lake (1979), and Witherbee (1978). Even though reduced fifty percent, it should be adequate for all trails and most bushwhacks.

BEARS

Bears have become a problem throughout the Adirondacks, and they are especially bothersome to campers in the High Peaks region. There are some things you can do to foil bears: keep all food in sealed containers and hang all food overnight in "bear bags," suspended on a rope thrown between two trees at least 15 feet apart, with the bear bag at least 10 feet from the ground. Do not keep food in your tent. A few bears have learned to attack ropes to get at the bags, so even this may not be a fool-proof solution. In some areas it is recommended that you not sleep in the clothing you wear while cooking. It may be wise to suspend your pack as well as your food sack, as even the pack carries food odors.

Bears are not a problem during the daytime and only at night if they detect food. If bears do come near your campsite, clanging pots and pans may scare them away.

FLAGGING

In several instances, the text refers to flags that have been placed on informal paths or herd paths. With the exception of the beginning of the trail to Allen, where flagging is essential to keep hikers on the only permitted route, all other flagging was done without the permission of the DEC. Since the first printing of this guide, those flags have been removed, but references to them have not been taken out of the text.

LEAN-TOS

The map does not show all existing lean-tos. It omits those that the DEC has considered removing or relocating; so you may find lean-tos that are not shown on the map. Be advised that the Unit Management Planning process, which is just beginning for the High Peaks region, may recommend further removals or relocations of lean-tos.

Nomenclature

Unravelling the source of Adirondack names reveals a history of the mountains and the men who found or enjoyed them. Naming geographic features has been a momentous part of Adirondack tradition, one that has provoked much controversy.

Early explorers named some of the highest peaks and more prominent features for people in the expeditions who first visited them. Early on, naming peaks for politicians became a custom. Many peaks took names from their characteristic shapes, such as Nippletop, Big Slide, and Haystack. Early Adirondack guides named a few peaks, among them Skylight and Gothics.

Verplanck Colvin named quite a few in the course of his Adirondack Survey, and he not only moved a few names around in the process, he added a few more politicians to the roster. Some names have been switched over the years by the USGS.

A few names were suggested by the Marshalls and others by Russell Carson, who not only wrote a history of the names, but chronicled the first ascents of the forty-six peaks. You should read his *Peaks and People* to learn more about those mountains. The Forty-sixers also have suggested names to the state geographical group responsible for names. Currently a few changes have been proposed, as noted in the text.

This guide emphasizes the naming of many of the lesser features. Names are a part of Adirondack lore that is continually growing, and this guide uses a few names that have made their way into Adirondack tradition. Some new names are also used to describe branches of streams and such, not to impose those names, but to make descriptions easier.

The names used in this guide are spelled as in the USGS metric maps, with some significant exceptions. The guide follows traditional patterns for Wolf Jaws, which never was one word until the map gave it that way. The trails and mountain named for Henry Van Hoevenberg are spelled -berg, unlike the USGS -burg, because that is how his name is spelled. Occasionally this guide uses names that are clearly more accepted than those given in the new metric maps; for example, Seward Brook is usually known as Ouluska Pass Brook.

MacIntyre, the mountain range, is spelled as in the USGS, but the man for whom the mountain is named spelled it McIntyre. This error was made a long time ago. There also has long been a discussion about the naming of Mount Colden, which was at one time McMartin. Because of the family relationship, I have woven Warder Cadbury's recent research into the story of the naming. A footnote to that story is the fact that there were four McMartin brothers, the sons of Duncan. One son was involved in the mine, and one was my great-great-grandfather. All four brothers married McIntyre girls, two pairs of first cousins, sisters and cousins of the McIntyre for whom the MacIntyre Range is named.

Instead of always addressing peaks formally as Mount So-and-so or Such-and-such Mountain, this guide generally refers to them by their proper names alone, unless there might be confusion with similarly named lakes or ponds. This, too, seems to be a part of Adirondack tradition, for most hikers develop the anthropomorphic view that the peaks are just old friends, to be referred to casually. Where there is no chance of confusion, this guide does just that, and so will you, after you have met a few of these great old friends.

Tahawus—The Iron Mine

EVERY HIKER SHOULD read *The Story of Adirondac*, by Arthur A. Masten, before walking the trails from Tahawus. It tells how in 1826 Malcolm McMartin, Dyer Thompson, John McIntyre, David Henderson, Enoch (a "negro servant"), and the Indian Lewis Elijah traveled south through Indian Pass (then called the Notch in the South Mountains and later Adirondack Pass). Their goal was the Indians' source of iron ore, but what they discovered exceeded their expectations. They found rich ore beds and veins, even a ledge five feet high of pure ore running into the infant Hudson River near Lake Sanford.

They immediately sought to purchase Township 47 of the Totten and Crossfield Purchase, which stretched west to Santanoni and Panther Peak, and the Gore East of Township 47, which included part of Indian Pass and the southwesterly part of the MacIntyre Range. The latter 6080-acre tract was surveyed in the summer of 1827 by Major Reuben Sanford and John Richards and appraised at ten cents an acre.

Archibald McIntyre, Duncan McMartin, and David Henderson were the leading men in the development of the property and the formation of the McIntyre Iron Company. In 1828, Judge McMartin secured the passage of an act appointing Commissioners to explore and lay out a road from the ore beds to Cedar Point (Port Henry). The early years were devoted to building this road. Building at the Tahawus works began in 1832. In 1833 the iron company acquired the Gore Around Lake Colden, which added the rest of Calamity Brook and the Opalescent River, Flowed Lands, Lake Colden, Avalanche Lake, and Mount Colden to their holdings. As early as 1834, however, when the road was built to the outlet of Henderson Lake, it was apparent that the iron mine would be fraught with trouble.

The company established farms, sawmills, and a community to support the workers who constructed forges and worked the mines. To supply water power, a dam was built across the Hudson near the Upper Works, where the community of Adirondac was built. The Great Dam, 1700 feet long, was built across the Hudson near the Lower Works (Tahawus), which is near the present bridge across the Hudson. That dam flooded the Hudson and provided a flatwater route through Lake Sanford. Both dams washed away in the flood of 1856.

Surrounding forests were cut for charcoal and a blast furnace forty-eight feet tall and thirty-six feet square at the base was fired up in 1854. But the difficulty of transporting iron to Lake Champlain and problems of making the iron compounded the lack of leadership caused by the untimely death in 1845 of David Henderson. This combination proved disastrous for the company. By the time Lossing visited Adirondac in 1859, it was already a "deserted village."

Cold River above Millers Falls

Houses still stand along the road near the Upper Works Trailhead and the magnificent stone furnace is a startling sight in the forest beside the road to the south.

By the late 1800s, all the pine had been cut from the company lands. In 1876, some of the principals in the Adirondack Steel Manufacturing Company (successor to the McIntyre Iron Company) formed the Preston Ponds Club and leased the company lands for hunting and fishing. It continued as a summer retreat known as the Adirondack Club, and finally became the Tahawus Club in 1897. In 1920, the state appropriated the Gore Around Lake Colden and a portion of the Gore East of Township 47, which included Indian Pass. Other lands were sold to Finch, Pruyn and Company.

Of the holdings west of Tahawus, the state acquired the west slopes of Santanoni, Panther, and Couchsachraga and the Morse Gore in Cold River country in 1907. The headwaters of the Cold River were purchased with 1916 Bond Act funds. In 1955, Finch Pruyn gave the state 2500 acres in two parcels on the east slopes of Panther and Santanoni. These parcels were to be managed by the state, but were not to be part of the Forest Preserve. In 1960, the state finally acquired the Cold River Gore and with it the dam at Duck Hole. Currently, the state is negotiating to buy the tract that stretches from Lake Henderson north to Duck Hole and which includes the Preston Ponds, a vitally important acquisition that will greatly expand the hiking and camping opportunities described in this chapter.

In the 1940s, the mine was reopened to ship processed titanium, the constituent in the mineral ilmenite that had made the iron so difficult to process. Titanium was so valuable to the war effort that the railroad was finally extended to the mine from North Creek in 1944. The tailings piles visible on the road to the Upper Works and the mine pits are evidence of this later effort. However, all that remains of that operation today is the enormous hole in the ground and the tailings piles. National Lead Industries, the current owners, continue to ship magnetite by train, but it is used in other industries, and no longer is the ore processed for iron.

Several trailheads are located along the road that leads past the National Lead Industries operations at Tahawus. To find them, turn off the Blue Ridge Road, 0 mile, pass the entrance to the Tahawus Club at 0.4 mile, cross the railroad tracks and the Hudson at 0.6 mile, and drive through posted lands to a fork at 6.25 miles. Straight ahead across the bridge over the Hudson River is the mine. Turn left before the bridge for the Marcy trails. The left fork passes ponds and tailings piles and High Peaks views. A left turn at 8.3 miles takes you to the parking area for the Santanoni Trails. Watch closely at 9.15 miles for the enormous McIntyre furnace beside the road. The parking area on the right at 9.3 miles serves the trails to Flowed Lands via the Opalescent River, section 42, and the bushwhack to Allen. The Upper Works Parking Area and the end of the road is at 9.9 miles.

At present, the beginning of all the trails radiating from this road are on private land, where no camping or straying from the marked routes is permitted. Trail descriptions note when the trails reach state land.

1 Indian Pass

4.4 miles, 2¹/₄ hours, 1050-foot elevation change, yellow and red markers

David Henderson wrote of his first trip through Indian Pass that it was "a fatiguing journey through as wild a place as the writer had ever seen." The pass quickly became a much visited and described place. The English actor William Macready called it a wild scene of terrible beauty. No one has matched the florid prose of Alfred Billings Street's book, *The Indian Pass*. Still, the pass remains almost as they saw it, and every bit as wonderful as they described.

The yellow trail to Indian Pass heads north from the Upper Works Parking Area at Tahawus, angles left, and crosses the outlet of Henderson Lake, which is the beginning of the Hudson River. Just beyond, a private road forks left. The way right leads to a junction at 0.25 mile, where the Calamity Brook Trail forks right. Stay straight, passing a wetland, which is off to the left. The trail follows a wide roadway, a rough, sometimes muddy, mine field of rocks with a slight grade, to a height-of-land above Lake Henderson, then descends with glimpses of the lake. A path heads left to water at an old ford, and, shortly beyond, the red trail to Duck Hole (section 2) branches left to cross Indian Pass Brook at 1.55 miles.

Continue straight ahead following the old roadway. The trail is now marked with red disks. Another road forks left, but the trail continues straight, generally north. You quickly reach state land—there is a small meadow where people have camped, but the Henderson Lean-to is a minute or so away at 1.75 miles. The forest has changed to mature stands of maple and yellow birch with spruce emerging. The trail circles a muddy spot and reaches a grass clearing at 2.05 miles, forty-five minutes from the start. The trail leaves the clearing, and the Blue Bypass Trail (section 44) continues along the roadway, to connect with the Calamity Brook Trail.

You angle left, staying on the red trail, which is now a narrow, relatively new footpath that leads across Indian Pass Brook on a high new bridge, one side of which is supported by a huge boulder. The path winds back to the old roadway. (If you are going south on this route, a bridge sign would alert you to this left turn; the continuing roadway is blocked by a brush pile.) The trail rejoins a roadway to continue north, angling right. There are lots of boulders beside the rugged and rolling trail. Slopes of the MacIntyre Range are visible through the trees.

Proximity to the brook makes stretches of the trail very handsome, though you are not close to its banks again until you approach Wallface Lean-to at 2.75 miles. Paths lead to water here. The trail starts uphill, veering away from the brook, to follow a shelf higher on the west side of the valley. A bit more than five minutes past the lean-to, the trail returns to brook level again. There is a camping spot on the east shore, but it is too close to the water. You cross an intermittent stream—a broad wallow—with glimpses of Wallface ahead. The trail stays close to the brook and at 3.2 miles makes two hop-a-rock crossings of the split outlet of Wallface Ponds.

The valley is very steep up to your left now as you come close to the flanks of Wallface. A very muddy stretch follows—you are in a small stream for 50 feet. As the valley narrows, you cross an overflow from Indian Pass Brook. Precariously perched boulders line the slopes above to your left. Huge rocks line the right side of the valley. At about 2100 feet, just short of 3.9 miles, a huge boulder almost blocks the valley ahead. A path continues straight to a camping spot. The trail turns right to make a rough crossing of Indian Pass Brook just downstream from the boulder.

If you like to bushwhack, you can head due east to east-southeast around the edge of the flat area to a stream and follow it up ten or fifteen minutes to a spectacular series of pools, falls, and open rock slabs. The most imposing feature is much farther up, a ravine on the slopes of the MacIntyre Range that Henderson noticed from the lake named for him. He explored it in 1844, describing its wild and abrupt scenery as equaling anything he had seen before, "the stream running for over a mile on a steep inclined plane of smooth, solid rock from 50 to 100 feet wide. This inclined plane is broken every few hundred feet by perpendicular precipices over which the river runs."

The trail continues north from the crossing along the east bank of the brook. Look to the west side of the valley where a huge, slanted rock pierces the slopes. It looks like a giant arrowhead. You scramble up and around overhanging boulders—a little bit of protection from the rain here. Now you have a good view of Wallface. You slide down a rock chute beneath vertical slabs, then, at the 2300-foot level, you angle sharply right, uphill, scrambling around rock ledges. The valley of Indian Pass Brook is way below you as you approach a fairly new, steep staircase and a ladder. On top of the ladder, angle briefly left to rejoin the old route, then make a right angle turn to the right, east, uphill. Paths lead straight ahead here, disappearing among the monster boulders of the pass. Many people have strayed from the trail here to wind beneath overhanging rocks.

The trail climbs steeply now, then turns north again through a rock-walled, narrow draw to circle a knob on the valley wall. On top of it, the trail again heads steeply up, then slides down to the base of a huge outcrop and heads up an enormous ladder. On top of the ladder, a path forks left to Summit Rock. The last 0.5 mile from the Indian Pass Brook crossing is rugged enough that it requires a half hour.

The view from Summit Rock was first painted by Charles C. Ingham after his 1837 visit with the geologist Ebenezer Emmons and it was popularized as an engraving in Headley's *The Adirondacks* in 1849. From here, you can explore the pass ahead, and either walk through to Adirondak Loj (section 34) or return to Tahawus.

2 Duck Hole via Preston Ponds

7.4 miles, 4½ hours, 1000-foot cumulative elevation change, yellow and red markers

This shortest route to Duck Hole is also the easiest way to the Cold River, which begins as that man-made pond's outlet. The first dam at Duck Hole was constructed by the Santa Clara Lumber Company in 1912, creating the large, shallow lake that covers what was originally marshlands. The present dam was built by the Civilian Conservation Corps (CCC) in 1934–35.

Walk the first 1.55 miles of the Indian Pass Trail and turn left across the bridge over Indian Pass Brook. The trail, now marked with red, heads back south along the brook, which flows into Henderson Lake. (The sign says it is now 4.2 miles to state land, but the distance appears to be about 0.4 longer.)

The trail briefly follows the brook, then turns away to cross a small stream with a beaver meadow above to the right. The trail is atop the beaver dam and across a couple of sagging logs. Continuing through once flooded beaver meadows and over some mud wallows, signs warn you away from Henderson Lake. After crossing over a knoll, the trail intersects an old tote road at 2.25 miles, where an arrow directs you to turn right.

Chains of treated lumber take you through a wet marsh beside a stream. You turn left to cross a bridge with high cribs in a balsam and spruce swamp. There is a second bridge over a smaller stream 130 feet farther along. The trail now follows the banks of the larger stream for 100 yards to a third bridge, a fourth in 100 yards, and a fifth in 60 yards, where the stream drops over a rock slide into a pool. After one more small bridge over a tributary, you finally reach high ground. The trail is close to an old beaver marsh. You cross its outlet and follow alongside it on rocks and stringers, rough footing again. The trail descends to the head of the grassy meadow with standing skeletons of trees. You follow a small brook and twenty minutes from the beginning of the road cross yet another bridge. You cross a small stream, then follow another to cross it on a remarkably big bridge.

Gradually the trail angles away from the stream valley, which is now down to your left and you begin a gentle climb. You cross a small draw, then cross a second on a small log bridge. Chains of treated lumber lead you into the valley, with mountains rising steeply from it. Soon you can see the cliffs on the lower slopes of Henderson Mountain.

Duck Hole and MacNaughton

Preston Ponds Pass is encased in cliffs from which slabs have fallen and lie jagged in the ferns of the wet meadow. Passing boulders on chains of logs, posted signs warn you away from caves secreted in the cliffs. Remember, all *but* the route of the trail is posted! Finally at 2230 feet, you start to descend. The pass is small, but lovely, and it marks a significant divide—waters so far have been flowing to the Hudson; now the drainage leads to the Raquette River and the St. Lawrence. You cross the small stream that drains the west side of the pass and descend through bogs on more long chains of logs.

Contemplate for a moment David Henderson's trek through the pass in 1833 and wonder at his proposal to blast the pass and dam and divert the Preston Ponds to Lake Henderson to increase the mine's water supply.

The trail turns right at 4.05 miles, two hours, just before the shores of the Upper Preston Pond, and climbs, following a little stream in a small gorge that is a wild place, with rocks and cliffs above and little cascades in the stream. Angling west again, and still following the stream, the trail rounds a sharp knob that is to the left and reaches an overlook of Hunters Pond at 4.5 miles. The trail rounds the north side of this pretty pond with a big beaver house by winding between boulders that have fallen from the steep slopes above. You climb high above the pond to a little pass, then descend a steep chute to a muddy col and immediately there is a stream, flowing northwest, which you cross twice.

A long, gentle, sometimes wet descent follows, first past a beaver marsh, then below jagged ledges and around boulder shards down to marsh level again. Below its beaver dam, the trail is again rubbly and steep along the stream, which you cross. An old logging clearing follows, then you come down to a much larger stream at 5.2 miles. This stream comes from high up on MacNaughton and it turns now to take on the same northwest direction the trail has been following. You immediately cross it without benefit of a bridge and continue the gentle descent.

The trail here is quite close to the state land boundary and hikers have trespassed for a few yards to begin the bushwhack up MacNaughton. The shortest route, with this currently illegal beginning, follows the east side of this stream. There is something of a path along the stream already. Since the state is negotiating to buy the Preston Ponds Tract, there is the possibility that this route will be open to the public shortly. In any event, the trail enters a corner of state land shortly after crossing the stream, so a legal approach is possible, even though the first two hundred yards following the west side of the stream are dense and horrible. See section 37 for more details of MacNaughton.

From a bank high above the water, you have a fleeting glimpse of Lower Preston Pond. The trail, still along an old roadway lined with corduroy, is very wet and difficult to walk as it descends to traverse marshes to the northeast of the pond. At 6 miles, the trail rounds the end of the pond without ever coming near its shores.

Climbing away from the Lower Pond, the trail rises moderately, crosses a spruce bog where there is a knob out to the left between it and the pond, and somewhere, unmarked in this lovely forest, reaches state land. After descending steeply through a balsam slope (the trail is densely grown in) the trail reaches a log-filled, narrow bay of Duck Hole, at 6.45 miles. You climb moderately for 180 feet, cross a lovely height, then drop steeply to a small marsh with views to the north. In 100 yards and one more rise you reach Roaring Brook, which you also ford. The intersection with the Northville-Placid Trail is on the far bank at nearly 6.9 miles.

Turn left on the blue trail; just past intersection, the trail is close to a marshy finger of Duck Hole, over which there is a view toward Panther Mountain. The trail winds beneath rock outcrops to an open field, 0.5 mile from the intersection. Here there is another intersection, with the truck trail to Coreys heading right, northwest from the field. One of Duck Hole's lean-tos sits on a wooded promontory to the left; the second is in the field almost at the dam, which has as many snakes as the site of French Louie's camp on West Canada Lake, many miles south on the Northville-Placid Trail. (See *Discover the West Central Adirondacks*.) Nevertheless, this is one of the better camping destinations. The fishing is good, the islands are charming, and the views of Mac-Naughton, Henderson, and Panther above the dense spruce-covered shoreline are most attractive. Because of its proximity to five major routes, it is also a very popular place.

Duck Hole Bridge

3 Duck Hole to Moose Pond

3.8 miles from the dam at Duck Hole, 2 hours, blue markers

Another of the very pretty wooded segments of the Northville-Placid Trail lies north of Duck Hole. Enjoy it either as a through route to the end of the trail, adding section 32, or as a round-trip walk from a campsite at Duck Hole.

Walk 0.5 mile back along the shore of Duck Hole to the intersection with the red trail (section 2). The blue trail continues along Roaring Brook, heading uphill, beside the wildly tumbling stream. Cliffs face the ledges on the east side. The stream becomes gravelly, then opens to a flatwater. Above the meander you can see the sharp cliffs on the knob below Henderson. The forest is lovely, the walking occasionally mucky. Steep slopes rise above to your left and big boulders fill the narrow valley. The trail is very narrow. Thirty-five minutes from the intersection, at 1.6 miles, and a rock-hop across Roaring Brook, there is a campsite—too close to water. Upstream, Roaring Brook makes a sharp turn to the east. The trail does not cross the brook, but beyond this point, it angles west into a draw, five minutes from the top.

The narrow valley through which you descend is filled with lush ferns, mostly woodferns, but watch—after descending for about ten minutes—for there are magnificent specimens of the uncommon Braun's holly fern, *Polystichum braunii*. The trail crosses to the right, east, side of the valley and traverses along it. Cliffs rise above the trail to the east. You have glimpses of mountains across the valley as the trail rolls along beneath tall spruce.

The trail crosses a small stream, heads into a spruce swamp, then makes a hairpin turn back southeast to cross the tiny stream again. You climb slightly to a ridge with a wetland below to your left. The Sawtooth Mountains are visible through openings created by dying spruce.

A beaver flow interrupts the trail—there is a marker on a tree out in the water. Head left to cross on the first dam below the old trail crossing. More dams impede the stream below, just above its confluence with Moose Creek; flooding extends well upstream, so the dam is probably the best way to cross, even if it is difficult.

The trail draws close to Moose Creek shortly beyond, within a ten-minute walk of the lean-to, but you still have more streams and wetlands to cross. The lean-to, on a knoll above the pond, is a great place to sit and study the craggy profile of the Sawtooth Mountains, as well as a great place to camp.

4 Duck Hole via Santanoni Brook and Bradley Pond Lean-to

4.5 miles, 2½ hours to the lean-to, 1210-foot elevation change, 3.65 miles, 2 hours lean-to to Duck Hole, 820-foot elevation change, blue markers

Someone wrote in the trailhead register that the trail to Bradley Pond (Santanoni) Lean-to was a swamp. Other comments were less polite, but equally correct. For a trail that starts dryly along a gravel road and continues on high ground nearly to the pass, all anyone remembers is the mess in the last mile below the lean-to. Oh, for waterbars!

Still, the trail down the north side of the pass is even worse! It is lined with old corduroy, indicating that it really was a road, unbelievable as it may seem. Very steep, eroded, almost dangerous with a pack, this trail needs a major rerouting.

Almost all of the trail from the Upper Works to Bradley Pond Lean-to is on private land. You will need to hike almost to the lean-to if you plan to bushwhack to the Santanoni Range (section 5) for a point near the lean-to on state land is the only permitted approach. The old herd path, which headed directly to Santanoni from a point almost 1 mile short of the lean-to, is definitely off limits. The southern part of the trail to the lean-to is routine and easy to follow, and except for two spots, not terribly attractive.

You might also consider the through route as an alternative to Duck Hole; and a long, but good, day hike involves a loop to Duck Hole via Preston Ponds with a return on this route. It may also be easier to negotiate when climbing with a pack if you are headed into the pass from Duck Hole, rather than descending from it to the north. That's why the trail is described from north to south.

The trail crosses the dam at Duck Hole and immediately there is a path left to a campsite. In 250 yards the trail emerges from a balsam-walled corridor at a dam/causeway with slippery planks, a marsh to the right, and a great view of MacNaughton. Briefly following the shore, a path left leads to a campsite too close to water beside an inlet bay. The trail right climbs over a knoll to avoid wet areas and by the time it has returned to this nameless inlet stream, it is a charming babbling brook. Let's call it North Panther Brook, since its origins are high on the slopes beneath Panther Mountain and the name Panther Brook is attached to a tributary of Santanoni Brook. Almost immediately, you ford the brook, crossing to private land to turn to follow the brook upstream. You reach Forest Preserve again shortly after the crossing.

North Panther Brook is lovely, here overhung with cedars. The trail, passing through stands of spruce and balsam, soon reaches a quiet oxbow. It makes a hairpin turn heading east around a second oxbow, then at 1.65 miles, twenty-five minutes from the previous crossing, again crosses the brook, which here makes a bend to the east.

Heading southwest, the trail enters a meadow, crosses an old logging settlement site, then heads southeast along the meadow, making a hairpin turn now to the east. Many of these sharp turns have undoubtedly resulted from past beaver ponds, built on the level floodplain.

You stay fairly close to the brook then move away from it to circle marshes and cross several little streams, returning to North Panther Brook at the oxbows. At one point the trail climbs a knoll to the right, west, of the brook. A huge disrupted area follows—a hillside of dead spruce and balsam. The trail rises slightly over a small hillock where balsam all but conceal the way. Without clearing, parts of this trail may soon be lost. There is a big wetland off to the southwest with good views of Panther now. Birch cover the next knoll, then there is a big meadow that has been flooded in the past, either by man or beaver. At 1.95 miles, the trail goes right out into the meadow on an old beaver dam, from which you can see both Henderson and Panther. The trail is finally more open and easy to walk. That last 0.7 mile takes thirty-five minutes, perhaps because the trail wanders about in the marshes more than the map indicates.

Beyond the meadow you hop rocks to cross a major tributary that flows from the slopes of Panther, then negotiate the mudholes in yet another beaver meadow. You cross a muddy stream on old logs before this 0.7 mile stretch ends in an open meadow where you turn sharply left to cross the main brook again.

The trail stays off to the east of North Panther Brook, following its course gradually uphill until the east side of the valley becomes increasingly steep, forcing the trail close to the brook. At 3.1 miles you cross the brook again. Just upstream there is an old logging clearing with many artifacts to the right of the

Panther from Duck Hole Bay

trail. An immense old iron bucket—a pig-sticking bucket—is curious, unless you know that loggers used them to pack snow along their roads in winter.

You cross back to the east side of the brook again in 150 yards, elevation about 2460 feet, an hour and three quarters from Duck Hole. The next 500-foot climb in just over 0.6 mile is along one of the wildest and most improbable stretches of road ever built. Even as a trail, parts are astonishing. The trail climbs immediately to a tributary stream, which shortly runs down the trail. Muddy old logs bridge it in places, corduroy stairs lead upward, through the pretty, but very rugged, gorge. As the grade eases you emerge on the west side of a freshet. The trail is still gullied and rocky. Where the trail rejoins the main tributary, water has wiped out the roadway, which becomes rubbly, steep, and dangerous. The mess of rocks and old cedar corduroy seems unending. In some places, the corduroy holds the water in the trail. A final hop-a-rock climb brings you to the pass, elevation 2952 feet, and the decrepit lean-to is to the south, just below the pass.

Log stringers take you through some of the mud below the lean-to. A wet meadow follows; you can see across it to Panther and southwest to Santanoni. The trail follows the meadow. At the beaver dam at the southern end of the meadow, a path forks west across the dam. It leads around private land to the paths on Santanoni (section 5). Even as the trail begins to descend, it remains wet and muddy. After descending to the level of another marsh, the trail makes a rubbly climb up to a bank above Santanoni Brook and comes to the point, close to the brook, where the old and currently illegal route to Santanoni began. Log stringers now make the going easier, but the rest of the trail is a rough boulder-field as it descends for a few more minutes to views at 2650 feet of a series of waterfalls and chutes on Santanoni Brook.

You hardly need directions for the rest of the descent from the bottom of the falls at 5.65 miles, but be warned the trail is still full of boulders and moderately steep. In twenty minutes, just short of 2300 feet, a mess of logging roads crosses the one the trail follows. Stay on the one with the corduroy. A little over fifteen minutes more brings you to the edge of the cedar-and-hemlock gorge that surrounds the brook. The trail turns right onto a narrow footpath to cross Santanoni Brook on a high bridge just above its confluence with an unnamed tributary coming from the southwest. The trail heads through a field, follows this tributary upstream (wonderful cedar here) and turns left to cross it on a good bridge. Shortly, at 5.9 miles, you reach a T with a gravel road. Turn left. The road crosses the outlet of Harkness Lake at 6.5 miles, just above marshes that continue all the way to Henderson Lake, providing an opening to the north with a fine view of Wallface. It is only 1.2 miles farther down the road to the gate and the Santanoni parking area.

5 Santanoni Mountains

Paths

Although there are no maintained trails on the Santanoni Range, there are well-used paths connecting Santanoni, Panther, and Couchsachraga, its three principal summits. The most easily reached jumping-off point for any of the peaks is a beaver dam on the blue trail to Bradley Pond (section 4). This point is 4.3 miles and a good two hours from the parking area, 350 yards short of Bradley Pond Lean-to. It is currently the only permitted approach to the Santanoni Mountains. The more direct approach to Santanoni Peak, which was used for many years, crossed private lands and is currently posted and off limits to hikers. The Bradley Pond (Santanoni) Lean-to is the only available nearby—if not especially pleasant—campsite for the approach to the range from the east side.

In normal summer conditions it is easy to cross the beaver dam, but if you happen to come along right after a great downpour, you may have difficulty keeping your feet dry. On the far side, bear slightly right to find the beginning of the path up onto the range. Here, and for the next 0.75 mile, you will find yellow paint blazes marking the route. This is not the state land boundary, as yellow blazes often are, but it is a survey route from the right-of-way on the blue trail, across Finch Pruyn property. About ten minutes from the beaver dam along the survey route, you pass the northern edge of Bradley Pond and then climb steeply, then more moderately along the base of cliffs lining the south side of the prominent ridge extending east from the summit of Panther down to the pond. At the end of the survey line, find the path angling sharply left and follow it for ten minutes around the base of this east ridge into Panther Brook. If you continue up in the westerly direction of the survey line, as many hikers mistakenly have, you will be traveling up Panther's east ridge through an area that was among those most severely devastated by the 1950 hurricane. And, while the intervening decades have tempered this experience significantly, you will conserve considerable energy by finding the usual route up the brook. A quick scan of comments in the Panther register will probably suffice to satisfy your curiosity about conditions on the east ridge.

Panther Brook will take you up about 400 vertical feet before it disappears underground, still 600 feet below the high ridge connecting Santanoni and Panther Peaks. A heavily used path, 15 years older than the survey route and cutover, quickly appears as the brook disappears. About two and a quarter hours from the blue trail, it will bring you to well-trampled Times Square, a staging area between a small knoll and a large boulder on the crest of the ridge. From here it is 500 yards to Panther, to the north, beyond the knoll. Santanoni is a little more than a mile away, beyond the boulder to the south. And it is 1.5 miles to Couchsachraga, down the long ridge dropping slowly away to the west. Take your pick. A moderately strong party will use much of an hour getting to Panther and back, two hours or more on the round trip to Santanoni, and over three hours for Couchsachraga. But if you are inclined to climb more than one, you will return here to Times Square from each peak before starting on to the next. *There are no shortcuts.*

SANTANONI

More than half of your hike to Santanoni follows the ridge crest south from Times Square, arriving at the base of Santanoni Peak with less than a 200-foot drop. It will not pay for you to rush here, for the path has been pushed through sturdy spruce-fir scrub, which at this elevation does not shrink from pushing back. If you try to hurry, you will almost certainly find some of your clothing, if not your flesh, torn up by or left behind on the broken limbs that form the jagged edges of much of the path. From the low point on the ridge, the path climbs steeply to the first of three false summits. There are good views west and north and east from several lookout points on these bumps, while the peak itself, elevation 4605 feet, 1404 meters, is occupied by a sharp boulder surrounded by thicket. Clamber a few feet past the summit boulder to find a perch with excellent views east toward the main jumble of the High Peaks. There is a particularly fine view of Indian Pass and Wallface to the northeast.

On your return to Times Square, watch out for a path that you passed between the first and second false summits as you climbed up. As you head north, it branches right and descends steeply to the east. This is the old Santanoni Trail, which was originally marked and kept somewhat cleared by the Santanoni Club. Where the trail crosses land owned by Finch Pruyn, the route is posted and closed to the public. It is evident that not all hikers have been respecting this posting, whether innocently or by design; and in following this path, they risk embarrassment and arrest.

PANTHER

Panther has two summits, the higher, elevation 4441 feet, 1354 meters, being the southwest peak, which is the first one you will reach on the easy walk from Times Square. The ascent is little over 150 feet, complicated only by a very soggy area (look for paths to your left here) as you approach the rock face southwest of the summit. Open rock slabs near the top, providing wide views to the west, make Panther a favored spot on the range for spending a few extra minutes. The view down onto Couchsachraga allows hikers on their way there to really savor the dimension of the experience ahead.

Curiously, Henderson was originally Panther, and this peak was called Henderson; the names were switched by the USGS for no apparent reason.

COUCHSACHRAGA

The Indian name Couchsachraga, land of the beavers, was bestowed on the mountain by Bob and George Marshall, who were the first to climb this peak, thinking it was over 4000 feet. The new metric map gives its elevation as 1156 meters (3791 feet). Couchsachraga tops out over 600 feet below the summit of Panther, and almost 500 feet below your elevation at Times Square, and the path to it crosses its low point over 800 feet down. If you find yourself wondering why you are bothering with the hike to Couchie, be assured you are by no means the first to do so. Viewed from Panther, it is the virtual essence of insignificance. And, although there is a good lookout as you approach the top of Couchie, south over Calahan Brook toward Santanoni and Little Santanoni, the stand-up views from the top itself are too far from anywhere to be remarkable. That very situation, however, contributes to the mystique of Couchsachraga. As you descend from the Panther-Santanoni Ridge you are sinking into a truly remote and wild territory, and the path you are following is almost ephemeral in its narrow and wandering penetration of the forest. Finally, if you are not enchanted by the bryophyte park that hangs quietly between Couchie's two gentle summits, then indeed you should have stayed home and gotten your day's workout on an exercise machine.

On your return from Times Square down to Bradley Pond, beware of false starts on paths leading strongly south of east out of the square. Your path down should take a sharp left turn almost immediately, and then bend slowly right to descend almost due east down to Panther Brook. Remember to watch as you descend along the brook for the cutover path to the survey line (marked in 1988 by a rock cairn on the right side of the brook, and survey tape on the left side).

Newcomb

NEWCOMB WAS ORIGINALLY called Pendleton for a Judge Pendleton who built a gristmill at the foot of Rich Lake in 1810. D. T. Newcomb farmed along the road that leads to the lake that now bears his name. Newcomb was convinced that his land held deposits of silver, but its riches were in its forest cover, which remained little touched when Robert C. Pruyn of Finch, Pruyn and Company acquired the farm in 1893. Pruyn assembled an 11,205-acre parcel of lands in Totten and Crossfield Townships 27 and 28 that included Newcomb Lake and Moose Ponds. He built an enormous log home on the shore of Newcomb Lake. It has 5000 square feet of covered porches connecting several log structures—the porches were needed so his guests would not feel claustrophobic in the gloom of all the Adirondack rain.

The entire property was sold to the Melvin family of Syracuse in the 1960s and in 1972 the state acquired all the land, but not before it had been heavily logged. Because the land is in the Forest Preserve, the buildings will eventually be torn down.

Today the estate roads are hiking trails that are also open to horses. It is possible to hire a horse at Newcomb to take you and your family by cart to Newcomb Lake. Your canoe can also be transported there, and this is a delightful way to begin a canoe camping expedition to Newcomb Lake.

Groups of horseback riders regularly camp at Moose Pond (section 9) and the hard road surface makes this delightful. Good roads continue north of Moose Pond to Calahan Brook. Past this crossing, parts of the roads are not well graded, so stretches can be muddy quagmires, a truly discouraging situation for hikers seeking to share the trails. The worst stretch of horse trail is just south of the Cold River crossing. It was cut expressly for use by horses in an area of typical Adirondack muck, not the sandy gravelly soils of the rest of the horse trail network. It is a disaster.

6 Newcomb Lake—Santanoni Preserve

Hiking, skiing, canoeing, fishing, swimming, camping, horseback riding
4.8 miles, just over 2 hours, relatively level

Santanoni Preserve Trailhead is less than a mile east of the High Peaks View Rest Stop in Newcomb. The marked access road crosses the outlet of Rich Lake and the parking area is to the right of the roadway, just short of the gate and the registration booth. With very easy walking on the continuing roadway, which is barred to all but DEC maintenance vehicles, you cruise along beside marshes that are out to your right along the outlet of Newcomb Lake. Wonderful forests of hemlock shelter the road. Beyond, there are patches of noble hardwoods. All along this stretch there are spectacular forests, tall and open beneath. Note that these are the best forests you will encounter on the entire preserve purchase tract, for all the rest, except the corridor to the camp and the immediate shores of the lake, were logged shortly before the state acquired them.

In twenty-five minutes, you pass barns and a stone house, then traverse an open field, and cross two small streams. In fifty-five minutes, there is a large bridge; and shortly, at 2.2 miles, you reach an intersection. The way left leads to Moose Pond (section 9). You go right, relatively level at first, then descend gently. You cross a second stone bridge, then at 3.9 miles the red trail (section 8) turns off to the left. At 4.2 miles you are at a picnic area on a bluff. The road descends to cross the bridge and turn sharply left. It passes several numbered campsites along the shore before reaching Camp Santanoni at 4.8 miles.

Note that there are more truly lovely campsites on the north shore beyond the camp—a path leads to these numbered sites (see below).

7 North Shore of Newcomb Lake

2.3 miles, 1½ hours, 150-foot rise, yellow markers

The trail that circles the north shore of Newcomb Lake has not been cleared in recent years—it is filling in with thick stands of raspberries, small trees, and tall weeds. The fate of this route, much of which follows old logging roads, will be decided by the Unit Management Plan.

The trail begins to the north of the camp, heading out between an outhouse and one of the collapsed structures. It follows close to shoreline and what a shore it is! Exquisite sandy beaches, overhanging cedars, lovely campsites, even a bathhouse border the pathway. I know no other walk in the Park with such lovely cedars. The last campsite, number 8, 0.3 mile from Camp Santanoni, is beside Sucker Brook. The yellow trail leads out the back of that campsite away from shore to join a logging road. Turn left on it and immediately cross the brook on a collapsing bridge.

The trail now winds uphill, reaching ledges high above the lake in a forest that was heavily logged. You are so far from the lake you can barely see it through the trees. You reach a height-of-land, then climb again, with sparse yellow markers to assure you that this overgrown route is the right course. A gentle descent follows, then a sharp curve to the north and a steeper descent leads to a marsh. The trail leads out into the marsh and at 1.5 miles crosses Santanoni Brook (one of two so named in the area) on a precarious two-log bridge. Continue through the marsh into a spruce forest where a left turn at 1.6 miles leads to the Ward Pond Brook Lean-to on the shore of Newcomb Lake. The sandy beach, the lovely forest, vistas of islands, and quiet shores all make this a lovely campsite. The walk from the bridge, past the camps to the lean-to, takes about an hour.

The trail continues behind the lean-to, entering one of the best parts of the trail. After crossing Ward Pond Brook, the yellow trail, now a very narrow footpath, leads for 0.7 mile through a mature spruce and cedar swamp. It is generally close enough to shore so you can occasionally glimpse the water. Just short of 2.3 miles, you reach an intersection with the red trail (section 8), within sight of the marshes along the inlet that drains Shaw Pond. The new bridge over this inlet to the left permits you to complete the circuit.

8 South Shore of Newcomb Lake

2 miles to the yellow trail, 6 miles to Shaw Pond, 1 hour to the yellow trail, relatively level, red markers

The last 4 miles of this route from Newcomb Lake to Shaw Pond and on to the Moose Pond Horse Trail are not now an official or maintained trail, although you can still walk along them. The lack of care is only a minor problem along the southern portion of these 4 miles, but the trail gradually becomes more and more obscure to the north. There are no markers directing you to the trail at its northern terminus, near the horse trail beyond Moose Pond. A ranger speculates that the trail may be routed to the horse trail 0.7 mile south of the Moose Pond Intersection (see section 9), but its fate awaits the Unit Management Plan.

The red trail begins 0.4 mile south of the Newcomb Lake bridge and heads west on high ground traversing a hardwood ridge. Cedar swamps lie between the trail and the lake and you never do get a view of the lake while on this trail. After a fifteen-minute walk, the trail curves downhill to cross a two-log bridge. After climbing over a ridge, it continues on a bank above yet another marsh. After an easy thirty-minute walk, you pass the last of the marshes and reach an intersection at 1.5 miles. Here a blue trail heads 200 yards sharply downhill to a rocky promontory on the lake. A lean-to and several campsites grace this choice spot, with its views of the Santanoni Range and Newcomb Lake's islands. Lovely cedar-capped rocks clasp the bay to the east of the promontory.

West of the intersection, the red trail continues briefly on the ridge above the lake. You immediately pass an enormous glacial erratic lying below the ledge you are traversing. As the trail descends to lake level, the going gets wetter. The trail continues west through swamps filled with jewel weed, along a ferny bottom land with tall spruce and balsam, and across an old corduroy road to reach the bridge at 2 miles, less than fifteen minutes from the lean-to intersection.

After crossing the bridge, the trail winds through the marsh, then heads up into the spruce swamp to the intersection—at 2 miles—with the yellow trail (section 7). The red trail, the left fork, heads slightly uphill and continues on dry ground, paralleling the inlet stream. Marshes lie off to the west all along this stretch, which is alternately a narrow footpath or the bed of an old logging road. It is confusing and will get worse without remarking. You cross a beaver dam 0.8 mile from the bridge and circle a large swamp. After crossing two more streams, at 4.1 miles, the trail is on a ridge above Shaw Pond Outlet at the outlet's closest approach to the Moose Pond Horse Trail. There is speculation that the official red trail will ultimately end here, at a logging road that leads 150 yards to the horse trail.

At present, the red trail, fainter now, begins to climb, and in 0.15 mile turns left, west, and crosses the outlet stream. No marker or sign of path is visible on the far side, so you will have to search about for the vague footpath that continues uphill, generally heading north, then west around the south end of Shaw Pond. At 5.9 miles, the trail curves north to a beaver dam, which the red trail used to cross. Do not cross the beaver dam, but leave the red markers and skirt left, west, around the swamp to the horse trail. See section 10 for clues to finding this north end of the red trail from the horse trail.

The red trail used to continue north past Shaw Pond to intersect the blue horse trail south of the Northern Lean-tos (section 11). That stretch has been closed so long that it is virtually impossible to follow.

9 Moose Pond

Hiking, swimming, camping, horseback riding, skiing
7 miles, under 3 hours, small hills, blue horse-trail markers

The left fork, 2.2 miles north on the road into the Santanoni Preserve, is the route to Moose Pond. The trail follows an excellent old logging road that is marked as a horse trail. The road bed is sufficiently well filled with gravel that horses do not chew up the surface. However, it is a circuitous route if you also want to visit Newcomb Lake. (See section 8 for problems along the alternate hikers route.)

The road crosses several small streams that drain marshy areas, but there is little good water until you reach Moose Pond. The roadway passes through huge open fields—hot places in summer. The only good thing about the road is that you can walk the last 4.8 miles in two hours, even with a pack.

From the intersection, the road winds on high ground for nearly a mile to a bridge—there is a campsite nearby. There is a second bridge shortly beyond at 3.3 miles, then a rise to a height-of-land. A long, gentle 200-foot descent follows. At 4.3 miles, less than half an hour from the intersection, you cross a stream, then emerge in the open fields with views of Baldwin Mountain behind you and a sharp, unnamed cone to the west. Marshes, small stream crossings, and a gravel pit are about all the excitement this stretch has to offer, though there are views of Moose Mountain ahead and from one marsh just off the trail to the left there are good views of the Santanoni Range including the Ermine Brook slide. This 1.6-mile segment takes thirty-five minutes to walk. At 5.9 miles you cross a very small stream and start uphill. A little more than 100 yards into the climb, a road forks right. It leads to a campsite above Shaw Pond Outlet and is a logical place for the red trail from Newcomb Lake (section 8) to join the horse trail. The red trail is to the east, up the ridge, here.

The Moose Pond Horse Trail continues a gradual climb to the col between Moose Mountain and an unnamed hill to the north, then descends slightly, traversing the side of the hill, above a draw, to reach an intersection in twenty minutes more. Here at 6.7 miles, the blue horse trail (section 10) forks right. Another roadway heads sharply downhill to round the southern end of Moose Pond. This road ends by a large campsite in a field. Two paths lead to shoreline, one heading off just before the field, the other from the field. The latter leads to a wonderful view of the Santanoni Range and the best place from which to study the new Ermine Brook slide (section 12).

10 Moose Pond to Shattuck Clearing via Moose Pond Creek

Hiking, skiing, horseback riding
7.9 miles, 4 hours, relatively level, blue horse-trail markers

From the Intersection above Moose Pond, the blue horse trail heads north, winding gently up on the hillside high above Moose Pond, which is barely visible from the trail. About ten minutes from the intersection, the trail swings sharply left and you pass a gravel pit and a pile of small boulders lying to the left side of the trail. If you are interested in finding the north end of the red trail to Newcomb Lake (section 8) or Shaw Pond, this is the point to leave the horse trail. There is a small swamp to the right. Bushwhack along the right edge of this swamp through a tiny grove of young balsams for 150 yards to the red trail. This point is at the beaver dam mentioned in section 8. Red markers lead you south toward Newcomb Lake; the old trail north (across the dam) quickly fades.

Just beyond, on the horse trail, at 0.6 mile, a huge marsh opens off to your right. Then you cross a sand pit and a second marsh with upturned roots and a bridge over the stream that flows through the middle of the marsh. The trail continues on the edge of a hill, climbing slightly, rounding a bend, then heading downhill to a broad meadow at 1.4 miles. Ermine Brook flows through this meadow—it is the beginning of the exciting bushwhack of section 12. The crossing, a ford, is thirty-five minutes from the Moose Pond Intersection.

The trail winds through the meadows—there are lots of campsites here— then begins to climb slightly to cross a little brook. On the next rise, wet

places appear in the trail. You can see big marshes through the trees to your
left. A gradual downhill follows, but not much else of interest until you round
the crest of a small hill, descend steeply to a sharp hairpin turn, then continue
for ten more minutes to the descent to Calahan Brook. It takes less than an
hour to walk the 2.3 miles from Ermine Brook to Calahan Brook, which is 3.7
miles from the Moose Pond Intersection. There is no level ground for camping
in the vicinity of Calahan Brook, but there are pools to swim in near the
crossing and plenty of good, cold water. (For the intrepid explorer, Calahan
Brook is a challenging route toward Couchsachraga and the western slopes of
the Santanoni Range. Part way up, we are told, there is a spectacular waterfall
on the brook.)

You hop rocks to follow the trail across Calahan Brook and it can be wet!
The trail starts uphill, and at 4.1 miles the trail bends left to a narrow stretch
of trail, then at 4.3 miles intersects a road again and turns sharply right.
(When you head south on this stretch of trail, you may find this point is
confusing, because then it appears as if the proper route would be the continuing roadway.) For all the turns, the trail is basically curving west to round a
small hill. The trail descends, then becomes a quagmire—a horrible mess.
Muddy, unpleasant walking continues to the intersection with the yellow
Horse Trail at 5.2 miles. This point is forty-five minutes from Calahan Brook.

Heading west, straight ahead, from the intersection, the trail traverses
gently down a side hill for 250 feet in elevation to a big opening with two lean-
tos. The field, at 6 miles, twenty minutes from the intersection, is right beside
Moose Pond Creek. A very substantial bridge crosses the creek. The trail
continues west through scrub forests for another mile to a marked intersection
with yet another old logging road. The way south, left, leads to private land.
The trail turns north for 0.7 mile to the right fork for the Northville-Placid
Trail, a turn which is slightly concealed. It is almost within sight of a second
fork on the road, where, at 6.8 miles, the right fork leads to the Cold River
ford and the horse trail north to Coreys. The way left leads in 0.1 mile to the
middle of the field at Shattuck Clearing where the Northville-Placid Trail
(section 15) heads left, due south.

11 Horse Trail to Duck Hole

8.6 miles, 3½ hours, relatively level, yellow horse-trail markers

The Horse Trail, connecting the trail described in section 10 with the Cold
River 0.9 mile west of Duck Hole, should be a good access to the western
slopes of the Santanoni Range. The southern part is a fairly well-graded road,
suitable for horses; but, as noted in the introduction, the northern 2.4 miles
are terrible for the hiker. There has been discussion of closing this trail to
horses, and if waterbars and needed drainage were added to the northern

portion, it would become a good route for hikers. Because it can serve as the return of the loop from Shattuck Clearing to Duck Hole via the Northville-Placid Trail (section 17) the route is described from north to south. An additional reason for choosing this direction is that you will know immediately if water is low enough to cross the Cold River at the ford, instead of being disappointed at the end of a long walk.

In dry times, the ford south of the Northville-Placid Trail is an easy crossing. The river bed is wide, gravelly, and not usually deeper than a foot and a half. Take off your boots and wear sneakers if needed.

You immediately climb a small hill on a very muddy, chewed up trail. A second rise takes you to a height-of-land way above the river. In fifteen minutes you reach a rocky and muddy roadway, which leads back right—an abandoned route. The trail follows the road to the left, climbing another hill. It is routed even higher on the hillside, avoiding one particularly bad stretch of road. The trail continues now on a rolling course around the side of a hill, with a steep drop to the right. You cross a small stream beside an outstandingly large cedar, then continue through surprisingly good woods. A grove of hemlocks gives way to a hardwood hill, then the forest changes—most of what follows has all been logged. You will see only patches of good forest all the way back to Newcomb!

Maples as tall as your head fill the trail, which is gradually descending. There is a horrible muddy stretch, then you hear the river again and are finally, at just short of 2 miles, back beside it. Watch closely through the dense spruce that line the trail for the deep, walled flume just beyond—this is the stretch Colvin named the Cold River Canyon. It lasts for only about 200 yards, then the river broadens out again and the trail finally becomes drier, though it is filling with brambles. At 2.4 miles, you enter a large field with the two Northern Lean-tos perched beside a rocky stretch of river. In spite of all the rough walking, it takes about an hour and a quarter to reach this point from the crossing.

The trail, now wider and easier, continues beside the broad river for ten minutes, until at just over 2.8 miles the river turns sharply north and the trail turns left, south. The old route northwest to the ford forked right here (see section 17 for its intersection to the north with the Northville-Placid Trail). Huge swamps lie to the right of the trail, which crosses a swampy inlet on a large bridge built for horses. The road was obviously built with heavy equipment and has a dry course on a ledge above swamp level. Signs of logging abound, though there are stands of significant hardwoods with spruce and a few large cedars.

This 1.3-mile stretch is easy walking, requiring but forty-five minutes. At various points between the Northern Lean-tos and the bridge over the small stream that drains a shoulder of Couchsachraga you have great views of the Seward Range. This brook has many forks, so using it as an ascent route to Couchsachraga is tricky; but if you do not relish backtracking Panther's summit ridge (section 5), you can simply head north from Couchie and follow the drainage to this trail.

Just across that bridge at 4.1 miles was the beginning of the abandoned red foot trail—even its beginning is now hard to find. Beyond there is a stand of old growth forest, huge hemlock, and spruce, then a gradual climb to a height-of-land. Some impressive cedars line this grassy segment of trail. You cross a small stream, walk past a grassy opening with a beaver marsh off to your left, and climb a short rise to an esker ridge. Look carefully among the small spruce and balsam that line both sides of the ridge for the huge stumps of the fallen giants that once dotted these lowlands. The trail continues its rolling course to a big new horse bridge over a very small flow. You reach this point at 5.8 miles in another fifty minutes.

Little changes as you continue. Beaver marshes lie to the right now as the trail heads southwest. An old logging road forks right, but you turn left—it is unmarked. A marsh with huge cedar stumps borders the road next, then you reach a log staging area and cross another creek in another twenty minutes, at 6.6 miles.

The roadway is so open there is little shade on a hot day. In ten minutes you recross the tiny creek—it is now flowing to your left—on a huge new bridge. Past it, the trail begins to climb—there is a huge boulder at the head of a cirque on your left. Then another log landing, many signs of logging, and open fields. You cross another small stream at 7.4 miles. Beyond there are lots of logging roads intersecting your route, which turns distinctly south. A long but gradual uphill brings you at 8.4 miles to the intersection with the Moose Pond-Shattuck Clearing Trail (section 10). Assuming forty minutes for the last segment, the walk can be done in about three and a half hours, though needed rests and lunch will add to this time.

12 Ermine Brook Slide on Santanoni

Bushwhack, slide-climb

The massive new slide on Ermine Brook offers one of the most exciting bushwhacks in the High Peaks. Torrential rains brought by Hurricane Gloria in September 1985 created the slide. Though not one of the widest or steepest in the Adirondacks, it may well be the longest. It begins at a headwall, or vertical rock face, nearly on top of the Santanoni Range at an elevation of almost 4200 feet. It courses sinuously down the western side of the range for over a mile, turns south, and diminishes gradually back to an ordinary brook. Ermine Brook then resumes a westerly course to the Moose Pond-Shattuck Clearing Horse Trail (section 10), where the bushwhack begins.

Since it is a 16.2-mile round-trip walk to the beginning of the 6-mile round-trip bushwhack, you may want to camp at Moose Pond or at Ermine Brook.

Ermine Brook Slide from the Headwall

Otherwise count on a ten- to twelve-hour day and a possible walk out on the horse trail after dark. You certainly do not want to bypass Moose Pond, for the view of the slide from the shore will give you an excellent indication of the route you will be following.

Walk toward Moose Pond (section 9) and continue north at 6.7 miles on the blue Horse Trail of section 10 to Ermine Brook, another 1.4 miles. Begin the bushwhack by heading upstream along the south side of Ermine Brook. There are vestiges of an old tote road at first, but this shortly becomes swampy and overgrown, and from here on, rock-hopping is almost always the best route. Within fifteen minutes a tributary comes in on your left. Avoid it, for it leads to the east side of Little Santanoni. Note that this brook is incorrectly shown on the 1953 USGS 15' map as the main fork of Ermine Brook.

You continue upstream, bearing right at this point with the larger flow of water; the going is surprisingly easy with relatively few blowdowns across the picturesque stream. In a few minutes the first of numerous pretty waterfalls appears. There is an inviting flat rock to rest on at this point.

Beyond this first falls, the grade steepens as you travel through a small gorge. There are more falls and one is a most interesting triple, with double chock-stones separating the three cascades. Beautiful moss-covered cliffs, more than fifty feet high, overhang the right side of the stream at this dramatic point. Near the top of the gorge is a good swimming hole. The grade slackens somewhat beyond the pool as the brook bed becomes less cobble-filled and more smooth and slabby.

Cobble soon returns, however, as Ermine Brook becomes quite flat; after an hour you find more places to rest as the brook begins to slide over wide,

Waterfall on Ermine Brook Slide

smooth slabs. Later, the going becomes steeper and more difficult as the brook is punctuated again by numerous cascades and cataracts of all types. In one place, the brook courses narrowly down a ramp-like flume.

Except in very high water, there is almost always room to stay with the brook. At a few spots with deep pools, you may have to detour away from the brook, but these detours are short and not very obstructed with blowdown. Be aware, however, that the mosses and rocks in the stream are slippery.

Past the most picturesque series of falls, the brook flattens somewhat and you have a taste of what is ahead. Debris piled at bends in the brook indicate the forces at work above. When you have traveled about 1.4 miles upstream, another tributary appears on your right. Avoid it, again staying with the larger flow of water. Within an hour and a half from the horse trail, piles of trees, branches, roots, and mud become larger and more numerous. At first they are confined to the bends of Ermine Brook; now they line all the banks.

At a bend heading north, the sun pours in; this is the result of the first obvious widening of the brook. Freshly exposed boulders litter the bed and banks; larger trees lay prostrate along the banks. Because of the force of the water and debris, virtually all of the trees are parallel to the flow of the stream and present surprisingly little impediment to the bushwhack. Already it is difficult to comprehend the power with which the side of the mountain moved through here.

Soon the bed bends east and becomes wider. Gigantic piles of debris line the way. You can begin to look back to distant hills. A hundred-foot bare wall appears ahead. This marks the beginning of the mile-long, nearly 2000-foot climb up the slide proper (up to now you have been walking in the widened brook bed) and the beginning of steady, steep climbing. The brook is still carrying a good flow of water and falls spectacularly down the left side of the wall.

The safest route up the bare wall is at the extreme right, where there are sufficient handholds; if in doubt, however, take to the trees at the side and avoid the bare rock. Above this point you are now slide-climbing. Be careful, though, for the going varies between steep, smooth slabs and areas of dangerously loose rock. It is usually safest to pick smooth slabs and zigzag up the slope.

The top of the slide begins to put in an occasional appearance; it is a grand sight with the headwall frowning down on those who would climb the slide. The slide track is now about 200 feet wide, with a mostly moderately steep grade. Looking back, you have glimpses of Moose Pond. Santanoni is soon visible dead ahead as the grade steepens and the bed becomes ever wider. At a swing to the right, the slide becomes over 300 feet wide. Dikes cut across the massive white slabs of anorthosite. Wide views to the south open up; Snowy Mountain is prominent on the skyline. The rest of the slide to the top is now visible. Only a few forlorn islands of vegetation dot the upper reaches of the slide. Bluets and bottle gentian contrast starkly with the surrounding bedrock.

Headwall of Ermine Brook Slide

Soon a tributary from the left side of the track cuts Ermine Brook's flow by about half; but even in dry times, the main brook has a surprisingly good flow, even within a few hundred yards of the headwall.

Views now include Long Lake beyond Catlin Lake, with Little Santanoni near at hand to the west. Small cliff faces dot its eastern slopes and suggest to the bushwhacker the possibility of exploring the western fork of Ermine Brook.

The grade now becomes very steep; your boots must be able to grip securely. Views west and northwest open up with the gained elevation. You see Mount Morris, the village of Tupper Lake, and Mount Emmons beyond the slopes of Santanoni. At one point it is possible to see Donaldson. As the headwall gets nearer, the slide track narrows somewhat. The panorama below includes most of the slide, the lakes and mountains already named, plus Goodnow, Blue, and Kempshall mountains.

When you are about 50 yards from the base of the headwall, the going becomes tricky; the slide is covered with a great deal of mud and loose rock, all of it unstable and very slippery. Use caution! There is no reason to continue beyond the base of the headwall, for the headwall is almost vertical and requires technical skills to climb. Further, the push through the scrub around the sides is difficult and there are no additional rewards, since the view from the top is the same as from the base.

If you should consider climbing to Santanoni's summit from here, note that although the distance north along the ridge top is only a little over a mile, the cripplebush is exceedingly thick, requiring two to three hours. Better to turn around, for the views are even better going down and the return to the horse trail takes only about two hours.

Long Lake Portal

THE DAGGER OF state land thrust southwest from the High Peaks approaches Long Lake Village and provides a corridor by which to approach the heart of the western High Peaks, the Cold River country. The Cold River is backpackers' territory—remote, seemingly difficult to reach, yet anything but inaccessible. Canoes plying Long Lake—and sharing the extraordinarily beautiful lean-tos and campsites along the lake's eastern shore—can bring backpackers to within 2.7 miles of Shattuck Clearing (see the Pine Point Trail, section 16). Horseback riders from either Axton-Coreys or Newcomb have a network of trails into this interior; at key campsites, the backpacker often encounters large groups of horses and riders. Backpackers also share some of the horse trails as routes to other foot trails, and the experience is not always pleasant. Those bent on shortening the routes into the recesses of the Cold River can arrange to fly to Plumley Point with Helms Aviation, reducing the trip by 7.6 miles.

The Cold River begins at the dam at the outlet of Duck Hole. Old timers like Clarence Petty, who knew the river well, remember that it ran cold in summer, in years after the first Duck Hole dam was built and the adjacent land was logged. But sometime in the '20s or '30s, the river warmed, and no one seems to be able to explain the change. The river is broad and open for most of its thirteen-mile course (as the crow flies). Meanders through swamps and marshes stretch the actual length to seventeen miles. For most of its length the river is wide, lined with huge boulders, and filled with boulders large and small. The river cuts through a glacial valley and the shores of the lower stretches are banks of sand and gravel. The mouth of the Cold River is at one of the quiet loops of the Raquette River.

Lowland glacial soils and access to a major river such as the Raquette made the Cold River a prime source of lumber. The lower stretches were logged early in the nineteenth century, and Shattuck Clearing was the hub of lumbering activity through 1920, when the state completed acquisition of this land. By then, logging for pulp had been so severe that whole stretches required reforesting by the Civilian Conservation Corps (CCC) in the 1930s, when a large CCC camp stood in Shattuck Clearing.

The full brunt of the 1950 hurricane fell upon the western High Peaks, destroying the cover on whole mountainsides. Roads were pushed into the interior to remove some of this timber, which was considered a fire hazard.

Except for one stretch of Northville-Placid Trail along the Cold River, and a segment of horse trail south of the river, all the trails follow these logging or fire roads. They are broad, easy to walk, generally dry, and good routes into the interior, though with one or two exceptions, they pass through scrub forests and plantations.

13 Northville-Placid Trail to Plumley Point

7.6 miles, 3¹/₂ hours, relatively level, blue markers

There is a parking lot for the Northville-Placid Trail on NY 28N, 1.5 miles east of Long Lake, 12.4 miles west of the Santanoni Preserve in Newcomb. A road opposite the parking area leads north 0.7 mile to a second parking area for those headed north. The trail, 100 feet beyond the parking area, immediately heads downhill. (The descent to lake level will be quite noticeable if you return on this route with a pack!) You begin by descending through a hardwood forest to reach the boundary of the High Peaks Wilderness Area in a nice stand of hemlocks with ferns underneath. Then you walk through a wetland and cross the stream that drains it, the outlet of Polliwog Pond, on a wide bridge at 0.6 mile. The trail continues a rolling course through an exceptionally beautiful hemlock forest that is open underneath. A sharp descent follows, then a more gradual descent to a second wetland. Here, at 1.1 miles, log stringers carry the trail and you can begin to see the lakeshore.

Less than half an hour from the trailhead, a path leads left across a tiny stream to the shores of Catlin Bay, a beautiful, deep bay with a lovely campsite sheltered by hemlock, cedar, and spruce. A path leads north along the shore to the lean-tos.

The trail continues rolling north, staying fairly close to lakeshore. At a height-of-land, the trail crosses an old road, then a very small stream. Here another path leads to a boulder-enclosed bay with one campsite, and the trail leads down to a point on the north side of the bay where a fire ring marks a second campsite.

The trail stays close to the cedar-lined shore beside a very handsome sandy bay. Hop rocks to cross the stream that flows into the bay. Suddenly the cover changes—birch and bracken along the shore attest to previous fires. The trail now begins to climb through a scrubby hardwood forest, reaching, at 3.3 miles, a knob 200 feet above the lake. A minor zigzag marks the descent from this knob. Back at lake level, at 4 miles, a three-log bridge takes you across a stream. Shortly beyond, a path leads to shoreline and a pretty campsite among the cedars and rocks. The trail enters a field (with raspberries and old foundations and modern privies) and stays to the east side of it. To the west are the two lean-tos on the wooded promontory of Kelly Point.

At 4.5 miles, no more than a two-hour walk (unless you have stopped to explore the bays and campsites), you reach the trail intersection at Kempshall Landing. The way right, east, is the abandoned trail on which to begin a bushwhack to Blueberry Mountain (see section 14).

There are several good campsites beneath the tall hemlock that cap the heights of the gorge beside the stream that flows into the lake here. The shore broadens into a sandy spit from which you can see the Seward Range as it descends west toward the Raquette River. Ampersand rises behind, on the horizon.

Fifty feet beyond the intersection, you cross the stream beneath some magnificent hemlocks. The trail, with gentle ups and downs, reaches a small bridge, then climbs slightly to a knoll of unbelievably tall, straight maples. There is a small grassy clearing with log stringers, a rocky stream, and then 200 yards beyond, a small cairn marking a path to the left. The path, at 5.5 miles, leads steeply down to lean-tos on the shore.

The trail continues to climb slightly, then begins a long, gradual downhill almost to lake level at a bridge over a small stream. The trail is, however, well back from the shore because of the private camps that line the lake here. You encounter several paths leading left to the camps, some posted signs, a spring-house surrounded by a wire fence, and many wet places in the trail. The spectacular forest of enormous maples and yellow birch makes up for the uncomfortable walking.

You have a glimpse of the lake just before the trail reaches a big and very handsome swamp, which lies to the right of the trail. Several paths, marked with posted signs, intersect the trail that stays close to the swamp. A sign stating "public lean-to ½ mile" keeps you on the proper route. You walk beside the marsh for a good ten minutes, enter the woods, then reach another, but very small, marsh. Here, you angle right, using a log to cross the stream, which drains the marshes. At this spot, which is not well marked, you turn almost east across the stream before curving back to continue north. Five minutes later, at 7.6 miles, you reach an intersection. A path heading toward lakeshore here or one just a hundred feet north both lead about 200 yards to the pine-covered, rocky knoll called Plumley Point. There is one lean-to on the point and a second 200 yards north along the shore. Views toward the north end of the lake show several points and islands and many sandy beaches.

14 Blueberry Mountain

Bushwhack

The fire tower on Kempshall Mountain used to offer wonderful views of the lake as well as northwest to the High Peaks. There is no view without the tower and the trail is officially closed. There are superb views from Blueberry, however, for its summit and southwestern slopes are bare. They were burned in 1913 in one of the fire storms that burned the organic soils right down to rock and mineral soil. Huge patches of the southwest flank of the mountain remain covered with no more than mosses and lichens. Either of two routes make a fairly easy bushwhack to the summit, suggesting that the best way to enjoy the mountain is a loop using both routes.

Start along the abandoned Kempshall Trail. It has grown in, but is definitely followable. The disturbed forest is dense with young maples and beech and witch hobble, making a thick understory. Generally following the stream, the route is remarkably straight. The trail climbs, then crosses a stream bed on a slippery log before beginning to climb quite steeply. After about a mile, and a half-hour walk, the trail descends slightly to cross the stream it has been following. Here, not far from the col between Kempshall and Blueberry, you turn away from the trail, heading generally southwest and uphill.

At first you have to fight through the witch hobble, then the forest opens a bit. It is fairly steep. As the grade eases, angle a bit more to the west. Again you encounter patches of witch hobble. After about a half hour you emerge on the ridgeline. Follow the open lichen-covered prong west to a slope that overlooks the south end of the lake. You can see the bridge, with Owls Head beyond.

From the summit, your route down is generally west, winding between the open slopes, looking for more views of the lake. From one patch, Lake Eaton is clearly visible. Mosses and lichens carpet the open patches, which become more steep as you descend. A leisurely twenty minutes will take you to the edge of the burn. Entering the woods again, you reach very steep slopes and a few small cliffs. Some you can descend, some you have to walk around. It is a lovely forest of taller spruce and balsam. A very tall cliff faces a long stretch of Blueberry's flanks and there are only a few places where you can descend it. At the bottom of the cliff a draw angles left. Cross it and continue west through an area of big stumps. You should intersect an old logging road. Turn right to follow it, for it is an easy route close under the steepest of Blueberry's slopes. Stay on it until it turns away from the lake. Here you are only a hundred feet or so from the trail and no more than 200 yards south of the trail intersection where you started. The descent takes about an hour even if you do not follow the route described, but take any route around the cliffs heading west toward the lake.

15 Plumley Point to Shattuck Clearing

4.1 miles, 2 hours with a pack, relatively level, blue markers

At the marked intersection near Plumley Point, the Northville-Placid Trail angles right, east, curving with the shoreline. A path leads directly to the northern lean-to and another to a campsite farther north along the shore. The trail curves east and crosses a sluggish stream. It continues through a very wet area with the aid of fairly new and very welcome stringers built by ADK. After a second set of stringers, the trail begins a gentle uphill, heading east.

The trail traverses the hardwood hill then gradually descends as land begins to slope away on both sides. Hardwoods give way to stands of pine and you begin to see a swamp two hundred yards to the left of the trail. You continue on the pine ridge, which becomes sort of a prong thrust out into a marsh.

Cold River from High Bridge east of Shattuck Clearing

Alders line the north side of the prong, open marsh lines the left. Finally, after less than an hour walk from Plumley Point, the prong leads to the edge of a marsh. You cross the open marsh on log stringers. This point, at 1.8 miles, was flooded just a few years ago, requiring a long detour to the north. Flags marking a path around the marsh are still visible, as are the large beaver houses of those responsible for the flooding.

Just beyond the marsh, the trail again mounts a pine knoll and within 100 yards you see a sign saying "trail," which indicates you should angle left to stay with it. At this point, a very faint path heads south. It gets even fainter as it crosses the marshes and it used to lead about 0.5 mile to the shores of Round Pond. It is a deceptive 0.5 mile, requiring as much as an hour of tough bushwhacking, but the pond has its rewards. The northwest shore of Round Pond's upper bay has a lovely sandy beach; the northeast shore has an excellent campsite on a pine-covered rise above the pond.

The trail now follows high ground, either a long esker or glacial ridge. A second marsh follows; it has some open water and two beaver houses. Then you mount another low ridge, this one covered with a pine plantation. Descending now to swamp level again, you cross the end of a marsh, hopping rocks to cross a small stream, then Pine Brook at 2.3 miles.

The very handsome and narrow trail continues along a spruce knoll with a carpet of lycopodia beneath. To the north there is a grassy marsh with standing snags, then a second beaver marsh. The trail enters spruce plantation and continues winding along an esker ridge. Beyond a pine knoll, you reach a big meadow to the right of the trail. There is a small open pond which has been larger. As a result two trails swing left around the meadow, but they rejoin in a raspberry patch. The trail circles around this point to a boulder, then crosses the outlet below the pond—without benefit of a bridge.

Popple and soft maple cover the next esker. You head down off it, then through a wooded draw to a red pine plantation on a knoll. To the left you can see a grassy marsh surrounding open water. A second red pine knoll leads to a clearing with a trail sign at the far end. The spot is 4 miles from the intersection near Plumley Point. A blue-marked trail turns left, west, to Pine Point (section 16). Straight ahead, the roadway leads to the much larger fields of Shattuck Clearing, where you will find fire rings and a picnic table and a hub of old gravel roads. The spot is 4.1 miles from Plumley Point intersection, 11.7 miles from the Northville-Placid Trailhead near Long Lake.

The fields of Shattuck Clearing were once the center of a major lumber operation and from them you have a superb view of the Seward Range. In the 1930s, there was a CCC camp here and its workers were responsible for the Scotch, red, and white pine plantations you just walked through. There is a ford across the river at the end of a dirt road to the east of the clearing and a sign warning you the weight limit on the bridge is three tons. There is no bridge. It and another that once stood three hundred yards downstream have washed away.

Cold River near Pine Point

16 Pine Point from Shattuck Clearing

2.6 miles, 1¼ hours, relatively level, blue markers

The sign at the intersection 0.1 mile south of Shattuck Clearing says, "3 miles to Pine Point," but the trail is definitely shorter. It needs clearing and obviously receives little use. Nevertheless, it is a handsome walk, and is quite useful to those hiking to Shattuck Clearing after a canoe trip to Pine Point, which is just upstream from the first rapids on the Cold River.

The trail begins along an old road and heads downhill to the river bank, near the site of one of the old bridges. A scrub forest surrounds the trail, which is filling in with brambles, asters, raspberries, meadowsweet, native dogwood, and bracken. The trail heads away from the river and up slopes covered with popple, then crosses a pine plantation. After dropping down to cross a small stream, the trail rises to a knoll planted more than fifty years ago with spruce. After winding through a balsam thicket, the trail finally returns to the river near an island.

The trail remains by the river, passing clumps of large cedars. There is a gravel bank on the far shore. Much of the trail is overgrown with alders crowding in various places. At just over 2 miles, there is a log bridge over a small stream. The trail turns away from the river, becomes obscure near a blowdown in a wet area, but continues not far from the river. Within an hour from the intersection, there is a slight rise to a balsam-covered knoll with one giant, straight pine. Several equally big pines stand nearby. An unmarked path leads along the shore to the point, just below the rapids, which you can reach by canoe. The river bend, the pines, and the approaching rapids make the spot obvious to those approaching from the Raquette by canoe.

Cold River Rocks below High Bridge

A word of caution: Two yellow jackets' nests are buried in the middle of the trail where it is close to the shore, not far from a stand of cedars. The point is approximately 1.4 miles from Pine Point, about 0.15 mile past the western end of the large island. Such an ephemeral thing would not ordinarily belong in a guide, except for the fact they have persisted for years and several people have reported stings. If you detour too far inland, south, to avoid the spot, you encounter a messy swamp, though you will find giant purple fringed orchis blooming in it in the first week of August.

17 Shattuck Clearing past Rondeau's to Duck Hole

11.9 miles, 7 hours, 480-foot total elevation gain plus an additional two small hills with 200 and 300 feet to climb, blue markers

This trail takes you through the heart of the Cold River wilds. Once past the roads built for fires and to harvest timber after the 1950 hurricane and disturbed forests east of Shattuck Clearing, the Northville-Placid Trail becomes a narrow route, cut expressly for that trail. You pass a lovely waterfall, two beautifully sited lean-tos, and the most undisturbed stretch of this river. Farther north, the trail passes the site of Noah John Rondeau's Hermitage; from there on to Duck Hole, the route is again along logging roads. But as anyone who has walked the route along the river will tell you, this is the best part of the northern segment of the Northville-Placid Trail.

From Shattuck Clearing, head east along the gravel road for 150 yards past the left fork that once led to a bridge. The Northville-Placid Trail forks inconspicuously left from the road. It is a very narrow trail, leading 0.1 mile past a campsite with a picnic table, through a bramble patch, and down, zigzagging through pine trees, to a spectacular wood and cable swinging bridge over Moose Pond Creek. (This creek is so designated to differentiate it from the Moose Creek which flows into the Cold River, not far from its beginning. That Moose Creek is, however, also the outlet of a Moose Pond.)

The trail winds across a spruce-covered knoll for another 0.6 mile to reach a second spectacular bridge that spans a narrow gorge high above the Cold River. The view from the bridge is of the Santanoni Range. It takes little more than twenty minutes to reach the gorge, with its waterfalls, deep pools, chutes, and potholes. The bridge's iron beams and cables are an anomaly in this wilderness setting. A guideboard with mileages stands on the north side of the bridge where a narrow path leads 100 feet uphill to join the tote road that used to be the principal route west from Shattuck Clearing. (Note that southbound hikers should watch for an arrow on a birch pointing to this path; it is easy to miss.)

Cold River Lean-tos Three and Four are west of this bridge, one within sight of it, the other 0.2 mile farther west along the roadway. The downstream lean-to sits above the river, with a magnificent view upstream to the bridge and the Santanoni Range beyond. (If you continue west to a point opposite Shattuck Clearing for just over 0.4 mile past the western lean-to, you reach a clearing regularly used by campers on horseback who approach along the main trail from Coreys. See section 27. Horses are technically restricted to this clearing, but careless riders have camped and tied up horses near the lean-to by the bridge, creating a mess that will take some time to disappear.

The blue-marked trail east along the gravel road climbs to a ledge high above the water which is here very wide, with a steep bank sloping to the boulder-strewn river. The forest cover is very scrubby, so there is no shade. You can see the cluster of islands in the river. At 1.6 miles, 0.8 from the Cold River Bridge, the trail crosses the stream that drains the shoulder of Emmons, then descends almost to river level. At 1.8 miles you are opposite a little rock ledge topped with cedar, then the river opens into the wide pool of Big Eddy, which lies at the foot of a wide waterfall.

All along this stretch of river there are views of slide-scarred slopes. The river is flowing from the north here, so in this stretch of trail, the rocky slope you see ahead is a shoulder of Emmons. The trail continues wide, mostly grassy underfoot with lycopodia and blueberries and thick carpets of trailing arbutus and creeping white winterberry, with clumps of bunchberry and twinflower to liven the walk. Pause to observe a long finger of boulders that angles into a now narrower and rockier river. The trail, filled with alders and meadowsweet, climbs to a bank forty feet above the stream, with views of a narrow gorge downstream and another widening upstream. The river has resumed its east-west course, so opposite this widening, the distant views are of the Santanoni Range. Just beyond, at 3.2 miles, you cross a stream that drains the ponds above on the shoulder of Emmons. For all there is to see, it will take under an hour to walk from the bridge to this point.

Santanoni Mountains from below Rondeaus

The trail now climbs to an esker-like ridge high above the river. Soon you reach the end of the road the trail has been following. The road was built to harvest timber after the 1950 hurricane. The trail beyond is one of the few stretches of the Northville-Placid Trail cut expressly for foot travel. The narrow footpath heads down and makes a sharp left turn, at a point where if you walk a few feet to the right there is an outcrop with excellent views of the river far below. Continuing with sharp ups and downs through balsam thickets, your pace slows. It takes nearly a half hour to reach, at 3.9 miles, the Millers Falls (Seward) Lean-to, which sits above the falls on a spruce knoll. Potholes and pools for swimming dent the smooth rock slabs that form the falls, making this a lovely spot to rest or camp. This is even a good campsite in bug season and you will find an excellent spring on the left side of the trail 100 yards beyond the lean-to. From the river bank above the falls there are good views of Couchsachraga and Panther.

Back on the trail, which is now quite narrow and rougher underfoot, you traverse a sprucy bank with cedars in a much deeper woods. The next hour between lean-tos is the most pleasant imaginable. The size of the forest—the towering hemlocks—contrasts sharply with the earlier part of the walk. A lovely stretch of trail hugs the river bank. Huge cedars overhang the river and enormous boulders fill its course. The scene is incredibly beautiful. You approach a bend with views south to Couchsachraga, then as the river bends north again you can look north to Emmons with its slide and Seward with all its rock patches.

Continuing close to the river, the trail makes another sharp bend, and there is a second chance to view Emmons. The trail pulls briefly away from the river to cross Ouluska Pass Brook (the new metric map calls it Seward Brook, but the former is the accepted name). There is no bridge, but a chain of rocks between the site of the old bridge and the confluence with the Cold River helps; however, this is a large stream and in high water will be difficult to cross. Just beyond, at 6 miles, you reach Ouluska Pass Lean-to, which sits right beside a broad stretch of shallow river. The many standing kettleholes in nearby marshes breed hordes of mosquitos that bedevil this site in July and August.

Upstream, the river makes another big curve to the north. You pass a survey marker, then reach a trail sign pointing you right. The trail is now back on a roadway and used to continue straight to bypass the Hermitage. You reach the bluff just short of 6.5 miles, less than fifteen minutes past the lean-to, where Rondeau's tent city of pole-like structures once stood. The hermit, who built his hut from lumber scavenged from Santa Clara Lumber Company camps, was resident here in the 1930s and '40s. Visitors and hikers who regularly brought him treats and mail were attracted to his camp.

In the raspberry field that was his city, you can find cultivated flowers which survive, among them *lychnis* with its red blooms. There are no summer views from the bluffs, but a path leads east, downhill to the river just above the point where the high dam was constructed. This flood dam was built in 1912 by John J. Anderson, a logger from Long Lake, who owned many tracts along the Cold River, all of which were sold to the state in the early decades of this century.

Beaver have flooded the marshes to the north and if you walk out on the beaver dam you can enjoy two wonderful panoramas. To the south you see Couchsachraga to the east of Panther. To the north you see Emmons on the left, the cut for Ouluska Pass with Donaldson and its slides behind, then Seymour to the right.

Leaving the bluff, the trail makes a right angle turn to the north and quickly descends to the old roadway again. Continuing northeast, the trail rounds the beaver marsh, crosses a little stream on a rickety bridge, and makes a sharp left turn. The old trail southeast to the river, which branched off here, is no longer visible. The trail bends right, then left again; and 1 mile from the Hermitage you reach the spot where another old road used to angle back west. It led to a lumber camp site (even now it is an open field) and if you can find it, it is one of the easier ways to reach Ouluska Pass Brook for a bushwhack up along it to the slide on Emmons (section 29).

Tall, straight maples crown the ridge you climb, winding north, then east. You continue climbing, passing beneath ledges to the north of the trail, then entering a draw that continues up. It takes nearly an hour to walk the 1.4 miles from the Hermitage to the height-of-land above a tiny unnamed pond. Seymour rises above the pond. A gentle traverse down the hillside leads to a stream crossing (the outlet of the pond) at 8.5 miles. Fifteen minutes of ups and downs lead to a second stream crossing. Here a field to the east of the stream marks the site of a lumber camp. Angle left through the field (raspberries again!) and continue to a second field. At 10.5 miles, you cross a third stream

Seymour and Sawtooth Range from Mountain Pond

(the outlet of Mountain Pond) on stones that replace a washed out bridge. There is an enormous amount of rubble in the trail, which now climbs a hillside southeast of the pond. Corduroy lines the roadway, which curves around the pond. Stones, put in the low spot in the trail at its closest approach to the pond, mark the easiest place to leave the trail. Walk no more than 150 feet to the marshy bordered pond with its stumps and snags. It was much larger in the past.

A rise in the trail leads quickly to the Ward Brook Truck Trail (section 25) from Coreys at 10.2 miles. Guide boards give distances for all three directions from this point. Turning right, east, the wide road makes a gentle descent through pretty woods. Soon you hear the river again and at 10.6 miles reach the first Cold River Lean-to. It sits on a knoll high above the confluence with Moose Creek. The pools and chutes below the confluence are a great place to cool off!

The second lean-to is to the left of the trail, 50 feet beyond the first. The bridge over Moose Creek is down a short grade just beyond. The trail climbs a small hill east of the crossing, then descends to river level and a fork right at 11 miles to the ford over Cold River (section 11). The wide road continues high and dry to the north of the river, descending slightly to the big clearing at Duck Hole. One lean-to sits hidden in the trees on a small bluff to the left of the roadway. The second is to the right, immediately above the dam that creates Duck Hole. You reach the dam at 11.9 miles, after walking for six and a half hours from Shattuck Clearing, though stops to enjoy the sights will add at least two or three hours.

Confusingly, the trail to Bradley Pond (section 4) is blue-marked, like the Northville-Placid Trail. Northbound hikers bear left at the end of the road, while those headed for Bradley Pond cross the dam.

Coreys Road

The Northwestern Region

THE RAQUETTE RIVER enters Tupper Lake in a wide, marshy expanse along NY 30, at the southern edge of the village of Tupper Lake. If you look east from the highway across the still waters, the rugged profile of the Seward Range rises steeply above the river's basin. These two most prominent features on the western edge of the High Peaks region are contrasts in more than just elevation. This stretch of the Raquette River is one of the most popular canoe routes in the park, and each year thousands enjoy the easily accessible, scenic paddling between Long Lake and Tupper Lake. The Seward Range, on the other hand, remains one of the least traveled areas in the state. Though it is encircled by a network of trails, the range's size, rough contours, and dense forest cover make it a challenge to explore. Four summits exceed 4000 feet, and those climbing to them must use usually well-defined, but unmaintained, herd paths or face a grueling bushwhack for which careful planning is a must.

The main access to the adventures described in this chapter is along Coreys Road, which turns south off NY 3, 2.6 miles east of the junction of NY 30, between the villages of Tupper Lake and Saranac Lake. A large DEC sign at its beginning tells you that this is the western approach to Duck Hole and the High Peaks. The road is named after Jesse Corey, the first white settler in the area, who ran the Rustic Lodge in the 1800s. Mileages from NY 3 are as follows:

0.0 Junction, Coreys Road and NY 3
0.5 Canoe access at edge of Stony Creek Ponds
0.6 Canoe carry to Stony Creek Ponds
1.2 Pavement ends
1.9 Side road leading 0.2 mile to Axton Landing canoe access
2.0 Side road leading 0.1 mile to Axton Landing canoe access
2.5 Iron bridge over Stony Creek and state land boundary
2.7 Trailhead for Raquette River trails
3.3 Rock Pond trailhead
3.8 Pickerel Pond trailhead
5.7 Trailhead for trails around the Seward Range
5.8 Gate where road enters private property (road ends at Ampersand Lake)

Large camping areas are located on both sides of the road at the south end of the iron bridge over Stony Creek. This is a popular spot for trucks, campers, and families with large tents, but there are no facilities and impact can be heavy. There are also several turnoffs of varying size where parking and camping are allowed between this point and the Seward trailhead. No camping of any kind is allowed at trailheads. An iron gate just past the Raquette River trailhead marks the limit of winter maintenance and the road is closed in winter and early spring.

In addition to the points of access for the Raquette River at Axton Landing and Stony Creek, there is a public access facility on NY 3, 1.5 miles west of its junction with NY 30.

Most of the trails in this region are horse trails or combination horse and foot trails and tend to be long and uneventful. In dry seasons, the churned-up sandy sections can be hot and dusty, but more often than not, your greatest inconvenience will be the extensive muddy stretches that make foot travel quite unpleasant. Add to this the animal waste at lean-tos and other stopping points, and you may wish to reserve travel through the area until winter. That is not a bad idea since the wide horse trails make excellent cross-country ski routes, and if you have the proper skills and equipment many extended wilderness ski tours are possible.

The keen-eyed hiker will note numerous old logging and tote roads fading in and out of the woods, and their history is the story of the region. In 1890, 400,000 acres owned by William West Durant were bought by a group of lumber companies. Of that total, 35,000 High Peaks acres were controlled by the Santa Clara Lumber Company, which existed from 1888 to 1938. The company purchased valuable stands of pine, spruce, hemlock, and hardwoods for $1.50 an acre. Their tract included all of Township 26, which spans the Raquette River from Coreys almost to the Cold River, and Township 27, which stretches from Ampersand Lake to Duck Hole and includes Mount Seward, Mount Donaldson, Seymour Mountain, and the Sawtooth Mountains.

In 1903, Titus Meigs, president of Santa Clara, traveled with guide and woodlands manager Gene Bruce the breadth of the holding, following a route Bruce pioneered. He was the first white man to traverse the unbroken virgin forest in the notch between the Seward Range and the Sawtooth Mountains. Their trek took them to Preston Ponds and out to the Upper Works at Tahawus, to meet Verplanck Colvin. Colvin had been called on to help settle the boundaries of the Gore North of Township 47. This gore, like many in the Adirondacks, resulted from patent lines that did not meet. The state claimed that Santa Clara did not own the Gore and assessed the company a trespassing fine of $500,000 for cutting timber on the tract. Clarence Petty, who grew up in one of Santa Clara's camps, thinks this was not the company's only trespass of state lands.

"What a wonderful forest it was," wrote Meigs, "so largely comprised of spruce that the other species were rare by comparison. The soft humus, the moss, the blackness, relieved and intensified by an occasional shaft of sunlight, the brilliant water of the streams, rushing over the rocks and pebbles in virgin purity." He claimed the company cut only the larger spruce, but the forest still yielded 66 cords per acre.

The company was proud that only two small fires ever burned in these tracts, one at a camp at Seward (Ouluska Pass) Brook, inadvertently set by the Health Department, the other at a camp near Ward Brook, accidently set by the careless pipe of a member of the USGS crew.

In later years the company logged high on the steep, rocky slopes where roads were too steep (over 40°) to permit hauling by teams. The company built roads with alternate steep and level stretches, and used engines to haul up teams and empty sleds, then lower them, attached to cables. Later the company devised a modified Barrenger brake to hold back the teams.

After logging the heavily wooded slopes of Township 26 for twenty years, the land west of the Raquette was sold to the state in 1916 for $23 an acre. Most of Township 27, the Seward Tract, was sold to the state in 1920, with 18,000 acres bringing over a half-million dollars.

Most of the company's roads have faded—those well-built roads that serve as today's horse trails were logging company roads improved as fire roads by the old Conservation Department in a controversial program that lasted from 1934 to 1936. Some were rebuilt with modern equipment to salvage timber blown down by the hurricane of November 1950. The Seward Range and Cold River Valley were two of the hardest hit areas during that "Big Blow."

18 Stony Creek Ponds and Ampersand Brook

Canoeing, camping, fishing, paths

Stony Creek Ponds with their many lobes and bays have been a strategic link between the Raquette and Saranac river systems for centuries; Indians paddled this way long before white men began to use this route over 160 years ago. As early as 1858, a party reported fishing the creek, which "winds and twists like a boa constrictor, in a flat meadow overgrown with swamp maples and alders." That is a better description of the creek than its name, Stony.

From the confluence of Stony Creek and the Raquette River, a paddle of 2.5 miles will take you to the upper end of the Stony Creek Ponds in under an hour. A 1.6-mile portage will then take you to the southern end of Upper Saranac Lake along a route known as the Indian Carry. If you choose this route instead of beginning the carry at Axton Landing (section 19), you will have about 2 miles of additional paddling, but the carry distance to Upper Saranac Lake is reduced by 1.4 miles.

You can enter one of the upper ponds from Coreys Road 0.5 mile from NY 3.

The roadside is private, but the owner has granted permission for canoeists to cross. Careful attention to parking and access signs will allow this convenience to continue. At 0.6 mile, a marked carry leads 150 yards to a put-in point on the south shore of the pond.

It is also possible to launch your canoe into Stony Creek at the campsite area at 2.5 miles, where Coreys Road crosses the creek on an iron bridge. Paddling 0.3 mile southwest, downstream, takes you through a marshy area to the Raquette River, 0.5 mile above Axton Landing. Paddling upstream, Stony Creek swings north and winds its way into a peaceful alder- and willow-lined stretch. As of 1988, there was only one low beaver dam to negotiate. However, in times of low water, you may have to drag your canoe over some spots.

After thirty minutes and 1.2 miles, Stony Creek opens up into the lower pond, with Ampersand Brook flowing in on the right. The surrounding land is private and several camps and homes line the west bank. Ahead to the right is a wide channel that will take you under a road and into the upper ponds which are, for the most part, bays of a large central pond. To reach the carry, proceed 0.3 mile northwest to a narrow channel that leads to the small pond where the western bay access points can be found on the southern and western edges.

State land borders most of the northern portion of the ponds. Seven designated campsites, easily accessible by canoe, provide a little more privacy than those at Coreys Road. Campsites one and two are found on the south and north banks of the narrow channel. Sites three through six, as well as an unnumbered one between three and four, are situated clockwise around the northernmost bay, which is separated from the main pond by an island. Campsite five has an especially nice sand beach.

Ampersand Brook can be canoed for a little over 1.5 miles before an increasing number of snags make navigation frustrating. This little side trip may seem insignificant and it is probably overlooked by most paddlers, but the lack of traffic adds to its quiet, deep-woods character. From the pond, paddle south then east past a sandy bank on the left to a long beaver dam at 0.3 mile. Above the dam, a large wetland extends east toward Stony Creek Mountain. To continue up the brook, turn right and you will soon pass through the remains of an old dam constructed of posts. The way leads south, then east through dense forest where you may see remains of old rowboats and broken cable crossings. About a mile past the dam, blowdown and snags become annoying and you will probably not wish to continue much farther.

From the camping areas at Coreys Road, paths follow the east banks of Stony Creek. One heads southwest for 0.3 mile to the Raquette River and four more campsites. Another follows an old road east and north for ten minutes to the limit of vehicle use, after which the path narrows and becomes hard to find. It ends less than ten minutes later at a nondescript point on the creek.

Raquette River near falls

19 Raquette River Access

Canoeing

You can reach the Raquette River from Axton Landing by turning right at the Axton Landing sign on Coreys Road, 1.9 miles from NY 3. A dirt road leads 0.2 mile to a large clearing and sandy beach on the river, then loops back to rejoin Coreys Road in 0.1 mile. Axton is a shortened version of "axe town," the name given to the Santa Clara Lumber Camp that once occupied the spot. Around 1900, the site was taken over by the Cornell School of Forestry, which accounts for the numerous plantations of various evergreens found throughout the area. No buildings remain today, but in the summer, the landing is frequently congested with hoards of canoeists.

Heading downstream from Axton Landing, it is 8 miles to the lean-tos at Trombley Landing, 9.5 miles to the public access facility on NY 3, and 16.5 miles to Tupper Lake. Upstream, it is 0.5 mile to the confluence of Stony Creek, 6.5 miles to the foot of Raquette Falls, 7.8 miles to the upper end of the falls, 13.8 miles to Long Lake, and 23.3 miles to Long Lake village. The only carry between the two lakes is 1.3 miles along the southeast shore around Raquette Falls. Due to the sinuous nature of the river, these mileages are approximate. Your judgment can easily be thrown off by the many secondary channels, side washes, and oxbows you will encounter, so pay careful attention to your position and direction of travel.

You can also put in on Stony Creek at the iron bridge and paddle 0.3 mile downstream to the river. This way takes 0.2 mile off the upstream trip, but adds 0.8 mile to the downstream journey.

20 Raquette Falls and Carry by Trail

Horse trail, hiking, cross-country skiing, waterfall, camping, lean-tos, swimming, picnicking, fishing
4.5 miles to base of falls, 2¼ hours; 5.8 miles to top of falls, 2¾ hours, easy grades, yellow markers

The Horse Trail to Raquette Falls begins at a large parking area on the right side of Coreys Road, 2.7 miles from NY 3. A wide, sandy road, marked with yellow horse-trail markers heads south from the register, reaching a fork in 150 feet. The foot trail right follows red markers to a lean-to 200 yards away. The trail goes past the lean-to to the sandy edge of the river and the four campsites reached by the path from the iron bridge (section 18).

The Horse Trail continues south along the old dirt road through a mixed woods, passing a large, split glacial erratic on the left after twenty minutes.

Markers are almost nonexistent, but the way is obvious. The river is never visible, although the forest on the right occasionally opens up near wetlands and side channels. After one hour, you should notice an old sign on the right that marks the side trail to the Hemlock Hill Lean-to. At 2.2 miles, this is the halfway point on the trail and the 0.5 mile hike to the lean-to is a pleasant diversion. Descending west along an old road, swing right and avoid a faint road that forks left into blowdown. The trail levels, narrows, and heads north, passing a flooded area on the left. Not far beyond, the lean-to, in good condition, sits high above the river and a path to the right drops steeply down to the water's edge.

Beyond the junction, the Horse Trail swings southeast and arrives at another junction at 2.3 miles. Straight ahead is the link trail (section 22), which will take you to the Calkins Brook Truck Trail. Turn right here and drop to a wide wooden bridge crossing Palmer Brook. After fifteen minutes, the trail descends to a low area with a grassy marsh on the right. An ascent returns you to the woods and as the trail levels off, look for an unmarked path to the right. It will take you 300 feet to a lean-to and several adjacent tent sites above a large sandy beach on the river. A path leads 200 feet upstream to a knoll where a second lean-to and tent site area are situated. Both sites have outhouses and all structures are in good shape.

Several side paths lead right from the Horse Trail to the upstream lean-to, 100 feet away, but your attention will likely be focused on the trail itself since it has suddenly become very muddy. After fifteen minutes, the worst is over and you cross a stream. A short rise is followed by a steady switchback descent with a few more mud holes. Several old roads are evident as the trail levels out. A path along one to the right leads 150 feet to a campsite by the river. Just beyond, the trail crosses the outlet of Dawson Pond (section 21), then comes to an intersection. A hitching rail and sign mark the end of horse travel.

The left fork at the intersection leads to a large clearing, the site of a former inn and homestead. When the area passed into the ownership of the state, a commodious interior ranger station was built here. It is manned roughly from May to October. The right fork leads to a register at the lower end of the carry and a large sandy beach at the foot of Raquette Falls. The river is filled with large boulders and is quite scenic. During the summer months, this area is frequently congested with visitors arriving by foot, horse, canoe, or—from Tupper Lake—motorboat.

The carry passes between the clearing and the river through open woods with several campsites and one lean-to. It steadily ascends to the southwest for fifteen minutes before reaching the height-of-land, 0.9 mile from the clearing. It then descends the final 0.4 mile to the wide, sandy take-out area above the falls. An outhouse is located on the east side of the carry, 100 yards from the river; a lean-to, accessible by canoe, sits on the west side of the river.

Raquette Falls is actually a series of rapids and falls that is not visible from the trails. Many paths lead through the woods to the banks high above the churning waters, so be careful if you choose to follow them. Occasionally, someone tries to "shoot the falls" in a canoe. The ranger says that he first learns of these attempts when he sees pieces of gear and canoe fragments washing down the river near his station. A mangled canoe near a maintenance shed reminds everyone that the carry is the safe route.

21 Dawson Pond

Path, hiking, fishing
1 mile, 20 minutes, slight ascent

This pond is said to have been named for George Dawson, editor of the Albany Journal, who was among the first to call for the establishment of an Adirondack Park.

The path to Dawson Pond is unmarked, but is such a popular side trip that the way is well worn. It begins at the southeastern corner of the clearing and ascends easily, crossing one small wet area. It ends at the edge of the pond near its outlet. The depth of the pond and the cold spring that feeds it appear to make good fishing. Its shoreline is quite brushy, so the best way to fish it is from a canoe or raft. The remains of several old rowboats can be found near the pond's outlet.

22 Link Trail
Between Raquette River and Calkins Brook Horse Trails

Horse trail, hiking, cross-country skiing
3.4 miles, 1¹/₂ hours, 600-foot vertical rise to height-of-land, followed by 300-foot descent, yellow horse-trail markers

This is a useful connector between the two major trails west of the Seward Range, but most of the time it is not visually interesting. With the numerous muddy sections and a long, steady ascent, you may wish you had a horse under you. Yellow horse-trail markers are rarely seen. Leaving the Raquette River Horse Trail from the junction near Palmer Brook, this trail heads west-southwest, paralleling the brook for 0.6 mile before crossing it on a wooden bridge in a wetland. A short rise takes you to a vly where you cross a stream on its far side. The trail now heads south-southeast and slowly begins to climb through a mature hardwood forest. The route becomes muddier and steeper, finally reaching the height-of-land after one hour and 2.7 miles. A brief level stretch is followed by a steep, muddy descent where you will lose half of the elevation you gained in the past hour. Arriving at the Calkins Brook Trail, you will be relieved to leave the mud behind.

23 Rock Pond

Hiking, canoeing, fishing
0.4 mile, 10 minutes, level, blue markers

The trail to Rock Pond is a delightful little wilderness route that, despite its shortness, gives you a true sense of being in the deep woods. Old blue DEC markers are very rare, but the foot tread is well defined. A small sign marks its beginning on the south side of Coreys Road, 3.3 miles from NY 3. There is room for two or three vehicles on the widened shoulder of the road. Beginning in a mixed woods, you will notice a few old, deteriorating log treadways. After a muddy crossing of a small stream, the forest becomes dominated by tall hemlocks and cedars. A slight rise ahead, however, takes you into a mature hardwood section with many nice maples and yellow birches. The trail then drops through a tall hemlock grove to the grassy edge of the pond. Its banks are lined with large rocks and dead, fallen timber. A path continues on to the left, through the grove for 300 feet, passing areas where people have camped. Camping is not recommended, though, because the open ground is quite uneven and too close to the water. If you take this trail at dawn, you may be rewarded by the sight of ducks gliding on the water or a beaver making its morning rounds.

24 Pickerel Pond

Path, hiking, canoeing, fishing
0.3 mile, 10 minutes

Pickerel Pond is almost identical to Rock Pond in size and approach. At a turnoff for two or three vehicles on the south side of Coreys Road, 3.8 miles from NY 3, a small sign marks the trailhead. There are no markers. The trail starts off easily, ascending an old road that quickly levels off before swinging right into blowdown. The path leaves the road at the outside of the curve, drops down to the left, and passes over the remains of old log walkways. You soon arrive at the brushy edge of the pond where it is possible to put a canoe in. A western shoulder of the Seward Range looms over the coniferous swamp on the opposite side.

25   Blueberry Foot Trail and Ward Brook Truck Trail

Hiking, cross-country skiing, camping, lean-tos
8.7 miles, 4¹/₂ hours to the Northville-Placid, Trail, 400-foot
elevation change over easy grades, red markers

Though it follows fragments of old logging roads along much of its 4.6 miles, the Blueberry Foot Trail is the only exclusive foot trail in the region. Since it is the principal access route into the High Peaks interior from the northwest, it is wide and usually well maintained, making it a good ski trail as well. It ends at an intersection with the Ward Brook Truck Trail, a DEC service road that comes in from private lands to the north. The route to Duck Hole continues on the truck trail, and at the 8.7-mile point, it merges with the Northville-Placid Trail and the two continue east an additional 1.7 miles to Duck Hole. Red DEC markers are found frequently on the Blueberry Trail, but are scarce on the Ward Brook Truck Trail section.

The trail begins at a large parking area on the south side of Coreys Road, 5.7 miles from NY 3. This is also the trailhead for a horse trail (section 26) that parallels the Blueberry Foot Trail. A sign just to the right of the register marks its beginning. Following red DEC markers, you dip into a dense spruce bog where ladies tresses orchids rise up out of the sphagnum and spruce grouse hide in the shadows. Several sections of log and plank walkways are provided here and you should make every effort to use them to protect the bog community. They can be extremely slippery, though, so use care—especially if you have a full pack. After ten minutes, the trail rises into a drier, mature hardwood section. A moderately steep pitch is followed by a level stretch where you enter private land. Both sides of the trail are private, but only the left is posted.

After thirty-five minutes, 1.3 miles from the trailhead, the trail descends to a junction with a DEC service road coming in from the north. That road, barred by an iron gate north of the Blueberry Trail, connects with the private road extension of the Coreys Road toward Ampersand Lake. It continues south for almost 10 miles to Shattuck Clearing on the Cold River and was once used by the rangers to reach the interior station that was located there. It now serves as the Calkins Brook Horse Trail (section 27). After the Blueberry Foot Trail crosses the road, it dips to cross a stream, and begins following the route of a grassy old road through open woods. You cross several streams in the next forty-five minutes and you should catch glimpses of Blueberry Pond through the trees to the left. A large boulder soon appears on the left and a tall yellow birch growing on its top has sent down roots so big that they have formed a bark covering of their own. An annoying wet section follows and it signals the end of both private land and the old road. Another boulder and tree arrangement, this one dead, lies off to the left at the end of the wet area.

Height-of-land is at 2.5 miles after one and a half hours and you drop steeply to cross the largest stream on the trail on a haphazard pile of logs. Gradually descending, you cross another stream and come to some recently constructed planking that rises in steps over a wet area. Now Blueberry Lean-to is not far ahead, at 4.5 miles. A stream just beyond has the remains of a small wooden trough, presumably to aid in collecting water. The foot trail enters a grassy clearing at 4.6 miles, where it ends at a junction with the Ward Brook Truck Trail. Like the Calkins Brook Horse Trail before, this road comes in from private land near Ampersand Lake and was formerly used by rangers to reach the interior station that was located at Duck Hole.

Turning right on the Truck Trail (a misnomer, since vehicles are barred), you head southeast and, at 4.7 miles, pass the junction where the parallel Horse Trail (section 26) enters on the right. Horses, as well as hikers, are allowed to continue south to the Cold River region. Ahead, you can see a wide wood and iron bridge spanning a sizeable stream that drains the slopes of Seward. Before reaching it, you may notice a path turning left from the road that goes to some campsites. They are heavily used and not recommended. The stream is the one used for the ascent of Seward Mountain (section 28) and the path along it begins on the opposite side.

In the next ten minutes, you cross two more streams on wood and iron bridges. An easy climb then takes you to the Ward Brook Lean-to and its outhouse at 5.4 miles. Several paths surround the lean-to, but they lead nowhere. Two minutes beyond, on the opposite side of a stream that runs through a culvert under the road, the path up Seymour Mountain (section 31) begins. A long, gradual ascent in the trail lasts for fifteen minutes before leveling off at a clearing on the right where there are two lean-tos. At 6.1 miles, you come to the site of the Number Four lumber camp, Santa Clara's headquarters after the sale of Township 26. In a small clearing on the left, foundation posts and artifacts from it can still be seen. A small stream behind the lean-tos supplies water and an outhouse sits on a rise across the road.

The ascent continues for the next twenty minutes, passing a clearing on the left and crossing three major streams. After reaching height-of-land at 7 miles, you begin a gradual descent over a series of easy ups and downs, crossing several more streams, one of which has a wood and iron bridge. Beyond the lean-tos, the forest character has changed from open hardwoods to dense evergreens and back again. At 8.1 miles, the road enters a sizeable wetland with open water to the left. This area is prone to flooding, and as of 1988 up to six inches of water flooded the road for about 75 feet.

Beyond the wetland, the trail rises easily as it skirts a hill to the east, then drops to the well-marked junction at 8.7 miles where the Northville-Placid Trail (section 17) joins the Ward Brook Truck Trail from the right.

26 Horse Trail Parallel to Blueberry Foot Trail

Hiking, cross-country skiing
5.2 miles, 2²/₃ hours, 600-foot rise to height-of-land, followed by 300-foot drop to Ward Brook Truck Trail, moderate grades

This trail has several extremely muddy sections. It is also longer and has more tiring grades than the Blueberry Foot Trail. The only reason for the non-equestrian to take it is for the sake of curiosity or for a more challenging ski route. Yellow horse-trail markers are evident at the start, but soon become nonexistent. Beginning at the same parking area, the trail climbs slightly south past the register on an old logging road. After ten minutes, you bear right, avoiding an old trail ahead, then dip to a wet spot. A few minutes later, the trail splits for five hundred feet, the left fork being the drier route. You soon drop steeply to the Calkins Brook Horse Trail (section 27) at 1.5 miles. The Blueberry Foot Trail is a short five minutes to the left, north, if you've had enough.

If you choose to continue, cross the road and begin a gradual ascent, crossing a major stream after thirty minutes. At 2.7 miles, the trail levels off as it passes through an interesting draw near the 2400-foot level. A long, steady ascent begins at 3.2 miles, but it is straight and relatively dry. After climbing magnetic south for ten minutes, you turn sharp left and cross a stream, then resume your steady, straight climb for another five minutes. The trail then bends left, crosses a large stream at 3.7 miles and drops steeply toward magnetic north. You cross more streams as the trail works its way east-southeast, dropping finally to the Ward Brook Truck Trail at a point 0.1 mile south of the end of the Blueberry Foot Trail.

27 Calkins Brook Horse Trail
To Latham Pond and Shattuck Clearing

Horse trail, hiking, cross-country skiing, camping, lean-tos, swimming
8.7 miles, 3¹/₂ hours (10.1 or 10.3 miles, 4¹/₄ hours from parking area), long but easy grades

This trail is the longest in the area and is not very interesting. It is dry to a fault for most of its length and your hiking shoes may be dusty before you reach Shattuck Clearing. Access is by way of hiking the first 1.3 miles of the Blueberry Foot Trail (section 25) or the first sloppy 1.5 miles of the parallel Horse Trail (section 26). There are very few yellow horse-trail markers and rare yellow foot-trail markers. Several miles have no markers at all.

From the junction with the latter trail, head south past an old wagon on the left. A path beyond leads off to the left to a littered campsite. The trail gently ascends, passing a small clearing on the right. Twenty minutes and 1 mile past the junction, a height-of-land marks the beginning of a long, gradual descent. In the next mile, you cross a small stream on a concrete bridge, then approach Calkins Brook as it tumbles down from the Seward Range. The brook is spanned by a wood and iron bridge at 2.4 miles, only to be recrossed on a similar bridge five minutes later. The woods in this area are a noteworthy variety of balsam, spruce, cedar, hemlock, and white birch. The trail now levels out and you cross two small wooden bridges.

At 3.6 miles, the Link Trail (section 22) from the Raquette River Horse Trail comes in on the right. You have almost reached the halfway point between the parking area and Shattuck Clearing. Twenty minutes later, a moderate descent brings you to a clearing at 4.9 miles where the Calkins "Creek" Lean-tos sit off to the right. Each lean-to is in good shape and has its own fireplace and picnic table. A hitching rail stands just beyond and a single outhouse in fair shape is to the rear. Calkins Brook is across the road to the left.

Leaving the lean-tos, you immediately cross Calkins Brook on a wood and iron bridge, and begin a twenty-minute ascent that takes you past two sandpits and over a concrete bridge. After leveling off at 6.1 miles, you begin a steady descent that ends thirty-five minutes later at a wetland where the southern flanks of Mount Emmons are visible to the northeast.

At 7.3 miles, you cross Boulder Brook on a wooden bridge and, after fifteen minutes more of minor ups and downs, arrive at a junction at the 8.1-mile point. A side trail follows an old road to the left for four hundred feet to its end at the outlet of Latham Pond. The pond's shoreline is mostly brushy, interrupted by large rocks and dead timber. The mountain view across the far end of the pond includes Emmons and Donaldson, as well as several lesser summits of the range.

From the junction, the horse trail turns right, descending gently through a pine plantation to another junction where a large sandpit is visible to the right. There are several campsites in this area and the trail to the left leads to Cold River Lean-tos, numbers Three and Four. Ahead is the Cold River and the site of the former bridge crossing to Shattuck Clearing (see section 16).

28 The Seward Range
Seward, Donaldson, and Emmons from the Ward Brook Truck Trail

Strenuous climb along path
2.1 miles, 3 hours to Seward, 2340-foot vertical rise; 1 mile, 1 hour to Donaldson, 400-foot drop followed by 240-foot rise; 1 mile, 50 minutes to Emmons, 250-foot drop followed by 150-foot rise

Sometime before 1840, this mountain was named for William Henry Seward, governor of New York and secretary of state under President Lincoln. Colvin may have been the first to climb the mountain and he described it after his visit of October 15, 1870. "The view was magnificent, yet differing from the other of the loftier Adirondack mountains in that no clearing was discernible; wilderness everywhere; lake on lake, river on river, mountain on mountain, numberless." It was this peak that inspired Colvin to call for the formation of a park to ensure water and timber supplies. The view is little changed from his day, all because of the creation of that Park.

The Ward Brook Truck Trail leads to the favored approach to the Seward Range via a path that is generally well defined. The path is steep and eroded, however, and since it follows alongside, and frequently in, a stream, it can be quite wet, particularly in the upper reaches. With this in mind, plus the ups and downs between the three summits, it is a fatiguing route for most climbers. An additional problem is that if you proceed all the way to Emmons, you must either traverse the entire range in reverse to return to the Ward Brook Truck Trail or drop down into Ouluska Pass and return via the Northville-Placid Trail. This second option is described as an ascent route in section 29. Either way takes a full day and it is recommended that you pack in to the base on one day, begin your climb early on the second and pack out on the third. Remember to figure in rest stops and time for summit photography when making your plans.

The path begins on the eastern side of the first stream on the Ward Brook Truck Trail south of its junction with the Blueberry Foot Trail (section 25). Ten minutes after passing through some sites where camping is no longer allowed, you should pass a large boulder with trees on its top, and cross a muddy slope beyond. Ascending through a birch and maple section, you will come to a pretty flume where the nearby rock can be slippery. After fifty minutes, in an area of tall white birches and dense balsams, the path goes to the edge of the stream and you should notice several small waterfalls upstream. It is recommended that you cross the stream here. Ten minutes farther, the stream splits and you cross the right fork over the small mound that splits it. In less than five minutes you swing over to the edge of the left fork.

At this point, you must follow the path up the stream to another fork, where you turn left and leave the stream for two minutes before bearing around to the right to recross this fork. The path becomes exceedingly wet now and there are several small rivulets that may confuse you. By following the foot tread, you will return to the main stream, which is off to your right. Two hours will have passed and the woods have become increasingly thicker. Dense spruce and balsam, with patches of white birch and mountain ash seem to close in on all sides. Your first view occurs as you rise up on a high spot to overlook Ampersand Lake and the rugged Sawtooth Mountains, with Whiteface Mountain in the distance. From here, the path is almost entirely in the stream and the going is slippery and often muddy. This continues for at least half an hour until you reach a ten-foot headwall that forces you to turn left. There are three or four places where you can attempt to scale the headwall; the further you go to the left, the lower it gets. Once on top, the path turns right and follows the edge, giving you a field of view that extends from the Saranac Lakes in the north-northwest, past Ampersand Mountain, to far away Whiteface in the northeast. This is the only spot from which this view is possible.

The path now levels off, heading away from the headwall. After five minutes, a path forks off to the right and leads to a boulder with views off toward the Saranac Lakes. The main path continues straight ahead into dense growth, dips a little, then climbs up a rock to the left. Seward's canister is on a rise just ahead, at 4330 feet, 1320 meters. For views to the west and south, continue on the path as it starts to descend in a westerly direction. You will soon come to an open rock with a magnificent view out over Donaldson and Emmons. Long Lake stretches out to the horizon between the two summits and Tupper Lake can be seen in the west.

SEWARD TO DONALDSON

Seward has several summit nubbles. As the path continues on to Donaldson, it starts descending west, heading toward those nubbles, but quickly begins a steep, rough descent, curving around to the south-southeast past vertical rock walls. The path continues on the eastern side of the ridgeline to avoid these walls. A stream flows down the path for most of the descent, but the inconvenience is lessened when you get your first view down into the Cold River valley with the massive Santanoni Range beyond. Twenty-five minutes past the summit, the path levels off and a stream flows across it from right to left.

The ascent to the summit of Donaldson now begins, although you will encounter a few short drops. After thirty more minutes, the path nears the summit and splits. The right fork leads 75 feet to a lookout to the west. The left fork goes across a wet spot, then rises, passing the summit rock on the left. The canister is located on a tree on this rock, at 4108 feet, 1252 meters.

The mountain is the namesake of Alfred L. Donaldson, the early twentieth-century author who wrote the first comprehensive history of the Adirondacks. From this ledge, scarcely three feet across, is perhaps the finest view from the entire range. Facing east, a panorama unfolds before you, across Ouluska Pass and the Cold River valley. Seward and Seymour mountains rise to the northeast, the MacIntyre Range and Mount Marcy stand in the distant east, and the imposing Santanoni Range looms to the southeast.

DONALDSON TO EMMONS

The path on to Emmons does not have as great an elevation change, but as fatigue sets in, it may seem as rough. The path generally is to the west of the ridgeline. Dropping off the summit rock, turn left and head south through a muddy spot. The path becomes rougher and again descends below the ridgeline, this time to the west, giving you occasional views toward Tupper Lake. After thirty minutes, you have reached the low point and will begin the

final ascent. Twenty minutes later, the path turns a sharp left and climbs up the summit rock, 4038 feet, 1231 meters, to end at a tiny gap in the trees where the canister is.

The peak was named in honor of Professor Ebenezer Emmons, the New York State geologist who led the famous 1837 survey party that ascended Mount Marcy. The only view is a limited, yet unique one to the southeast, dominated by nearby Long Lake. Blue Mountain and a very distant West Mountain are two of the more recognizable summits beyond.

If you choose to descend to the Northville-Placid Trail via Ouluska Pass, retrace your steps 0.2 mile to a point where you can vaguely see through the trees to the east. Head east from this point on the ridgeline and within 50 feet or so you should find the well-defined descent path.

29 Emmons from the South

Strenuous bushwhack along intermittent paths, slide-climb
3 miles, 3½ hours to Mount Emmons, 2150-foot vertical rise

If you are hiking along the Northville-Placid Trail, an ascent of the Seward Range is possible using the Ouluska Lean-to as your base. You should allow a full day for the trip and possess strong navigational skills, because there is no continuous path and the upper reaches are very steep and dense. Along the way, however, you will be rewarded with a visit to an old lumber clearing and the option of climbing a slide.

Begin your journey by bushwhacking up the east bank of Ouluska Pass Brook, headed up into the pass that Colvin called a gloomy place of shadows. It is one of the deeper passes and its heights are virtually impenetrable because of the dense growth that followed the logging and because of the 1950 blowdown.

Even though this trek turns from the pass well before its high point, it is not an easy bushwhack. The banks are steep in places and you have to swing away from the brook from time to time. After twenty-five minutes, you may notice an old road coming in from the rear on your right. This road shows on the 1953 USGS Santanoni topographic map and you can try to follow its contours and corduroy remains north, but it fades out in places and is unreliable. One hour and a half later you should come to a large clearing where a logging camp once stood, 1.4 miles north of the Cold River. Old pieces of machinery and hardware are everywhere and it is intriguing to imagine the operations that went on here.

Looking north from the clearing, you see the steep southern flank of Seward. To the west-northwest, Emmons rises with its slide in plain sight. A small,

Looking up Emmons Slide

intervening summit hides Donaldson from view. To ascend the range, you must retrace your steps south along the edge of Ouluska Pass Brook just over 0.1 mile. A prominent stream tumbles down from the range on the opposite bank and this is your route. It is impossible to follow a continuous path along the stream, so once you cross the brook, you will have to choose your route carefully. The north side of the stream may offer the least resistance. An hour later, paths seem to be more in evidence and you come to a major source of the stream, the slide. The path bears right, away from the slide, but it is always within sight of it. Climbing becomes more difficult as the slopes get steeper, wetter, and more dense. Two major rock outcrops have to be negotiated and they can be hazardous, particularly on the descent. Finally, after three and a half hours, you reach the main path on the ridgeline, just over 0.2 mile north of Emmons' summit.

For those who like slides, this one is not difficult and offers an interesting panorama encompassing the Santanoni Range and several of the High Peaks beyond the Cold River valley. One dramatic presence is the sharp defile Ouluska Pass carves between Seward and Seymour mountains, with summits of the Sawtooth Mountains in the distance. The slide ends at a vertical headwall directly below the wooded summit, and to reach the path on the ridge you must enter the woods to the right and bushwhack your way to and across a small, steep slide. From there it is best to continue on contour around to the right until you reach the path descending from the ridge. It is possible to angle up to the ridgeline from the second slide, but thick growth and steepness make it undesirable.

30 Other Approaches to the Seward Range

Strenuous bushwhacks

The Seward Range is sometimes ascended from the west along Calkins Brook or Boulder Brook (an especially scenic route with its lovely waterfalls) and from the north along a major unnamed stream that crosses the Blueberry Foot Trail. It must be stated that these waterways are just guides and no continuous path exists along them. Their banks frequently become steep and densely forested, making them hazardous. As they diminish toward the top of the ridge, a very difficult bushwhack is required to reach the ridge path. Blowdowns, a tangled, mossy understory, and sheer cliffs are common problems. Such trips are an exciting challenge, but require advanced navigational skills and a high degree of stamina.

The old logging road, which parallels Boulder Brook along its southern banks, encounters a lot of blowdown past Seward Pond. This was the major route to Donaldson in the 1930s and '40s, but the hurricane virtually obliterated it.

On Seymour Slide

31 Seymour Mountain from the Ward Brook Truck Trail

Strenuous climb along path, slide-climb
1.5 miles, 1²/₃ hours, 2000-foot vertical rise

Seymour Mountain, originally Ragged, was renamed in honor of Horatio Seymour, who served two terms as governor of New York. Earlier, the name Seymour was given to a peak in the Sawtooth Mountains by Colvin, but the names were switched, apparently by the USGS. It was appropriate that Seymour was so honored, for unlike most politicians whose names grace the high peaks, he visited the mountain region and was involved in the state study, later phases of which resulted in the creation of the Forest Preserve.

This is the main approach and few attempt the climb from any other direction. As peaks without formal trails go, it is one of the easier ones, although it is likely to be muddy near the upper reaches and exposed rock along the way can be slippery.

The path begins on the east side of the first stream southeast of the Ward Brook Lean-to (section 25). Ascend along the stream for about ten minutes until you come to a fork in the stream marked by a large boulder. Circle behind the boulder and cross from the left fork over to the right. In three minutes, this fork splits and the path goes along the dry rise in the center for four minutes before crossing over to the left. Both forks rejoin and you bear left, away from the stream, then return to it in three minutes. The path now proceeds up the stream bed on large rocks and at a point about 0.6 mile from the trail, the route steepens, becoming a small slide. Paths exist just inside the woods to the right, where it becomes too difficult to remain on the exposed rock. As you climb higher, an ever-increasing view unfolds to the north, dominated by Ampersand Lake, Ampersand Mountain, and the northernmost summits of the Sawtooth Range.

The slide eventually becomes intermittent and too steep to navigate, causing the path to enter the woods to the right in under twenty minutes. Becoming steeper and muddier, the path splits at least three times as it winds its way up through the dense tangles. Try to choose the main route at all times to prevent further confusion and erosion of the slope. A little over one hour from the trail, the climb begins to lessen and you come to a lookout on the right. The view extends from Upper Saranac Lake in the northwest, past Azure and DeBar mountains in the distant north, to the rugged Sawtooth Range in the east. McKenzie and Whiteface mountains and the Sentinel Range define the far northeastern horizon.

The path splits again near the summit and the right fork leads fifty feet to a rock ledge with a breathtaking view of the entire Seward Range, with the view extending right to encompass the one from the previous lookout. The left fork leads one hundred feet to the wooded rise where the canister marks the 4090-foot (1247-meter) summit.

Averyville Road

ROADS SOUTH OF Lake Placid along the Chubb River are very old indeed, for the first settlement here dates back to 1803. The Averys, a farming family, arrived in 1819. Even though there was some logging along the Chubb, and Averyville Road was extended as a rude highway west toward Saranac Lake, much of the area south of the present road was never logged. One large tract south of Averyville and west of the river was acquired by the state in a tax sale of 1877, so it has not been disturbed since then; although land way south toward Moose Pond continued to be logged almost until 1920.

The northern forest portion of the Northville-Placid Trail is the principal route south from Averyville. That trail has been rerouted in recent years to avoid private land and now follows a course that is sometimes logging road, sometimes trail, on the east side of the Chubb River. The old portion of the trail—from the very end of Averyville Road, to the Chubb River below Wanika Falls—was abandoned because of parking problems at the trailhead. However, locals continue to use the former route and it is the preferred skiing track. The old road that became the Northville-Placid Trail is a very historic one and was used by local farmers to carry produce south to the Tahawus mine by way of Preston Ponds.

To reach the new trailhead, drive 1.1 miles south on Averyville Road from the Old Military Road. The trailhead and parking for a few cars are on the left side of the road, just short of the bridge over the Chubb River. There is a much larger parking area 0.2 mile beyond the trailhead on the right side of the road. Skiing access for the old trail, but no parking, is over 3 miles south, at the end of Averyville Road.

32 Wanika Falls and Moose Pond
Northville-Placid Trail
Hiking, skiing, camping, access to bushwhacks
8.3 miles, 4 hours, relatively level, blue markers

This stretch of trail is easy enough for a day-long round trip. The lean-tos at Wanika Falls and Moose Pond are good places to camp if you plan to bushwhack in the area, and three good bushwhacks are suggested. The rolling trail is wide enough to be popular with skiers in winter.

The trail briefly follows the east bank of the Chubb River. At 0.1 mile it comes to a register and veers left away from the river. Recent trail work, with contained gravel walkways, bridges, and log stringers, has raised the trail in the

View across Moose Pond to Sawtooth Range

wettest parts. You cross a number of streams that flow west toward the Chubb River; but on rainy days you may find the log stringers just too slippery to use.

The trail heads generally south with gentle ups and downs, skirting private property. At almost 3 miles, you cross Snow Brook (a local name). It has been dammed downstream by beaver, so the trail is now flooded. Angling west, the trail approaches a large stream and turns south to climb beside it. The trail stays east of a large marsh over which you have views of Ampersand Mountain. Shortly you have views of the new slide on Nye Mountain. At 4.5 miles you angle west again and at 4.7 miles cross another stream flowing down from the slopes of Nye.

A hundred yards beyond, you cross a stream that comes from the new slide on Nye. A 0.3-mile bushwhack uphill through open hardwoods takes you to the base of the slide, which was created by the earthquake of August 1983. The slide is about 1400 feet long and shallow, with a grade of about 25 percent. (This is a favorite destination for skiers, but the grade is steep enough that only expert skiers should attempt it.) The slide's course has quite a bit of debris—loose rocks and trees—but it is still fun for slide climbers, even in summer.

A second bridge, at almost 5.3 miles, crosses Big Brook (another local name). At 6.1 miles you reach the Chubb River crossing. This is worth a stop—a beautiful stretch of cascades livens the normally placid Chubb. Fifty feet beyond this third bridge, you come to the original Northville-Placid Trail. Turn left to follow the river upstream toward Wanika Falls.

At 6.7 miles you leave the trail for a short spur to the Wanika Falls Lean-to. There is no bridge to the east side of the river where the lean-to sits and during high water it is very difficult to get there. The falls are east of the lean-to and to get a full view of them, you must cross the Chubb, which is here turning east. Obviously, high water—the best time to see the falls—is the worst time to try to cross over for the view.

The Chubb River originates in a vly between Street and Nye mountains. In less than 2 miles, the river produces this awesome, high falls. Bushwhackers find that the Chubb is a great route to those mountains and offers a better challenge than the mess of herd paths from the east (section 38). You can follow the river and its northern fork all the way to the wet area in the saddle between Street and the Nye Ridge.

Back on the Northville-Placid Trail, turn south toward Moose Pond. This is a very pretty stretch of good trail. A little over half way, at about 7.5 miles, you see a pond below and to the west. Its outlet empties into Moose Pond. Just short of 8 miles you cross a small brook with a lovely little waterfall. The trail leads abruptly up to the lean-to, which sits on a bank above the pond. There is a gorgeous view of the pond fifty feet below and the Sawtooth Range beyond. Use the rest time to contemplate a bushwhack over the jagged peaks of that range. Those who climb it to its highest peak, about 3854 feet, will find that, as with almost every destination in the High Peaks, others have been there before. A canister records those climbs. The summit is just north of west from Moose Pond, 2 miles as the crow flies and 1500 feet above the pond. Although this approach is very rough, it is much better, I am told, than one from Duck Hole.

The Sawtooth Range remains the largest truly pathless mountain area in the Adirondacks. One summit was originally known as Seymour, another was named for Governor Levi P. Morton, but neither name stuck. The range has nearly a dozen peaks over 3300 feet, 1000 meters, in elevation, though none over 3900 as the Marshall brothers surmised from earlier and incorrect maps. They, with Herbert Clark, climbed two of the peaks in 1925 and named the two highest peaks Raker (the flatter eastern summit) and Cutter (the sharp western summit) for the similarly shaped teeth of a saw blade. These peaks do have views, and there is a third peak that is almost as tall. But all three, with the rest of the nearly dozen tallest knobs, sit in virtually inaccessible splendor atop this jagged ridge, waiting to be explored.

The Northville-Placid Trail continues 3.8 miles south to the dam and lean-tos at Duck Hole (section 3), with modest grades and lovely forest cover.

Wallface in Indian Pass

West of Adirondak Loj

HENRY VAN HOEVENBERG first visited the Adirondacks in 1877. He was an inventor with more than a hundred patents and chief electrician for the Baltimore and Ohio Railroad. All his money went into the purchase of the area around Heart Lake, which he and his fiancée Josephine Schofield had spied on a climbing trip shortly after they met. Josephine died within a year, never seeing the Adirondack Lodge that Henry built on the shore of the lake, with one of the most magnificent views in the High Peaks.

The Lodge was opened in 1880 and Henry served as a guide to the mountains. With others, he organized the Adirondack Tramp and Trail Club, which built trails and lean-tos from Heart Lake to the center of the High Peaks. One of those trails was to the small mountain with a magnificent view just behind the lodge—a mountain still known as Mount Jo.

Running the lodge sapped Henry of all his resources and he finally had to sell the property to the Lake Placid Club, which hired him as manager in 1900. Just three years later, in the worst fire year ever to hit that part of the Adirondacks, fires swept down from Mount Jo and south from South Meadow, forcing Henry to escape through Indian Pass.

Lands to the south and west of Adirondack Lodge have a mixed history. Tracts to the west around Street and Nye were acquired by the state in tax sales before 1885. Tracts along most of the Indian Pass Trail, the slopes of the MacIntyre Range, and from Scott Pond north to Lost Pond on the slopes of Street were lumbered by the J & J Rogers Company. These tracts did not become part of the Forest Preserve until 1921, explaining why the bushwhacker occasionally finds a corduroy road high on the slopes of MacIntyre or along the trail to Scott Pond. It also explains the variety of forests you encounter: the burned lands with their pioneering white birch reaching maturity, the logged lands with spruce becoming dominant, and tracts of old growth that were never logged except for a few softwoods, so today they appear untouched by man.

Looking at the slopes of MacIntyre from the shore of Heart Lake, it is difficult to imagine that they were burned black as high as 3400 feet after the fires of 1903.

The Adirondack Mountain Club acquired the Heart Lake tract and today runs its Adirondak Loj (spelling thanks to Melville Dewey, who belonged to the Lake Placid Club). Its large parking lots charge nonmembers a parking fee. Besides accommodations at the Loj, there are tent sites and lean-tos on Loj property for hire, and showers and a shop in the Campers and Hikers Building. You will usually encounter a forest ranger or interior ranger near the trailhead—their role is to help hikers be certain they are equipped for the hazards of high-mountain climbing.

33 Mount Jo

2-mile loop, 1½ hours, 695-foot climb, ADK markers

This peak at 2877 feet proves small is better. It has one of the most spectacular views in the east—a panorama of Marcy, Colden, MacIntyre, the slash of Indian Pass, and Wallface, plus peaks on either side, all mounted above the sparkling water of Heart Lake.

E. H. Ketchledge has written a small booklet that summarizes the natural history of the High Peaks from numbered observation posts on a climb along the western trail to Mount Jo. The booklet may be purchased at the Campers and Hikers Building, and you should take it on your walk up Mount Jo.

To find the trailhead, walk west from the parking lot across the Loj Road to the guide board that directs you onto the Indian Pass Trail. That trail curves around the Loj on a chain of boardwalk and turns right along an old roadway. The trail up Mount Jo is a right turn just beyond, 350 yards from the parking lot.

The trail climbs steeply for 150 yards and splits. The way left is the 0.3-mile-longer western loop, which heads nearly level over a shoulder of the little mountain, then turns northeast. A short spur to the left leads to the lower western summit. The way right climbs steeply through a draw and over rocks to intersect the western route. Both trails then join and angle east to the summit.

34 Indian Pass

6 miles to Summit Rock, 3½ hours, 690-foot elevation change, red markers

Indian Pass is the wildest pass in the Adirondacks—rock slabs and boulders the size of buses (broken from the cliffs of Wallface) choke the narrow valley. The steep slopes of MacIntyre rise from the east side of the pass. The trail through the pass winds along the slopes of MacIntyre, above the jumble of rock below. Crevices in the rock are filled with ice until late in the summer; fog and cold air emerge from holes between the rocks. Walking is not easy on the northern slopes of the pass, because the sides of the draw leading to it are so steep the trail has nowhere to go but through a stream that feeds Indian Pass Brook.

If you can arrange a car at either end, the through walk from Adirondak Loj to Summit Rock and on to Tahawus (see also section 1) is a wonderful one-day trip, 10.4 miles long.

The trail begins as for Mount Jo, above, but stays along the western shores of Heart Lake. The registration booth is just past the southwest corner of the lake. The Old Nye Ski Trail branches right immediately after the booth and another ski trail branches left at 0.6 mile, near the Wilderness boundary.

Rocks and corduroy make easy walking along this well-hardened trail. The forest is lovely, with big, old hemlocks among the maples. The bridges are wide enough to encourage skiers. After rolling along for 2.1 miles (forty-five minutes), a trail forks right to Rocky Falls Lean-to. That trail leads 0.1 mile to Indian Pass Brook, near lovely cascades. You can cross on the rocks 100 yards upstream near the lean-to, which sits on the west bank. The side trail then heads upstream and uphill, to rejoin the main trail after a detour of 0.25 mile.

The main trail starts uphill from the first turn-off, then levels off to rejoin the lean-to trail at 2.3 miles. You cross a gravel-bedded stream. The trail rises gently with some wet places. You cross the two small forks of a muddy stream. Marshes appear through the trees out to your right, then an unnamed stream is close right as the valley becomes narrower. You walk along the stream for a ways, then cross a wash that drains from MacIntyre. Paths lead left to campsites as you approach the Scotts Clearing Lean-to at 3.8 miles. Immediately in front of the lean-to, you cross another stream that drains from the slopes of MacIntyre near Boundary Peak. In another five minutes, at just over 4 miles, you reach Scotts Clearing and the rockwork of an old flood dam on Indian Pass Brook.

The trail to Scott and Wallface ponds (section 35) is a right turn here below the rockwork. For Indian Pass you can either turn left or go straight ahead, depending on the diligence of the beavers who try to replace the old dam. The way straight is often below water level. The way left climbs a knoll before rejoining the old roadway at nearly 4.5 miles. The trail now follows close beside the brook for 0.3 mile to the confluence with Iroquois Brook, which drains Iroquois Pass.

Shortly after crossing Iroquois Brook, at 4.9 miles, the yellow trail to Iroquois Pass turns left. The red Indian Pass Trail continues along Indian Pass Brook and crosses yet another tributary. Shortly, the trail fords Indian Pass Brook, crossing to its west bank just before that brook splits. Shortly, the trail crosses the western branch at a gravelly wash. This branch, which tumbles from the western side of the valley, is the outlet stream from Scott Pond, but it is designated Indian Pass Brook on the new metric map. The trail briefly follows this branch, then heads along the west bank of the much smaller stream that drains Indian Pass. You soon cross that stream on a bridge.

The walking becomes rough as the trail begins to climb beside the stream. After 100 feet of climbing, look for a path up to your left to a campsite. The trail continues to be rough as it climbs 250 feet in elevation through the streambed. A broken ladder is little help up a particularly steep pitch. The grade eases at 5.35 miles as you enter the pass. Walking between boulders you can feel cold air emerging from deep crevices that have ice in them almost all year long.

Scott Pond

Climbing to a height-of-land, you have views of Wallface cliffs. The lovely path continues through the pass, close to its eastern wall. Jog left, then right, still going up slightly, to cross a small stream at 5.55 miles. A fireplace marks another campsite, this one too close to both water and trail to be legal. You are still following the tiny stream. A small meadow surrounded by super boulders provides a great view of Wallface. Beyond this point you descend slightly, with frustrating, through-the-trees views of the cliffs above you. At 6 miles a path forks left to Summit Rock for the classic view of the pass. At this point, three and a half hours from the start, at elevation 2820 feet (860 meters), you can either turn around, or if you have arranged a car at Tahawus, continue on (section 1).

35 Wallface Ponds and Scott Pond

5.5 miles to Scott Pond, 6.7 miles to Wallface Ponds from Adirondak Loj, 4 hours, 1000-foot elevation change, red and blue markers

A half-dozen small ponds are nestled in the high plateau south of Street and north of MacNaughton and Wallface. Three of them have good campsites, so they are destinations in themselves as well as points from which to bushwhack to MacNaughton or to Lost Pond, perhaps the hardest to find of the Adirondacks' eight or so Lost Ponds.

Start as for Indian Pass, walking the red trail first for slightly more than 4 miles to Scotts Clearing. It takes less than two hours. Turn west below the rock dam at Scotts Clearing and downstream a few feet to the ford across Indian Pass Brook. Both the clearing and the pond were named after a Robert Scott, who worked for the McIntyre Iron Company in 1843, or for his father William, who claimed to have found silver on the slopes of Nye Mountain.

The blue trail starts steeply up beyond the brook, following an old logging road, heading southwest and clinging to the edge of the escarpment before turning west into a draw. Turn about for through-the-trees views that reveal Iroquois, Boundary, and Algonquin.

After climbing fairly steeply up the birch slopes, the trail reaches a height-of-land, descends slightly around a boulder, then heads up again, crossing a draw and a muddy stream bed. Thirty minutes into the climb you reach a stretch where the road is paved with cedar corduroy, which weathers to golden hues. Those who hiked this trail several decades ago remember fondly and vividly this golden road, though it is now weathering to muddy browns. The trail angles south across another draw, turns more westerly, but continues climbing on the golden road. The birch and balsam cover tells of fires as well as logging. The trail makes a long straight traverse leading to a col. You cross this height-of-land and head down beside a boulder-filled draw, which gradually develops into a rocky bed, way below the trail. A path leads right into the draw. The trail curves around and down to the outlet of Scott Pond, beside the huge dam and rockworks that once held back a much larger body of water before its 1929 collapse. Allow about an hour for the more than 1.5-mile walk from Scotts Clearing to this point.

Trail signs direct you downstream—it is really rough going for 100 feet, climbing over big boulders to a point where it is easy to cross the brook. Check out the breached dam or, in really low water, a beaver dam above the rock one; both crossings may be easier than the trail crossing, though all are scrambles. Note that there is a path left along the outlet—it is more obvious than the trail on the west side of the marked crossing. The correct route is northwest along the shore of the pond. As the trail turns west, chains of logs lead you uphill through muck on the side-hill; meadows that once were flooded parts of Scott Pond are visible through the trees, below to your right.

After crossing a draw and a sphagnum bog, you turn to go up along the watercourse that feeds the bog. It is also muddy at a second marsh upstream, then you walk right, up through the rubble-filled draw that drains into the marsh. Still climbing, you hug the side of a knob, circling around to see a very small, long, thin pond down on your left. The trail goes close to it and to a campsite that is too near water to be legal. You wind along, finding a little stream and a marsh and a trail sign 0.7 mile from Scott Pond. Shortly beyond, the trail crosses the stream on smooth rocks and heads along the side of another, much longer, marsh. This one is filled with Labrador tea, laurel, and meadowsweet. It has a small amount of open water. In 200 yards, the trail crosses its western end, allowing you a fine view of MacIntyre to the east across the marsh.

Turning away from the marsh, the trail follows the small stream that flows into the marsh. It is wet walking through the small draw that envelops this stream. Imperceptibly, a change of drainage occurs; Scott Pond and its tributaries flow into Lake Champlain, Wallface Ponds ahead flow south into the Hudson. It is ironic that such a small wet meadow as this one at 3150 feet elevation (960 meters) marks such a significant watershed boundary.

Heading west through the sphagnum meadow where this change occurs, the trail is supported by patches of corduroy. The trail ends at the northernmost of the Wallface Ponds, near rocks from which you can view MacNaughton. A path leads left toward the outlet and a good campsite, then continues along the short channel to the southern pond. This one is currently very flooded by a beaver dam. From this pond you can look through the cut by its outlet to the lower slopes of the MacIntyre Range.

36   Outlet Wallface Ponds

Bushwhack

A surprisingly good 2-mile bushwhack involves walking south along the Wallface Ponds to the outlet and following it to Indian Pass Brook. No matter how you approach this, if you are making a one-car loop, it requires walking through Indian Pass and along the trail to Wallface Ponds. It's a long trek for one day, but the rewards are great.

Spruce and balsam are thick near the outlet and on the first and steepest part of it, but the forest gradually opens up. In low water you can rock hop much of the way. There are numerous lovely cascades on the upper part of the stream. Stay on the west side and about halfway down, where the outlet levels out, there is a lovely moss meadow. A gorgeous waterfall tumbles down from a side stream that drops from a shoulder of MacNaughton. Cliffs edge these slopes above the outlet.

The stream becomes steep again, but not as steep as above and the forest changes to open hardwoods for the last half of the descent. The bushwhack takes about three hours and drops 1080 feet. You easily pick up the Indian Pass Trail from Tahawus (section 1) not far from the confluence of the outlet and Indian Pass Brook, south.

37 MacNaughton
Bushwhack

MacNaughton, originally called Henderson Mountain, was given its present name by Colvin after 1896. It may have been named for Dr. James Mac-Naughton, a son-in-law of Archibald McIntyre, but more likely was named for the latter's grandson, Archibald MacNaughton, who worked at the iron mine, or for the James MacNaughton, who served from 1880 on as a trustee of the Iron Company and later as its president until his death in 1905.

In spite of a fairly dense spruce-fir cover, MacNaughton has good to excellent views from different points along the summit ridge. The bushwhack from Wallface Ponds presents some problems in the lowlands near the ponds, but a compass route up the slopes can be fairly direct. Compounding the currently wet crossing of the channel between the Wallface Ponds is the marshy traverse south of the third pond. Nevertheless, it is only an 830-foot, 1-mile climb from the channel to the highest peak, which misses being one of the forty-six over 4000 feet by less than twenty feet (its elevation is 3981 feet, 1214 meters). A bushwhack west-southwest leads to the summit ridge and back in under two hours.

A shorter route—if you avoid the pitfalls described below—leads from the currently private land west of Hunters Pond (section 2). When the state acquires that tract, that route will undoubtedly supersede this one from Wallface Ponds. The bushwhack to MacNaughton is described as an ascent from Wallface Ponds with hints for the descent to the Preston Ponds Trail.

Across the channel between the Wallface Ponds, the first 0.5 mile consists of rough but not severe bushwhacking, depending on luck. There are thick areas, old blowdowns, and swampy areas to cross. Head generally southwest. (This portion is particularly challenging on the return trip.) The last 0.5 mile to the ridge is much easier going, but very steep. It is more open approaching the middle to southeast peak area. There is a well-set herd path from the middle to the northwest peak, where there is a register in a red canister. A less-used path leads to the southeast peak. There are good views north from the northwest peak and south and west from two lookouts on the middle peak. The first is on the northwest end where a short side path leads to an opening

Seward Range from Street

in the summit scrub; the second is on the southeast end, on a high rock ledge at the end of a long side path. The latter is the nicest spot on the long summit ridge.

Just southeast of the long side path to the cliff top, another path diverges south from the herd path along the ridge heading southeast, to the right of a very large boulder on the right side of the path. This leads down to the stream running southwest from MacNaughton to Preston Ponds. It is a great aid to route finding, but not often found by those going up from the Preston Ponds Trail. The south-southwest face of MacNaughton, in contrast to the north, is very difficult bushwhacking, being steep and thick and scratchy for the first 600-foot drop from the summit. Below that, once the stream drainage is organized, the going is much easier, with multiple paths on the left side of the stream as you descend.

On the way up from Preston Ponds, stay with the stream, described in section 2, until well after it has turned east, even following on to the south ridge before turning north, until you discover the path. The south face without the path is the worst thing on the mountain.

38 Street and Nye

Confusing paths, 8½-hour circuit

William B. Nye was Colvin's guide in 1873 and it was Colvin who named the mountain for him. Colvin also honored Alfred Billings Street, the author of *The Indian Pass* and *Woods and Waters*, two accounts of Adirondack travel, which did much to bring people to the Adirondacks.

Before attempting this seemingly short and easy bushwhack to the two peaks, there are several precautions for the hiker to consider:

1. The 1978 metric map shows the southerly peak on the Nye Ridge to be higher than the northern peak where the Forty-sixers have placed their register.

2. There are dozens of blowdowns near and on the summit. As a result there are many herd paths that lead nowhere or in confusing directions. There is even one that leads in a complete circle of about two hundred yards.

3. The number of herd paths can make this an exceptionally difficult bushwhack, especially if you find yourself in the clouds.

4. Many of the streams and marshes you encounter are not shown even on the most recent map, the metric one.

Of the several routes to the summits of these two mountains, the easiest and most obvious of the herd paths starts along the Old Nye Cross Country Ski Trail that was used during the 1932 Winter Olympics. From the Adirondak Loj parking lot walk west around Heart Lake as for the start of the Indian Pass Trail (section 34) and turn right at 0.6 mile at the start of the Old Nye Ski Trail.

You reach state land about 0.3 mile along this trail, where the route becomes an unmarked path. It is still very easy to follow as it descends toward Indian Pass Brook, though the number of blowdowns increases as you approach the brook. Skirt them, continuing generally west. About forty minutes from the parking lot, 0.9 mile from the Indian Pass Trail, you reach Indian Pass Brook. Here the path makes a sharp right and follows along the east bank of the brook, which is making a series of deep curves. About 1.5 miles from the Loj, the path descends to a small clearing next to the water beside a really big bend. Cross here. The spot is marked with two large cedar trees and a yellow birch on the left side where the path enters the water, with a cairn on a large boulder just ahead of the trees.

A path continues down the west bank of the brook for about 150 yards until it intersects the tributary from the west. Follow up the south side of the tributary, skirting the wide marshy area near its mouth. Shortly after the two banks of the stream come together, 200 yards later, the path crosses to the north bank of the tributary.

Now the path ascends gently following the north bank. After the ascent steepens, 0.2 mile from the crossing, there is a small clearing on the right side of the path with the remains of an old horse-drawn bobsled. The path recrosses the stream at this point to another clearing on the south side that contains some old enamel pots and pans and part of an old cast-iron stove. This crossing is about 1.8 miles and an hour and a quarter from the Loj.

The path now ascends at a moderate grade up the south side of the tributary, following an old road. Twenty-five minutes into the climb, the path starts to swing back and forth across the narrowing stream bed, then curves south. At approximately 2.8 miles, nearly two and a quarter hours, the path reaches a flat shoulder of Nye, actually a sag in a bump on the ridge. The area is poorly drained and contains many herd paths. From it you can see Street to the west-southwest. This bump on the shoulder of Nye drops slightly to the west, and the path to the summit is a sharp right out of the draw, through an opening in the brush heading about 320°.

This part of the path climbs moderately, then quite steeply, before leveling off as it approaches the summit ridge. Just over half an hour of climbing from the bump, the path enters an area of blowdowns where the path seems to split. Turn right, north, along Nye's summit ridge, and drop down a slight depression before ascending to Nye's wooded summit. If you miss the turn, the other part of the path will lead you in a couple of minutes to a large rock outcrop to the left of the path, near the site of the old register on Nye's highest summit. You can climb the outcrop to spot the Nye ridge to the north so you can orient yourself.

To head back along the Nye ridge toward Street, return along the herd path to the outcrop and continue on the path, descending slightly. Beyond some blowdown, the path splits. The way left leads off the ridge. The way right continues along the ridge amidst blowdowns and a number of confusing routes. There is no easy way to keep on the correct route, so keep checking your compass, heading generally south along the ridge. You drop off a small knoll and cross a marshy area where a fairly strong herd path begins to ascend Street. It requires about forty-five minutes to an hour to walk between the summits, depending on your luck in choosing herd paths.

About 20 yards before the summit of Street, there is a herd path to the right, west. Take it to an opening that gives an excellent view of the MacIntyre Range, the Seward Range, the Santanoni Range, and the Sawtooth Mountains.

You can retrace your steps north then west along the herd paths to descend. Or, choose one of the two other herd paths that begin a descent from the summit of Street. The one to the left leads back into the blowdown along the ridgeline. The one to the right is an old and excellent herd path that leads down the flank of Street to a draw that leads to Indian Pass Brook in the vicinity of Rocky Falls Lean-to. However, this route has fallen into such disuse that the herd path is not continually visible.

Tahawus—
The Cloudsplitter

NOT ONLY WAS the countryside near Tahawus shaped by the McIntyre Iron Mine, but the lakes and mountains were given the names of principals in the mine and events in their lives. Henderson Lake and Henderson Mountain were named for David Henderson, who valiantly tried to make the mine work; Calamity Brook (originally Ore Bed Stream) and Calamity Pond (originally another Duck Hole) were named for the sad event of Henderson's death by the accidental discharge of a pistol that took place at the pond; Sanford Lake was named for Major Reuben Sanford, a state senator from Wilmington, who surveyed and appraised the Gore East of Township 47 in 1833. No one knows for whom the lakes Jimmy and Sally were named. MacNaughton Mountain to the north was named for someone in that family who was tied to the McIntyres by marriage as well as in business.

The names of that trinity of mountain majesties—Marcy, Colden, and MacIntyre—all relate to the mine, but it is a curious twist of history that the central peak does not retain its original name, Mount McMartin. The privilege of bestowing names on geographical landmarks belongs, by common consent, to the first explorer. Further, in exercising this right, it is regarded as bad taste for the explorer to propose his own name for his discovery.

In this case there were two expeditions, in 1836 and 1837, with somewhat different personnel in each. The first party included Archibald McIntyre and Duncan McMartin, two members of the business enterprise that owned the land and iron mines; David Henderson, the partner who married into the McIntyre family; James Hall, assistant state geologist; William C. Redfield, scientist; and David C. Colden, sportsman and potential investor in the iron mines. This party of 1836 was hampered by wet weather and got only as far as the pretty body of water, to which "the party" gave the name of Lake Colden.

The expedition of 1837 did not include either Archibald McIntyre or Duncan McMartin, who was ill and died later that year after selling his interest in the mine. But it did include Ebenezer Emmons, who was the chief geologist for the state's northern district, as well as Hall, Redfield, Henderson, and a few others. On the 5th of August, 1837, the party stood on the summit of the highest mountain in the state; from that very place and date James Hall wrote a letter to an Albany newspaper to say that they had just been giving names to certain historic peaks: Marcy, after the governor who authorized the natural history survey, and McIntyre, to whose hospitality all were indebted. Hall's letter does not say so, but almost certainly Mount McMartin was named at the same time. In Redfield's third and final account of these expeditions, he mentions the naming of some of the mountains, including Mount McMartin: "In honor of one now deceased, who led the party of last year, and whose spirit of enterprise and persevering labors contributed to establishing the settlement at the great Ore Beds." Redfield's account included a map of the High Peaks, and Mounts McMartin and McIntyre are on it.

Early in the same year, 1838, Ebenezer Emmons published his official account of the 1837 expedition. In it he stated, "An isolated mountain, situated between Mount Marcy and Mt. McIntyre has been named Mt. McMartin, in honor of one now deceased." He described McMartin's contribution in words almost identical to Redfield's. In several of the fine lithographs, which accompanied the Emmons report, the profile and captioned name, Mt. McMartin, are unambiguous.

But the historical record is that the name McMartin did not stick, and about the 1850s or so it was gradually replaced on maps and in narrative by Mount Colden.

Matters were made much worse in 1869, when the rather brash twenty-two-year-old Verplanck Colvin, writing of a visit to the area, spoke of Mount Colden as "incorrectly known as Mt. McMartin." This was protested by a man who made the first visitors' map of the Adirondacks, Dr. W. W. Ely, but to no avail. For a while, Colvin argued that Caribou (Avalanche) Mountain was really McMartin, but eventually he abandoned that idea. As a consequence, the name of Mt. McMartin nowhere appears in the subsequent Colvin reports. If anybody could have straightened things out, it was Colvin; but he did not and so the name will remain Colden.

The name Tahawus, an Indian word meaning he who cleaves the sky, or cloudsplitter, was given to Mount Marcy by the writer C. F. Hoffman in 1837, shortly after it was named by the Emmons party. It is curious that this lovely name did not survive; but appropriate that the first explorer's name did. Only the mine, the deserted settlement, and a club are still called called Tahawus.

In 1877, the Adirondack Club, later the Tahawus Club, took title to 96,000 acres owned by the McIntyre Iron Company. Finch, Pruyn and Company began lumbering those lands in 1881, originally only for spruce and pine; and the company later acquired much of this land. Funds from the 1916 Bond Act were used to buy 75,000 acres of the tract, which included Indian Pass. In 1920, the state took title to 7820 acres of the Gore Around Lake Colden and 2000 acres of the Gore East of Township 47.

In 1948 the state acquired an easement for one dollar that gives public access to the trails to Mount Adams, along Calamity Brook, and the beginning of the Indian Pass trail. Finch Pruyn retains and leases much land to the west of Tahawus and along the Opalescent River. All land, except the marked trails, is posted, and no camping is permitted until you reach state land.

Because one trail from Tahawus is the shortest to Flowed Lands and Lake Colden, it is often used by campers heading to those destinations. Over the years, the shores, especially those at Lake Colden, were damaged by excessive

Colden and Avalanche across Flowed Lands

camping. Nearly a decade ago, camping in the area was limited, lean-tos too close to shore or trail were removed, campsites too close to shore were closed, other campsites were designated, and campsites away from water were created. The results are excellent. While there are few dead and downed trees and limbs near the lean-tos, the shorelines are recovering. The map shows the location of permitted campsites, as well as the lean-tos.

39 Calamity Brook to Flowed Lands

4.4 miles, 2 to 2½ hours, 1000-foot elevation change, mostly blue markers

Calamity Brook Trail offers the shortest route to Flowed Lands and Lake Colden. The trail follows a very old tote road, which was used when the dam at Flowed Lands was built, and later when the Henderson Monument was transported to Calamity Pond. The beginning of the trail is through very disturbed lands; in fact, a fisherman in 1890 reported that this route and all the land to the south was a barren waste. Over the years, the roadway became a quagmire. Work to place large stones in the mud have helped to dry the trail, but it is not an easy walking route, either heading uphill on the way in or on the way out, where the footing seems to negate the generally downhill course.

Starting from the Upper Works Parking Lot at Tahawus, you cross the Hudson at 0.2 mile on a bridge that is 200 yards from the river's source at Henderson Lake. Both red and yellow markers denote the trail, but very quickly the yellow Indian Pass Trail continues straight where you turn right on the red trail, still following a good road. Less distinct logging roads branch from the trail, which heads gently uphill with chains of logs and boardwalks to keep it dry. In twenty-five minutes, at 1.1 miles, a swinging bridge takes the trail over Calamity Brook. To the south you can see Mount Adams. Just beyond, look for the remains of an old rock crib dam sitting in the woods to the left of the trail.

Boulders and corduroy form the tread of the trail as it climbs, going over two little log bridges before reaching the second bridge over Calamity Brook at 1.6 miles. It is ten minutes between the first two bridges. This high bridge with tall cribs at either end has campsites nearby, but these are not on state land. At the intersection immediately across the bridge, the blue Bypass Trail (section 44) turns left, west. You go right, also with blue markers.

The trail parallels the brook and there is a campsite to the right. You cross a small stream, then a second. The trail is especially charming here, where it is close to Calamity Brook. Climbing now, the trail reaches a mucky, rocky spot at a height-of-land, then climbs some more. The state land boundary is in this stretch, but not well marked. At 2.6 miles the old road angles right to make a low-water crossing at a ford. The trail climbs steeply left around a knob to descend a ladder to the third bridge (a swinging one also) over Calamity Brook. The bridge is just upstream and within sight of the ford.

The trail/roadway is now very rocky. You can hear the brook, but not see it. Split logs, a washed out bridge, more rocks, more streams washing across the trail, and more climbing distinguish this stretch. Finally, you reach a height-of-land and descend to an open meadow. New chains of planking lead through the meadow. Now the way is swampy. Angle right as curved stringers take you over a little stream. The trail remains rocky, rooty, and muddy. You can see the flow surrounding Calamity Pond on your left. With lots of large rocks, root masses from cedars and spruce, and mosses, this is a most unusual and beautiful place. At the end of the flow, the trail angles right, but, at 4.05 miles, a narrow footpath leads left 60 feet to the edge of Calamity Pond and the Henderson Monument, which sits on high ground surrounded by water.

Before Henderson was shot, Calamity was known as East Brook and the pond was known as Duck Hole. Marshall is the mountain you see above the pond.

The trail continues close by the now dry, man-made portion of Calamity Brook. The iron mine never had an adequate and consistent supply of water for power. Among the many schemes for diversion, only the dam on the Opalescent was built. This huge dam, built by man and horsepower and probably completed in 1854, created a large flow where before only marshes had surrounded the Opalescent River to the west of Colden. A channel and a sluiceway were built at a low point on the west side of the Flowed Lands. Through it, the Opalescent was diverted west to join Calamity Brook, which empties into the Hudson immediately downstream from its beginning at Lake Henderson.

Erosion during the time waters from the Opalescent flowed this way has left an amazing bed of boulders. Moss on the rocks tells you little water has flowed this way in recent years. You climb to another height-of-land and in five minutes you can see Colden rising above Flowed Lands.

To your right as you approach Flowed Lands at 4.4 miles is the first Calamity Brook Lean-to. The second, just beyond, is up on a knoll opposite the sluiceway, almost at the edge of Flowed Lands, quite near the trail intersection. The way left, across the sluiceway, leads to Colden (section 40). The way right leads to the dam on the Opalescent and Hanging Spear Falls (section 42).

Today the dam is breached, so Flowed Lands are again smaller, though the remains of the dam still keep the water above the Opalescent's original level here. With the water low, you can often walk along the shoreline, enjoying views of Colden and Avalanche mountains and the MacIntyre Range.

40 Flowed Lands to Lake Colden and Avalanche Lake

2.4 miles, 1¹/₄ hours, relatively level, red, blue, and yellow markers

Tight restrictions limit camping in the vicinity of Flowed Lands, Lake Colden, and Avalanche Lake, though even with them, there are a number of camping spots and a dozen lean-tos. Five of the lean-tos are on Flowed Lands. From the end of the Calamity Brook Trail at Flowed Lands, cross the dry spillway of the man-made brook. The trail, marked with red, winds over several knolls and around the marsh at the head of a deep bay before climbing behind a headland faced with cliffs. The climb involves rough walking and a ladder on a trail hardened with stepping stones. The rocky trail winds over a number of small knolls before reaching the channel between Lake Colden and Flowed Lands, almost thirty minutes from the start.

Just at the beginning of the walk along the channel, you hop rocks to cross Herbert Brook. Shortly, you see a lean-to on the opposite shore of the channel, but there is no camping along your route. At 1.1 miles you pass a trail intersection near the bridge over Colden Outlet. Here a ladder descends to a walkway over the cribbing of Colden's dam. This is the beginning of the red trail along the Opalescent (section 46). From the end of the Calamity Brook Trail to this intersection, the trail is sufficiently tortuous as to require forty minutes.

Continuing east along the outlet, the trail to Lake Colden, also red, passes a path leading to several tent sites to the left, just before reaching the West Lean-to—the first of two on Beaver Point, at 1.4 miles on the southwest corner of Lake Colden. Beyond the lean-tos, the trail stays close to the shoreline. It passes a stairway leading uphill to more tent-sites. There are lovely views of the slides on Colden, rock slabs and unobtrusive hardening underfoot, and chains of logs along the shore. At 1.6 miles a sign points uphill to tent-sites along Cold Brook. The path to them is just before you reach a very civilized two-log bridge. Just past the brook, you come to a four-way intersection. Right leads quickly to the ranger's cabin; left is the yellow Iroquois Pass Trail (section 45); and straight ahead, the trail around Lake Colden, now marked with blue, continues for 0.1 mile to a bridge over a stream that drains the south slopes of Algonquin. Immediately across the bridge is the intersection with the yellow trail that heads up those slopes (section 141).

The blue trail continues close to Lake Colden, though you have to walk off the trail for the best views of Colden's slides. Arrows angle you across the outlet of Avalanche Lake through beaver-flooded wetlands to the intersection with a yellow trail. If you turn left, north, you reach the shores of Avalanche Lake in just over 0.3 mile. This ten-minute section along the outlet stream is rooty and mucky and lined with corduroy. As you approach Avalanche Lake, a spur trail to the right leads to a legal campsite, but there is no camping on the shoreline near the dock used by the ranger, nor is there camping anywhere else around the steep shores of the lake. This yellow trail along the shores of Avalanche Lake leading to Adirondak Loj is described in section 140. Even if you are not headed this way, continue along the shore as far as the first Hitch-up-Matilda for the view of the dike.

EAST SHORE LAKE COLDEN

If you turn right at the intersection and head south on the yellow trail along Colden's eastern shore, you reach one of the trails to Colden (section 141) in 0.4 mile. Another 0.4 mile takes you around the south shore of the lake to an intersection with the Opalescent Trail to Marcy (section 45). Two lean-tos are located to the left, along the start of that trail and there are nine designated campsites nearby. If you turn left for five minutes to the bridge across the Opalescent, a right turn across the bridge takes you to three more lean-tos and more than a dozen other designated campsites along the south side of Colden Outlet.

A right turn on the Opalescent Trail takes you across the bridge, over the dam at Colden's Outlet, to the red trail, completing a loop around Lake Colden.

41 Marshall

Herd path and route following a stream

Several names have been given the southern peak of the Algonquin Range that rises to over 4380 feet (1335 meters). It was first climbed by the Marshall brothers, so its present name is appropriate, but in the past it was called Clinton, for the governor, and later Herbert, for the Marshalls' guide, Herbert Clark.

The usual approach to Marshall begins where the red trail crosses Herbert Brook (section 40), about ten minutes west of Colden Dam. The brook at the crossing is sandy, not rocky, and too wide to jump. An excellent path along the north side of the brook will start you on your way. Take the time to make sure you have the right brook (it is possible to confuse it with others draining into Flowed Lands) and you will have an excellent path toward the summit.

The path follows very closely along the brook, around a sharp bend to the right, keeping mostly level to a second bend, back to the left at a cool, sunless pool and falls, about five minutes from the trail. The path climbs the steep bank to the right of the falls, and continues mostly on the right side of the brook—but sometimes in it—for about ten minutes to the base of open slabs. Through these first fifteen minutes from Flowed Lands, the route is delightfully varied as the brook wanders back and forth, at times almost level and at others descending mossy slabs or precipitous ledges. Beginning at the open slabs, you will be heading straight northwest for about 1 mile, climbing over 1000 feet to old beaver dams at the headwaters of Herbert Brook.

The preferred course from the base of the slabs is directly upstream, but high water may force you onto the banks. Either way, the route soon narrows into a steep cleft, mossy enough that you may prefer the woods to the streambed. Above the slabs, a path is more often found on the left side of the brook than the right. Above the steepest part, you may again be comfortable in the open stretches of the brook bed, but the path also becomes better defined. You will feel the ascent beginning to ease when you are still 0.5 mile from the summit, and the last several yards up to the beaver ponds tends to be rather wet underfoot. The path passes left, south, of the flowed area, and then climbs steeply up the last 300 feet to the register. It takes about two hours to reach it from Flowed Lands.

Marshall's summit is heavily wooded and not well defined, but if you poke around its edges you should find views in all directions except east. You will also find several paths leading down to the northeast, less than 200 feet apart. Take the path to the right as you leave the summit to return down Herbert Brook. Paths forking left lead toward Iroquois Pass.

An alternate path to Marshall crosses the 4160-foot ridge between Marshall and Iroquois Pass. To descend along it, take one of the competing paths leading northeast from the summit. Be alert for forks as you climb down from Marshall and cross the boggy saddle below it. You climb about 100 feet above the saddle to the top of the ridge, where the path seems to wander almost aimlessly for a while. It is winding through blowdowns that were much more substantial thirty years ago, when the path was first set. Be patient and stay with it. Once across the ridge, it will lead you very nearly down to Iroquois Pass, where a right turn leads you down Cold Brook to Lake Colden (section 45).

To take this path from the pass to Marshall, look for it just northwest (toward Indian Pass) of the group of very large boulders on the northeast side of the trail, in the vicinity of a thin but audible waterfall coming down over the cliffs on Iroquois. Although the path is distinct if you are looking for it at the right time, this is a dramatic section of Iroquois Pass and you can easily miss it if you are distracted.

42 The Opalescent River Trail
Hanging Spear Falls
8.45 miles between the Upper Works and the Calamity Brook Trail, 4 hours, 1015-foot elevation change, red markers north of Twin Brooks Lean-to, yellow markers south of it

You will walk the trail along the Opalescent to see Hanging Spear Falls, to make the longer of the two hikes to Flowed Lands, or to camp at the lean-to near the beginning of the route to Allen (section 43). Perhaps the most pleasant way to enjoy this trail is as part of a day-long loop to Flowed Lands via the Calamity Brook Trail, returning along this route past Hanging Spear Falls, so the trail is described in that direction.

The south end of the trail is at the old parking area which once served Mount Adams, 0.6 mile south of the Upper Works Parking Lot. Unless you have friends with a second car, that 0.6 mile additional makes this a 13.85-mile circuit.

Like all trails to waterfalls, this one is best enjoyed in wet times, but there is no bridge over the Opalescent at the outlet of Flowed Lands and it usually is a wet crossing. Carry sneakers so you can keep your boots dry.

Head south from the Calamity Brook Trail following the red markers. You pass the Flowed Lands Lean-to with its beautiful view, certainly one of the best in the High Peaks. Then continue beside the long, thin bay, to the dam, 0.4 mile from the Calamity Brook Trail. Just before the dam, a short trail leads uphill to a fourth lean-to (Griffin), which is secreted in the woods above the trail. With low water revealing a broad beach along the bay, most hikers seem to be using it instead of the trail.

There is a fifth lean-to on the shore of Flowed Lands, across the dam and 0.5 mile to the north along a yellow-marked spur on a point opposite the Calamity Brook lean-tos. It was recently rebuilt on a knoll back from shoreline, not far from tiny Livingston Pond and takes its name from that body of water. From here you can head north along a faint and fading path, bushwhacking toward the bridge over the outlet of Lake Colden (section 40).

The dam, with its beautiful stone work, was washed out by the hurricane of September 1942 and totally breeched in recent years. Cross below the dam— carefully hopping rocks if the water is low, fording otherwise. Signs on the north shore point you downstream along the Opalescent. From the narrow

Hanging Spear Falls on the Opalescent

trail, there are glimpses of the boulder-filled river and the cliff-faced slopes of Calamity Mountain above to the south. One side path leads to a slanted rock below a pretty cascade. The river is steep, mysterious, and very rugged.

A marked path points you right from the main trail at 0.95 mile, 0.55 mile from the dam. This narrow path leads to the edge of the cliffs above Hanging Spear Falls with its deep pool below, cascades above, and cliffs on the slopes of Calamity Mountain. It is hard to distinguish the rock slab shaped like a spear that supposedly inspired the naming of the falls. Easier to picture is a shining scimitar, with the jeweled cascades above as the hilt. Among the first to see the falls were David Henderson and Duncan McMartin who rock-hopped up the Opalescent in 1833 and climbed with difficulty the slide beside the falls and along the chutes above. (Rock-hopping below the falls in low water is still considered great sport.)

The side path to the falls continues down, intersecting the main trail at 1.05 miles. The trail is quite narrow and overgrown, though it has the feel of an old tote road. For a time it is near the bank of the river, then on ledges high above it. You can see a thin stream of water chuting down the side of Calamity Mountain. Even though the route is easy walking, it is filling with witch hobble and maples and may soon be obscure if no clearing is done. Beyond a steep descent you see Mount Adams. You return close to the river at the base of the gorge. Again you have views of Calamity Mountain; its south face and the fire tower on Adams to the south are clearly defined. The trail joins a small stream, which it crosses at an acute angle. Shortly beyond, at 2.3 miles, a privy and a big boulder beside the trail mark the turnoff to the Gorge Lean-to. Turn right, across a small stream to the lean-to that sits on a knoll beside the river.

The great forest continues along the trail—mature trees with an open understory make a lovely setting for the nice long level stretch that leads to a boundary marker and the edge of Tahawus Club lands. Shortly beyond, the trail joins a logging road and the trees are no longer as stately. The trail enters a log staging area, skirting to the right of the open field, then ducks into a pretty spruce-fir stand with big cedars. At 3.3 miles you cross Upper Twin Brook; big cedars make a pretty vista downstream from the shaky bridge. Just short of 3.4 miles you reach the Twin Brooks Lean-to. The closed trail between Cliff and Redfield heads northeast from this point; originally this yellow-marked trail led all the way from Tahawus to Marcy. Its route through private land was deeded to the state and it is closed only because it is no longer maintained (see section 51 for details).

The flagged beginning of the route to Allen (section 43) heads east from the lean-to.

The trail markings change to yellow south of the lean-to, which is just over 5 miles and little more than two hours from the trailhead, via a circuitous route that takes you on a big swing south of Mount Adams. Five minutes south of the lean-to, at 3.6 miles, you cross the log bridge over Lower Twin Brook, then cross a little stream on a washed-out bridge. In the next few miles you will pass

Opalescent Falls

herd paths leading from some of the camps on this private land. A tall, open forest provides the setting for a relatively level stretch that leads steeply down to the swinging bridge over the Opalescent at 4.65 miles. Across the river angle left to follow a new stretch of road along the river, passing the old ford at 4.8 miles.

The trail is close to the river, near a lovely oxbow, but watch for a trail rerouting to the west around a particularly wet section. At 5.85 miles you pass a view of Allen across the river (heading north, this is your first approach to the Opalescent). Leaving the river, the trail heads through a cedar corridor. It is occasionally muddy underfoot, but generally a nice narrow path through tall cedar, spruce, and balsam. The trail makes a distinct jog to the right and at 6.55 miles approaches Lake Sally. You continue north along that lake without ever coming close to it. Shortly after you leave Lake Sally, a sign points you to a sharp left turn up a grade, then a sharp right onto an old road. The way left is private.

Following the roadway, the trail is level and open, but soon angles left again to become a narrow route in the woods at 7.25 miles. The trail is rooty and muddy, rolling slightly, as it crosses several small streams in deep forest to reach an intersection at 7.75 miles. Right is the old trail to Mount Adams. The trail up Mount Adams is not described because its fire tower is closed and there is not even a hint of the great view of the High Peaks without it. Today, hikers can only enjoy the curious tale of the peak's name. Adams was some-times called Robinson, after a McIntyre relative who was associated with the mine. Members of the Tahawus Club remember calling it Iron Mountain early in this century, but it probably was named for an E. A. Adams, a founder of the Tahawian Society, a short-lived organization that in 1847 proposed building a "pedestrian road" from Keene Valley over Tahawus the mountain to Tahawus the mine.

You should angle left at this intersection and in 250 yards you reach the big floating bridge across the northern bay of beaver-raised, cedar-shored Lake Jimmy. Across the bridge, the road angles right, and the narrow trail leads left to another woods road. You walk beneath power lines and angle left at 8.35 miles to the bridge over the Hudson—a huge, iron, swinging affair. Across it the trail is briefly beside the Hudson, then left up a roadway to the parking area, 0.6 mile from the Upper Parking Area.

43 Allen Mountain
Paths, bushwhack, and slide-climb

This mountain was named for the Reverend Frederick B. Allen, who sketched and fished in the High Peaks during the summers of 1869 to 1871. There has never been a state trail to its summit, though you will find paths on the slopes.

The 2380-foot climb along a one-way, sometimes flagged, but occasionally poorly defined path of over 4.2 miles takes about four hours for the ascent, three hours for the return. This would be a full day's hiking, except for the fact that the path begins at the Twin Brooks Lean-to, 5 miles along the Opalescent Trail from the parking area on the road to the Upper Works. Hence climbing Allen is more than most hikers can manage in a day, though many hike in the first day and manage to hike out after conquering Allen on the second.

Before you start, consider the following:

1. Much of this flagged route/path, principally the first 2.3 miles, is over private land. You cannot camp or stray from the defined route.

2. The flagged route/path between Twin Brooks Lean-to and Skylight Brook is of relatively recent origin and follows a mixture of cut paths and old roads. If the surveyor's tape marking the path is not replaced when it finishes weathering away, the path could be very difficult to follow.

3. During high water it may be difficult to cross Skylight Brook.

4. When following Allen Brook, keep it on your left for most of the first two-thirds of the way. However, between 3700 and 3800 feet the path crosses the brook, so the edge of the slide is on your right. Do not try to climb the slide as it's messy and takes you away from the summit.

The yellow trail to the lean-to is described in the opposite direction in section 42. Reviewing the obvious points along the nearly 5.2 miles to the Twin Brooks Lean-to and starting at the parking area 0.6 mile south of the Upper Works Parking Area, the mileages are at 0.1 mile, the bridge over the Hudson; at 0.55 mile, the causeway over the arm of Lake Jimmy; at 0.7 mile, a right turn where the old Adams Trail continues straight ahead; at 1.2 miles, a right fork; at 1.9 miles, turn southeast away from Lake Sally; at 2.6 miles, reach the Opalescent River; trail rerouting in the flatlands makes for some confusion in this stretch, which is never far from the river; at 3.8 miles turn right to a path to a bridge over the Opalescent; nearly 5 miles, cross Lower Twin Brook on a log; the lean-to is just short of 5.2 miles. Hiking time is under two and a half hours.

The flagged route and the only legal way to cross the private lands begins at the guideboard near the lean-to. A variety of yellow, green, and blue tape and red yarn as well as red surveyor's tape marks the route. After passing to the right of the outhouse, the path twists and turns through the swamp surrounding Lower Twin Brook. At this point the path is easy to follow, but there are many roots and dead trees to step over and around. About five minutes from the lean-to the path reaches Lower Twin Brook and follows along that band for another five minutes or so before coming out on a gravel road about 75 yards from a camp, which is to the right, across the brook.

Turn left, follow the road for 60 feet as it enters an old gravel pit. Turn right; there should be a red flagged stick on top of a small rise. Ascend the rise and head toward an opening in the bushes, which is about 50 yards from the point the road enters the gravel pit. The path passes through a low, swampy area, climbs slightly, and, about 100 yards past the gravel pit, it intersects an old overgrown logging road. It follows this road for a few yards, cuts up a hillside and follows another overgrown road. This alternating pattern is continually repeated as the path ascends, keeping relatively near the brook. Each time the path levels off, it passes through a swampy section. Forty minutes from the lean-to, after a mile or so, elevation 2400 feet, the path reaches state land near a shallow pool at the base of a rock slab in Lower Twin Brook. The path crosses the brook at the outlet of the pool. The boundary is not well marked anywhere in the next stretch, but the trail remains on state land most of the time.

Across the brook, the path climbs slightly through a conifer stand, crosses a height-of-land, descends to cross a tributary, and enters a mixed hardwood forest. The path has been heading east and it now joins another old tote road for several yards, turns sharply left, leaving the road, to duck into conifers again. This path, swampy in places, undulates as it climbs a ridge, then makes a steep 20-foot descent to cross a tributary of Skylight Brook. Five minutes later the path reaches Skylight Brook at elevation 2200 feet, 1.3 miles from Lower Twin Brook, an hour and a half from the lean-to. During high water, crossing this brook can be difficult, if not impossible. Just after crossing Skylight Brook, you can find several good campsites, and the rest of the way is all on state land.

The path now begins its moderate ascent and in less than 100 feet intersects the old herd path to Allen. As the path ascends the mountain, there are occasional glimpses of Skylight Brook below on the left. In another half hour, after approximately 0.7 mile, the path reaches Allen Brook, 2600 feet elevation. Campsites near the confluence may be good, but it is difficult to get the required 150 feet from water. You are still a good hour and three-quarters from the summit.

Allen Brook follows a slide during most of its course down the mountain and there are several nice waterfalls near the confluence. The brook is on your left as you begin the steep ascent along it. After several yards, the climbing moderates, but there are occasional steep pitches along the lower two-thirds of the path. The path is to the right of the brook for the most part, but at about 3150 feet elevation, the path crosses to the right side, then back after 50 yards or so. At the same time, the width of the brook narrows.

Just after crossing back so the brook is on your left, at about 3200 feet, the path crosses a small gravel slide coming down from your right. There is a cairn marking the slide. Continue to follow the brook; do not go up the slide.

At between 3700 and 3800 feet the slide containing Allen Brook widens and becomes very steep. Be careful; the flagged path will shortly cross the slide and the brook, which is now only a seep. From here on, keep the slide on your right. The crossing is not well marked and a false herd path starts up the right side of this slide away from the summit. Avoid it.

Cross the slide, also the brook, and find the flagged herd path ascending on the north side. The path continues steeply up the left side of the slide, which is becoming wider. The path is bearing left, northeast. Steep climbing continues until you reach a saddle at the north foot of the south (lower) summit at 4200 feet. Here the path turns north along the ridge and you continue moderately for the last 0.1 mile to the wooded summit, 1.3 miles from Skylight Brook.

Views of Redfield begin at the junction of Skylight and Allen brooks. Near the summit, as you start down, you will see MacIntyre. Most of the rest of the trip is without views; but at the ends of short paths leading away from the canister on the summit, there are views east and north, the latter especially good.

44 Blue Bypass Trail

1.9 miles, 1 to 1½ hours, 440-foot elevation change, blue markers

This connector route between the Indian Pass and Calamity Brook trails crosses a low shoulder of the MacIntyre Range. It is rough walking and sometimes wet, enough so that if planning a trip between those two trails, you might consider a 1.3-mile longer, 3.2 mile route that continues on those trails to their intersection north of the Hudson crossing and the Upper Works Trailhead.

From Calamity Brook Trail, turn left, west, at the bridge onto the blue trail and the southern end of this route. New planking helps bridge the wet places as the trail traverses a cedar and spruce swamp. The trail has been rerouted to cross a creek, and here, after ten minutes, you have a view of the foothills of Marshall across a beaver flow. Soon you begin to climb, passing some notable erratics, and paralleling a small stream. You drop to a lowland with a brook and cross that brook three times before reaching a boulder garden near the head of the brook.

The trail cuts left to avoid a rock ledge just before it enters the top of the pass at 1.1 miles. The small pass, bordered with ledges, is quite pretty. The descent begins quickly—with a pack this stretch seems severe when walking north to south. Another little stream joins the trail, which levels out in a nice woods on a logging road to an intersection at 1.9 miles. The road straight leads back to Tahawus, while the narrow path right is the Indian Pass Trail to the north.

45 Iroquois Pass

3.3 miles, 2½ hours, almost 1400-foot elevation change, yellow markers

The pass that crosses the MacIntyre Range between Marshall and Iroquois peaks appears to be variously called Algonquin and Iroquois Pass, and either name is logical. What is not logical is the trail—parts of it are horrible—one writer referred to it as Algonquin Impasse, though it makes an exciting hike. It is often used as an alternate for backpackers returning to Adirondak Loj from Lake Colden, but as a backpack route it is quite a challenge.

For dedicated day hikers, this trail makes the middle leg of a triangle which circles from Tahawus over Indian Pass, over Iroquois Pass, and back along Colden and Flowed Lands and the Calamity Brook Trail. The two-pass triangle is 12.75 miles long, with an elevation change of 2450 feet, a substantial ten-hour trip even with few stops to enjoy the scenery.

The northern end of the trail is 4.9 miles south of Adirondack Loj or 5.5 miles north of Tahawus on the Indian Pass Trails, near the crossing of Iroquois Pass Brook (see section 34). The south end of the trail is 0.1 mile from Ranger Headquarters at Lake Colden. Walking from north to south, a path forks from the trail to cross to a campsite on the northeast side of Iroquois Brook. Actually, the trail stays on the southwest side, to climb steeply over a ridge and avoid high water and beaver problems, before it, too, crosses to the northeast side. In low water, hikers can bypass this climb and start on the path on the northeast side, because shortly both path and trail join to continue on that side.

Iroquois Brook tumbles steeply beside the trail, which begins in a lovely forest. A gentle uphill brings you to a waterfall that plunges beside a V-shaped rock, wedged between two boulders. Shortly beyond, at 0.5 mile, you cross to the southwest bank and head steeply up away from the brook, only to rejoin it as the brook slips over a rock slide. Turning away from the main brook a second time, you cross a tiny side stream on an old bridge, a very slippery, messy place with few markers. Heading northeast, the trail makes a sharp right turn at 2840 feet to pass a campsite. Angling back west, the trail zigzags near the tributary, which spills into the trail. Now the trail heads south of west beside a gorge, then traverses to rejoin the tributary, actually heading right upstream on rock slabs to a high col. Emerging from a narrow walled corridor of balsams into an open birch forest, you can glimpse the rocks that form the west side of the pass. Most spectacular is the 3600-foot rock knob on the shoulder of MacIntyre.

The trail stays on the sidehill, climbing steeply, still at least 100 feet above the valley cleft before it angles left to Iroquois Brook, then right up its bed. At 1.4 miles and 3240 feet, the trail crosses the brook at right angles. Climbing now on the northeast side of the pass, you have a view back to the rock knob as well as ahead to the rock cliffs on the Iroquois side of the pass.

The trail returns to the brook where it is badly eroded, with exposed roots and washouts making rough walking. The grade eases as sphagnum fills the pass. The pass, at 1.7 miles, has elevation just over 3850 feet. Do not be surprised if it takes as long as an hour and a half to climb to the pass. It is not an easy trail!

And it does not get better for a while. Starting down on the south side of the pass, the grade is gentle at first. Boardwalks keep you from falling in the muck. The rest is rooty and muddy and difficult. Even the neat little view of Marcy's summit and the top of Colden do not distract you from the awful boulder field that begins on the east side of the pass and continues for 0.5 mile. Along the eroded trail, you hop from rock to rock, barely descending, or cross marshy spots on slippery boardwalks. This trail was reopened in 1965 along an old route, one that may already have been old in 1922, when George Marshall and Herbert and Lloyd Clark were said to have cut it.

Finally, after descending for only 160 feet in that half mile, the trail becomes steeper. You hear a stream on your right—it is the headwaters of Cold Brook. The trail follows it all the way down to Lake Colden. At one point you can see Lake Colden, at another there is a good view of Colden's big slide. The descent is very steep for 500 feet, until at under 3200 feet it seems like a vertical chute quite close to the brook. Just below this chute in the trail and a waterfall in the brook, you cross the brook and continue descending steeply with more views of Colden's slides. Rock walls close in on the brook, forcing the trail close to it. The trail crosses back to the north side, rounds a boulder, and comes out into the brook. Shortly beyond there is a major rubble pile where gravel and rocks have washed down the streambed.

Beyond the rubble, 1.3 miles from the pass, you climb up the north bank and soon cross a stream flowing from left to right. As you return to the bank of Cold Brook, you can see a path leading across to a camping spot. Just beyond, 1.6 miles from the pass, you reach a registration booth and a major four-way intersection. Do not be surprised if that 1.6-mile descent takes over an hour.

The blue trail left leads in 0.1 mile to the Algonquin Trail (section 141), right leads to Flowed Lands (section 40).

46 Opalescent Trail
Lake Colden to Feldspar Brook
2.25 miles, 1 hour, 500-foot elevation change, red and yellow markers

With the closing of the yellow trail from Twin Brooks Lean-to to Uphill Brook in the late 1970s, the Opalescent Trail became the only maintained route to the interior High Peaks from the south. Even without the resulting additional traffic, the popularity of the Lake Colden and Flowed Lands area for camping ensures heavy use of the trail. That use, unfortunately, is apparent in its condition. You must expect a profusion of exposed roots and generous servings of mud; erosion-exposed rocks, when you encounter them, will be a relief rather than an eyesore. Heroic trail maintenance efforts since 1986 have greatly improved a bad situation, especially beyond Uphill Brook, and future effort will undoubtedly focus on stretches nearer to Lake Colden. Once you have this in mind, forget it and start hiking. This 2.25 miles along the route of the first ascent of Marcy transcends such trivia.

The trail begins at the junction and register 100 yards east of the Colden Dam and angles southeast behind the register. The yellow trail northeast from this junction along the east shore of Lake Colden is described in section 40. Less than a five-minute walk brings you past a lean-to on the right, through woods well-scoured for firewood, to a swinging bridge over the Opalescent. The crossing is at a delightful spot, over a deep pool, with a six-foot waterfall just upstream. To the right, at the far end of the bridge, is the high-water route leading downstream to the many campsites and lean-tos between Lake Colden and Flowed Lands. The red trail continues left, upstream, and in another two minutes drops down to the level of the spring gravel wash.

From here to the large pools below the flume, and from the top of the upper flume on to Uphill Brook, the preferred route would be right along the Opalescent, hopping rocks and walking slabs and climbing ledges, rather than staying with the trail. The choice, of course, requires low water, a little extra time, no backpack, and young and fairly long legs. If you are doubtful, try the first 200 yards anyway. The trail stays close by on your right here, and it is easy to clamber back up to it if you do not like conditions in the stream.

Either way, five minutes of travel brings you to a wide and spectacular arc of falls. From the middle of the open rock slabs at the top of the first falls, there are views back toward Iroquois. And 200 feet farther upstream, as the Opalescent again narrows, the more concentrated flow creates a more powerful and imposing falls. But this wild water is only an appetizer for the main course ahead.

Ten minutes farther up the trail, you reach the beginning of a series of pools in a deepening gorge. If you have been hiking up the stream, you will have to leave it here in favor of the trail. A ten-rung log ladder begins your ascent up the slope next to the gorge, and two more minutes up the trail brings you to a spectacular stretch—the trail is routed right next to the edge of the gorge, revealing a 40-foot drop into a deep pool, with a guard rail of minor brush. You continue to climb steeply another few minutes, passing a tributary flowing into the Opalescent, down the cliffs on the opposite side of the gorge, and finally crossing a lush, mossy, flat stretch before arriving at the top of the flume.

The flume is the machine that has created the succession of pools as it has cut back deeper and deeper, creating the gorge, now over one hundred feet deep at its active end. Not far upstream, visible from the top of the main flume, is a smaller one. Only half an hour from Lake Colden, this feature is certainly worth a side trip, even if your route is taking you elsewhere.

A few feet farther along the trail above the main flume, you pass an especially deep, green pool, just below the upper flume. Above that flume, the river is much quieter. You could return to it here in low water and follow it without any difficulty the remaining 0.6 mile to Uphill Brook, where the Opalescent Valley bends sharply northeast from the generally southeast course it has followed from Lake Colden. The rock-hopping and occasional scrambling along the banks around pools is definitely slower, if more satisfying, than staying with the trail.

Walking this stretch by trail, you follow around a hard bend to the left in the Opalescent, staying generally within 100 feet, but then angling away briefly after crossing a small feeder stream. About ten minutes from the flume, you are again within 100 feet of the Opalescent, before angling away to the right again, climbing up along the north shoulder of Cliff Mountain to a height-of-land on the trail in about ten minutes more. The open understory of the forest here permits glimpses back to the south shoulder and then to the summit of Mount Colden. Ahead, Gray Peak is briefly visible although the prominent feature is a high ridge extending northwest from Skylight that blocks views toward that peak and Mount Marcy.

From the high point on the trail, you quickly drop 100 feet down to cross the stream draining the saddle between Cliff and Redfield, then immediately pass the junction with the old yellow trail from Tahawus on the right and arrive at Uphill Lean-to, less than an hour's hike and 1.7 miles from Lake Colden. You should expect the lean-to to be occupied in summer, and although the area is generally damp, there is much evidence of overflow camping in the vicinity.

The trail continues, now with yellow markers, down in front of the lean-to to cross Uphill Brook, and you quickly find yourself on an extensive section of plank walkways that will carry you almost half the remaining distance to Feldspar Brook. The next 0.5 mile rises less than 100 feet and the ground is fundamentally wet. Stretches of the old, pre-boardwalk trail are visible alongside, and will help you appreciate the present condition of the trail. Less than a fifteen-minute walk from Uphill Brook brings you to Feldspar Brook, and a trail junction. Ahead, northeast, across the log bridge over the brook is the blue-marked Lake Arnold Trail, section 146. Feldspar Lean-to is only 100 yards away, across a second log that bridges the Opalescent. To the right, southeast, the yellow-marked Feldspar Trail leads up past Lake Tear to the Four Corners. No matter what way you head from here, whether along the Upper Opalescent or to Lake Arnold or Lake Tear, you will walk through old growth forests that have never been logged.

47 Feldspar Brook Trail

1.6 miles, 1 hour, 1027-foot elevation change, yellow markers

This section of the old yellow-marked trail from Tahawus to Marcy stretches from the Opalescent River to Four Corners. It parallels Feldspar Brook for the entire 1.3-mile length of the brook and continues on 0.3 mile to the intersection in the saddle between Skylight and Marcy, which is called Four Corners. This trail has the assignment of lifting you 1000 feet up from the Opalescent River to Lake Tear of the Clouds, and it does not coddle you in the execution of its task.

You begin by climbing southeast from the trail junction at the foot of Feldspar Brook, and almost immediately begin to diverge away from the brook, to the right, to cross a tributary within five minutes. This divergence puts you on the right, southwest, side of a steep ridge that separates Feldspar Brook from the tributary, and it is this ridge that you will follow through most of your climb, only occasionally traversing its crest where the brook is audible, if invisible, far down to your left. Although the forest is fairly open along the ridge, the trail is too steep to provide views ahead. Across Feldspar Brook, occasional glimpses of the ridges coming down from Gray Peak discouragingly seem to show that summit to be receding as you climb.

Most of your climbing is done in the first mile, as the trail reaches the top of the ridge and continues now through a sometimes level, sometimes slowly ascending area of mostly thick growth—an extensive area of old blowdown. You slowly angle back towards Feldspar Brook, which lagged behind your ascent and is now climbing rapidly to catch up. You finally pass quite near to the brook before climbing up over one last slight rise to drop down right next to its beginning at the outlet of Lake Tear.

The outlet provides the easiest and least muddy access to the edge of Lake Tear. The trail to Four Corners wisely avoids the boggy perimeter, although you will find several paths leading down to it as you pass, particularly in the vicinity of the old Lake Tear Lean-to site. Many strategically placed logs help you get through this generally wet area almost gracefully, and bring you quickly to the trail junction at the old Four Corners Lean-to site. (Both sites are too high and fragile to permit camping.) Straight ahead, southeast, the trail leads over 1000 feet down to Panther Gorge Lean-to (section 53) and the nearest camping area. To the left, northeast, the yellow trail climbs 1000 feet up to Mount Marcy. And to the right, southwest and south, a spur trail leads almost 600 feet up to the summit of Skylight (see also section 53).

48 Four Corners to Mount Marcy
0.8 mile, 45 minutes, 1000-foot vertical rise, yellow markers

The trail is all on bare rock now for the final ascent of Marcy from the south. It climbs moderately through spruce and balsam to a large, flat rock to the right of the trail, a little over halfway up. From the rock there are good views of Skylight, Haystack, and Panther Gorge. You shortly emerge above tree line, and 100 yards above the rock reach Schofield Cobble, a large, prominent outcrop, just over 0.3 mile below the summit. Marked with yellow blazes and a few cairns, the trail heads steeply northeast then back northwest to the summit.

If you are descending by this route, note that the trail heads toward the southeast shoulder of Marcy before zigzagging back toward the southwest. Sections 123 and 147 contain more on Marcy and continuing trails.

49 Gray Peak
Herd paths

Gray Peak was named for Asa Gray, the nineteenth-century botanist. It is a 4825-foot (1471-meter) projection on the western shoulder of the Marcy massif and it is the highest peak without a maintained trail in the Adirondacks. There are a number of paths leading to it, many of them leading from the summit of Marcy. In fact, it is quite difficult to find the correct one from this direction, so it is recommended that the first crossing of this ridge be from Gray to Marcy after an ascent to Gray from the outlet of Lake Tear.

You can spot the path that leads from the Feldspar Brook trail toward Gray from the trail. An obvious herd path crosses the outlet of Lake Tear and starts to climb at a moderate rate. It then drops down over an outcrop and continues the ascent, heading a little east of north. Shortly after going down the outcrop, the path reaches the site of a relatively new slide, which has been entirely caused by scrambling peak baggers since the late 1950s. Keep to the right of the slide.

The path alternates between moderate and steep, but the going is not terribly difficult. About 0.4 mile from the outlet of Lake Tear, the path levels off, bears right, and reaches the summit of Gray after climbing 495 feet. The top of Gray is a long ridge and the true summit is marked by a Forty-sixer canister.

Note that it is relatively easy to follow this path back down to Lake Tear,

Gray from Marcy with Cliff, Redfield, and Santanoni beyond

but much more difficult to follow the intermittent paths along the ridge line for 0.6 mile to Marcy's summit. The loop—from Marcy to Four Corners (with a side trip to Skylight) to Lake Tear and up over Gray—can be completed by the bushwhack along the ridgeline, but you need some experience with herd paths first. This is harder than Cliff or Redfield or Tabletop.

From Gray, head north of east on the ridge, over an outcrop, past a view spot, and drop down slightly to the col. The ascent toward Marcy is fairly steep, but quickly emerges from thick scrub onto open rock.

For those who want to go from Marcy to Gray, in spite of the fact that it is extremely difficult to find the herd path in this direction, head southwest from Marcy to the lowest point of the tree line, looking for an opening in the thick scrub. Take a compass heading toward the large rock outcrop that appears well below the summit of Gray. One herd path goes to the southeast corner of this outcrop, but scrub hides drop-offs on the ledges that ring the west shoulder of Marcy. Once you reach the outcrop, continue west, staying north of the outcrop. A path leads up the rock for a view, while another leads west, descends the outcrop, and ascends the summit of Gray.

50 Mount Redfield

Paths or following a stream

It was not until 1872 that Colvin named this peak after the geologist William C. Redfield, in spite of the fact Redfield was among the first explorers of several higher peaks. According to his son, Redfield thought of himself as the real leader of the 1836 and 1837 expeditions, and thus the proper authority to bestow names. In fact, the son wrote of the injustice of Marcy not being named after Redfield, who "first saw the peak, took its bearings, led a second expedition to its top, and made the first measurement of its height." He concluded that Colvin's action rendered "tardy and imperfect justice, by giving the name of Redfield to another lower peak lying in the wilderness of summits eastward (sic) of Mount Marcy."

Redfield, at 4505 feet (1404 meters), is almost always climbed from Uphill Brook Lean-to, which is also the usual starting point for Cliff, and round-trip travel time can be as little as two hours, so it is often climbed on the same day as the lower peak. But try not to be in a rush to get up and down Redfield. Most of the route is along Uphill Brook, which has the unique distinction of being entirely above 3200 feet in elevation. The first 0.5 mile of the route following Uphill Brook is worth lingering along, and you will want to spend extra time on the top, where there is a spectacular vista south past Allen Mountain and southeast toward the multitude of slides on the west side of the Dix Range.

You leave Uphill Lean-to going south on paths with Uphill Brook on your left. Stay left, near the brook, through the elaborate network of paths that spread out for the first five minutes, to where the brook bends southeast. Beyond the bend, there tends to be only a single good path, and occasional diverging paths merge in a few minutes. Five minutes beyond the bend, you arrive at the upper end of a large island in Uphill Brook, and the path brings you right to the bank so you can look straight southeast up the brook for four or five hundred feet. From this point, in low water, it is easier to follow the brook, although it is necessary to make a short bypass of a large pool about five minutes from the island. In high water, you have to follow the sometimes ragged paths that continue on the right side of the brook as you ascend.

Continuing along the brook, or next to it, you arrive at a magnificent sixty-foot falls, about twenty minutes from the lean-to. Cross the brook and climb next to the falls, or if there seems to be too much water to permit that, continue in the draw to the left to one of several high-water falls, where the rock is usually dry. Above the falls, Uphill Brook rises only slowly, flowing from one shallow pool to the next over slightly sloping rock slabs. About thirty minutes from the lean-to, you reach a major tributary that flows into a large pool from the right.

Above the pool, Uphill Brook tends to the east, eventually bending to reach Moss Pond, just 350 feet below the summit of Redfield. The usual route to Redfield continues from here along the tributary, the beginning usually marked by a cairn. Either climb up the stream bed, or find paths to the right of the stream as you climb. Five minutes from Uphill Brook, a strong feeder stream enters from the right; stay left with the main tributary here. Forty-five minutes from the lean-to, the tributary has begun to break up into its many small feeders and in another ten minutes you have climbed beyond the usual ends of all of them, well up the north face of Redfield.

About ten minutes from the top, you can step off the path onto a strategically placed boulder for views out to the north toward Colden and MacIntyre. The path splits a few moments beyond the lookout rock, but either choice will bring you quickly up to the summit and its small glacial erratic, an hour and a quarter from the lean-to.

51 Cliff Mountain

Path to a canister

In spite of the fact that the Adirondacks are rising, the recent USGS determined that several peaks are actually shorter than previous maps showed them to be. In this case, one of the Forty-six has shrunk to 58 feet below the requisite 4000 feet. The elevation of this trailless peak is currently given as 1202 meters.

When you look at Cliff to the southeast from the former outlet of Flowed Lands into Calamity Brook, it appears as an almost remarkably undramatic, if pleasant, backdrop to the Flowed Lands, with an unbroken mantle of gently rising forest. "That's Cliff?" is the most natural response to its identification. Had your approach to the mountain been up the old yellow trail to Marcy, along Upper Twin Brook, you would have seen no need to question its name. The southeast side of the mountain is lined with vertical rock. If you are coming to Cliff on this route from Twin Brooks Lean-to, there is an extensive rubble slide, obvious from the trail, that leads up through the cliffs to a notch just northeast of the summit, where you will find the herd track leading left up to the Forty-sixer register and canister. At the base of the slide, you are some 400 feet below the height-of-land in the saddle between Cliff and Redfield. Hikers from the north generally do not opt to nearly double the required ascent from the saddle by selecting this route up, but doing so provides the opportunity for an exciting and varied loop.

The usual route from the north begins by going south on the old yellow trail from the junction near Uphill Brook Lean-to. You can keep your feet a bit drier for the first few minutes if you pick paths staying nearer to Uphill Brook behind the lean-to, rather than trying to follow the old trail through the bogs,

which are continuous up to a sharp turn to the right, west, some 200 yards from the Opalescent Trail. Above the sharp turn, the trail slowly angles southwest up into the saddle, with somewhat drier footing, although there is often a stream sharing the corduroy track with you. About twelve minutes from the lean-to, you reach the beginning of the first of two competing paths that lead right toward Cliff, presently (1988) marked with red survey tape. The second is less than three minutes ahead, at the height-of-land in the saddle. Its beginning is marked by a cairn of small rocks.

Either path is adequate, and both may be confusing, since there are several paths linking the two, and abundant and dubious flagging does not tell you which is which. All of the reasonable choices merge within five or ten minutes, and bring you in fifteen minutes to the base of a very steep pitch. The traffic up this pitch is slowly removing the vegetation and threatens to turn it into another cliff. It is already open enough to allow views left toward Redfield and the long ridge connecting it with Skylight. Marcy becomes visible straight behind you as you climb.

The steep climbing ends abruptly after ten minutes, and although it is still a twenty-minute walk to the summit, about 0.4 mile, only minor ups and downs remain. You quickly pass over a boggy area, then climb past a group of very large boulders before crossing bumps on the crescent-shaped ridge that seem as if they ought to be the summit. A five-minute descent then takes you to an open notch, and less than ten minutes more brings you through a lushly mossy area and up to the summit register, about an hour and ten minutes from Uphill Lean-to. Nye's summit provides the standard for viewless summits, and this one closely approaches that standard, so do not expect to be wowed by the vista. If you want to see Marcy, push and peek through the scrub a few feet east of the register.

Hikers do make the round trip from Upper Works in one long day; but it takes more than twelve hours to hike to both Cliff and Redfield from the Upper Works.

NOTES ON THE UPPER TWIN BROOK TRAIL

This yellow-marked abandoned route from the Twin Brooks Lean-to (section 42) can still be followed, but with difficulty. Blowdowns have not been cleared, but detours are manageable. Because it has not been brushed out, you can get soaked in wet weather from the spruce and balsam-fir branches. There is an extensive stretch of side-sloping and very slippery corduroy. At the gravel Finch Pruyn tote road, near Twin Brooks Lean-to, there is a short jog left along the road, not a direct crossing.

In spite of these cautions, you may want to use the trail to reach Cliff by way of either the slide or as part of a long loop trip from the Upper Works to the Uphill and Feldspar brooks area.

Iroquois Pass, Shepherd's Tooth, and Iroquois from Uphill Brook above the falls

Elk Lake
to Panther Gorge

THE EARLIEST ROUTE, from Crown Point to the McIntyre Iron Mine went past Clear Pond, where the Johnsons kept a roadside house. Early visitors always noted the hospitality and the good fishing in the pond, and noted that there was a large body of water to the north called Mud Lake, today's Elk Lake.

In this century, a large holding was put together which included both Clear Pond and Elk Lake. In 1964, the owner, S. J. Bloomingdale, gave the state a restricted covenant that prevents further development within 1000 feet of Elk Lake's beautiful shores and bays. The state also has an easement on trails to state land over parts of the rest of the property, much of which is still logged. Elk Lake Lodge is an extraordinarily beautiful place to stay and a great base for hiking in the southern High Peaks. Except for two trunk trails, all trails are restricted to use by guests, including the trail up Sunrise Mountain, which has one of the best views of the High Peaks from the south.

The turnoff for Elk Lake Lodge is 4 miles west of Northway Exit 29 on the Blue Ridge Road. In just over 2 miles, macadam ends, and the entrance sign marking private land is 2.7 miles from the Blue Ridge Road. The trail to Boreas Mountain is at 4.2 miles and just beyond is a gate.

The last 1.9 miles to the parking area is closed the first weekend of hunting season and does not reopen until late in the spring, though you can ski along it throughout the non-hunting season months of winter. Further, all trails that cross the Elk Lake Preserve are closed during the deer hunting season.

You must stay on the trails, both where they cross the Elk Lake Preserve, as well as farther north, where they cross Adirondack Mountain Reserve (AMR) property. No camping is permitted on either property. See the introduction to the chapter on AMR for details of restrictions on the Reserve.

52 Panther Gorge

9.55 miles, 6 to 6½ hours with a pack, 2145-foot elevation change, blue markers

The very name Panther Gorge conjures all sorts of romantic notions of wilderness and indeed the gorge is one of the wildest places in the High Peaks. From it come two of the steepest trails in the High Peaks, leading to the third and fourth highest among the noble summits. While most of the eastern High

Haystack summit with Little Haystack

Peaks can be reached by day hikes, albeit sometimes long ones, it is almost impossible to explore the trails leading out of Panther Gorge unless you backpack in. The exceptions are a challenging walk to the gorge, up Haystack, and out past Johns Brook Lodge to Keene Valley, a distance of 19.9 miles; a 18.85-mile walk over Marcy to Adirondak Loj; or hike to Skylight, with a descent to Colden and out to Tahawus, a distance of 21.5 miles. This chapter suggests several day hikes from campsites in the gorge.

Even the backpack to the gorge is challenging for most people and this description suggests a way of breaking up the trip. Except for a small sliver at 5.2 miles, all of the first 7.1 miles of trail are on private land—the Elk Lake Preserve at first, AMR lands beyond. Camping is permitted only on state lands, which are at that sliver, or beyond 7.1 miles.

The trail heads west across the road from the parking area into a dense spruce and balsam thicket, gradually descending to cross The Branch, the outlet of Elk Lake, at 0.3 mile. Beyond the bridge, the trail briefly follows Nellie Brook, reaching a logging road at 0.4 mile. Here it turns left and immediately crosses Nellie Brook. A right turn 100 feet beyond the brook takes you away from the road to a narrow trail that angles first right, then left to join a logging road in less than five minutes.

The trail now follows the roadway, gradually uphill. Clear markings turn you right, away from an old road that forks left. At 1.1 miles, a bit more than twenty minutes, you cross Nellie Brook again. Signs keep you on the proper route as a trail forks right, a road crosses at right angles, and the yellow, private North Shore Trail forks right. The roadway is quite open—apt to be hot on a sunny day.

After forty minutes, you reach a beaver marsh on the right and a sign pointing left to Lightning Hill along another private trail. You cross Guideboard Brook 75 yards farther along, at 1.8 miles. The route is open and dull through logged forests, passing another trail right to Elk Lake. Clear markings again turn you right where a logging road branches left. Then, in an open field with no intersection, there is a guide board with mileages. A beaver marsh to the left, 0.3 mile farther along, has forced a trail rerouting. You cross a faint logging road, enter another field where the trail makes a sharp left before winding right, then go uphill around the marsh. A right angle turn to the right takes you onto a footpath along the roadway again at a point where it heads left, down into the marsh. Turn right through a draw. At 3.2 miles, an hour and a quarter, the trail crosses Guideboard Brook again—it is very small—and turns to follow it up a ridge.

Even though you are still following the route of an old logging road, the footpath is very narrow and your pace slows. The trail heads up fairly steeply, circles around the head of a draw, crosses to another draw so the steep slopes are now up to your left, then makes a rocky crossing of a rubbly gorge that slopes right, all the while climbing for thirty minutes to a height-of-land at 3.7 miles, elevation 2640 feet.

The woods change as you begin to descend—evergreens, big boulders, and big stumps are evident. You enter a ferny glen, then traverse with steep slopes to your left. In fifteen minutes an old bridge crosses a now dry drainage, then you climb for ten minutes to cross a draw with lots of boulders in it. The draw drops steeply left and you climb up to a little pass at just over 2600 feet and 4.6 miles. It takes nearly forty minutes for the 0.9 mile between the two heights-of-land.

Descending steeply at first, then more gently, the trail follows an intermittent stream downhill. Fifteen minutes from the pass, you make a sharp left in the vicinity of an old logging settlement, then turn right through a broad ferny meadow. The stream on your right now has water. An old wooden sign is all that indicates you have reached state land and two minutes later, at 5.35 miles, you reach the intersection with the ATIS Pinnacle Ridge Trail (section 58).

There is water in the stream 100 yards to the right along this trail, a hummock of dry but buggy ground where you could camp, then 200 yards farther along there is a second small stream. There is also an excellent campsite 0.75 miles to the east.

Beyond the intersection, the Panther Gorge Trail descends just over another 100 feet to marsh level. In five minutes you reach a trail intersection with the private trail that leads west to Panorama Bluff, east to Mud Pond Landing. (The profile of Gothics that is the symbol of ATIS, appearing on ATIS trail markers, is the view of that peak from Panorama Bluff.) Boardwalk takes you along an inlet; you turn sharply right to cross it near a boat landing. The uneven two-log bridge seems treacherous with your pack. (Only a small green arrow alerts you to the sharp left turn you must make to stay on the trail on the return.)

Across the bridge, you turn right to follow the meandering stream, then a boardwalk takes you through the edge of Marcy Swamp beside stagnant pools. You cross another small inlet stream, a slippery bridge here, to begin the five-minute, nearly 0.3-mile walk on a raised boardwalk that makes crossing the swamp possible. Although standing water fills this spruce and balsam swamp, it still supports trees tall enough to block distant mountain views.

The trail climbs into a balsam stand with more boardwalk. You may not even notice the point where the private Dividing Ridge Trail forks right to the upper lake. Your trail heads up into a tall woods with a pretty, ferny open understory. You have to jog left around some blowdown, then back east. Unless this stretch has been cleared you encounter brush, brambles, small beech, and blowdown. The trail then climbs through the dense forest northeast to an intersection at 7 miles, 1.65 miles from the Pinnacle Ridge Trail intersection. It takes about an hour for this segment, longer if the trail is not clear.

Signs at the intersection point east along the AMR private trail to Marcy Landing. (On the return, the latter is the much more obvious route—so watch

Marcy above Skylight's cairn

for the small green sign that marks the intersection, at a point where the trail starts to curve east.)

Here at 7 miles the trail angles northwest and in 100 yards crosses the state land boundary at elevation 2530 feet (770 meters). The trail climbs, then after a slight depression crosses a dry stream, and climbs again.

Climbing now with water in the trail, the tread soon becomes a rocky, rooty mess, gouged and messy. Every time the grade eases, the trail becomes muddy. You cross a small stream, then a larger one at 2870 feet. Notes on the 1.1-mile stretch to a larger stream crossing (forty minutes) just say mud, bad corduroy, mud, and so on. The trail, so obviously an old tote road, is now relatively level and more open, with views of Little Nippletop and back toward Allen. You walk along the 2870-foot level for some time, until a pile of brush in the trail alerts you to a sharp right turn onto a narrow path in the woods. A short rise leads you to another mud wallow and a stream crossing at 8.9 miles. For this one you cross a small brook and head downstream 20 feet to its confluence with a second stream, then you follow the second briefly upstream before crossing to its west bank.

Still keeping a gentle grade, the trail crosses a small stream in ten minutes. Soon you can see the slides on Marcy. The trail is now quite close to Marcy Brook. After walking through a section choked with spruce and balsam, you head over a knoll with enough level space for several tents, then descend to the decrepit lean-to right on the bank of Marcy Brook, elevation 3240 feet. The trail intersection with the Skylight and Haystack trails is a few feet beyond the lean-to.

The knoll and most of the surrounding valley is a wild scene of destruction—spruce deadfalls and blowdowns everywhere. It is little wonder the last portion of trail was so tangled with blowdown. And, combined with the dense stands of spruce and balsam, the blowdown makes traveling farther upstream to the headwall of Panther Gorge virtually impossible. No matter, great trails lead on, though the trail that used to lead up the headwall to the Phelps Trail (section 124) was never reopened after the 1950 blowdown, when some, but not all, of the destruction you see occurred.

53 Skylight

1.7 miles, 1²/₃ hours each way, 1678-foot vertical rise, yellow markers

Skylight, at 4923 feet (1501 meters), has the broadest expanse of open rock of any of the High Peaks. Several acres of open rock cover the gently rounded summit. Atop it are two rock piles—too big and diffuse to be called cairns—put there by hikers who over the years have heeded the superstition that if you do not carry up and add a rock to the pile, it will shortly rain. The mountain was named by the guide Old Mountain Phelps in 1857 when he and the artist Frederick S. Perkins studied its profile from Marcy; but it was not climbed until nearly two decades later, when Colvin made the first ascent as part of the Adirondack Survey.

Skylight's grade seems to be about average—100 feet of elevation gain for 0.1 mile of trail—just plain steep, but the trail from Panther Gorge to the Four Corners in the col between Skylight and Marcy is one of the really bad ones. Streams run down it for more than half its length. Nevertheless, the climb out of the gorge, the emerging cliffs on Marcy and Haystack, and the views to the head of the gorge make it a great climb.

The trail crosses Marcy Brook a few feet upstream from the lean-to and starts right up. There are No Camping signs on the slopes to the south, where a ledge of dead spruce creates a scene of devastation. In 240 yards you cross the stream that drains the col above and already the views begin! Beyond a smaller stream crossing, stop to marvel at the cliffs and slides on Marcy's lower slopes. After you cross the stream again, it begins to join the trail and it or a tributary stays with stretches of the trail for the next 700 feet of elevation gain.

Pause to look back to Nippletop, Dix and the Beckhorn, and Hough and Macomb. As the trail approaches the col, the grade eases and follows the small stream closely. Log bridges cross it and the wet meadow to the Four Corners, elevation 4346 feet (1325 meters), 1.2 miles from Panther Gorge. Straight ahead is the Feldspar Brook Trail of section 47 and to the right is Marcy.

Turning left toward Skylight, the trail is very rubbly at first, but very quickly you can see Schofield Cobble, the prominent knob on the slopes of

Basin, Saddleback, and Gothics from Haystack

Marcy. A steep rock traverse across a smooth slab ends in another patch of slippery rubble. Whiteface peeps up between Marcy and Gray. Even before you are out of the trees at elevation 4870 feet, you can see Haystack, Basin, Gothics, and Giant. Scanning to the left of Marcy, Wright is to the right of Colden, which is etched with three slides; MacIntyre slopes off to Algonquin Pass; and the many bumps past Marshall taper off to the Calamity Brook Valley.

Alpine plants cling to the border of the rock expanse and to niches between slabs. From the summit you can see the entire Pinnacle Ridge leading up to Blake and Colvin. The long flat ridge with one slide identifies East Dix, which peeks up between Hough and Macomb. Vanderwhacker rises above the Boreas Ponds, with Hoffman to the left in the distance. To the right of Vanderwhacker, but much closer, lie Cheney Cobble, the North River Mountains, then Allen. The Santanonis are on the horizon beyond Redfield, which is right below and just south of west. Over Redfield's shoulder you can see Calamity Mountain. The Sawtooth Range is above Algonquin Pass.

Colvin Bolt No. 17 was embedded in the summit in 1876. Descending from it, head toward Gray Peak, for cairns direct you along that course off the open rock.

54 Haystack

1.5 miles, 1¹/₂ to 2 hours, 1720-foot vertical rise, yellow markers

The top 400 feet of Haystack's cone are bare rock—green with map lichens—and it is perhaps the prettiest summit of all. Like its slightly shorter (by 36 feet) partner, Skylight, Haystack at 4969 feet (1512 meters), is a great mountain. Two trails approach its summit, suggesting several loops.

The statistics of its climb given above suggest the approach from Panther Gorge is only slightly steeper than Skylight's; but that is not true. For the first half of the distance to the summit, the trail zigzags up 516 feet to a saddle between the summit cone and Bartlett Ridge. It then turns north to climb nearly 1200 feet in 0.75 mile, making this the steepest trail in the Adirondacks.

The trail starts up from the intersection north of Panther Lean-to. The first pitch puts it on a plateau of blowdown—a wild scene of destruction. Glimpses of slides on Marcy appear as you zigzag up past big boulders, winding generally east. The col between Haystack and Bartlett Ridge is very pretty, with young spruce and balsam, though the trail becomes muddy in the level stretch just before the intersection at 0.75 mile, a thirty-minute climb. Here the trail turns north, left; the trail that descends Bartlett Ridge toward AMR and the Upper Lake (section 55) angles right.

Steep at first, Haystack's trail quickly becomes a mad scramble. Resting, you look back on the Boreas Ponds, then climb a sheer rock slab steeper than most of the slide-climbs in this guide. A level traverse at 4100 feet ends in another tough scramble. More smooth rock slabs at 4450 feet offer views of Allen and Skylight. Marcy appears as you pull yourself up through the last bit of scrub trees to emerge on the slopes of a wonderful rock knob. From here you see the fire tower on Boreas, Upper Ausable Lake and the Stillwater, the Boreas Ponds, Pinnacle Ridge, Hoffman, and Vanderwhacker.

There is a wonderful view across a boulder into Panther Gorge. Alpine plants, including three-leaf cinquefoil, mountain blueberry, bog wool, and Labrador tea, cling to crevices in the rocks. Cairns lead from here along the safest route to the summit, avoiding those rare alpine patches.

The summit reveals the two knobs of Basin; Saddleback, looking definitely shorter than Gothics; and Gothics, with its elephant-ear slides springing from the massive head, of which Pyramid appears to be the trunk. For those lowlanders who admire Gothics from a distance, this elephantine profile is much more characteristic of Gothics than the soaring arches suggested by views from points near the Ausable Lakes.

Tabletop lies to the north and the horizon beyond it includes McKenzie, Moose, the Sentinels, and Whiteface. The view of Marcy is tremendous! To the west you can see the slide on the east side of Santanoni, which unfortunately is out-of-bounds for the public. To the left of Skylight, the North River Mountains appear over Allen.

55   Snowbird and Bartlett Ridge Trails
As part of a loop over Haystack from Panther Gorge

Snowbird Trail 1.85 miles, descent 1160 feet, ATIS markers; Bartlett Ridge Trail 1.3 miles, ascent 860 feet, ATIS markers; loop 6.35 miles, 6 hours (The trail and lean-to are occasionally spelled Sno-bird.)

Certainly the trails on AMR maintained by ATIS are among the most beautiful in the High Peaks. The Snowbird, half on AMR, half on Forest Preserve, is one of their best. Superior forest cover, narrow foot tread, and infrequent use make this a true wilderness walk.

The Snowbird Trail is one of AMR's two approaches to Haystack, and with the Bartlett Ridge Trail and the Haystack Trail of section 54 members enjoy a great loop from Upper Ausable Lake. Difficulty in reaching the Snowbird Trail makes it unlikely that it will ever have much public use. However, campers in Panther Gorge can make a great day hike over Haystack, down over Little Haystack for 0.55 mile to the intersection with the Marcy Trail, and northeast and down for 0.4 mile to the Snowbird along the Upper Range Trail (see section 120 for more details). At the intersection with the Snowbird Trail and the Bartlett Ridge-Haystack Trail, the hiker can then turn west up the ridge to intersect the yellow trail of section 54 for the 0.75 mile return to the gorge.

This section describes a descent from Haystack to the Snowbird Trail, a descent along it, followed by a climb up the Bartlett Ridge Trail.

Head northwest from the summit of Haystack along the ridgeline to a col at 0.4 mile. Angle right, then left, following cairns to scramble steeply up Little Haystack and down it to a second col and a trail intersection at 0.55 mile. Turn right and descend the blue-marked Range Trail for 0.4 mile, twenty minutes and 460 feet down to a col. This stretch is a rough-footed, rock-hopping portion of the Range Trail that follows a small stream. At elevation 4060 feet, where the stream turns sharply right, south, to tumble down to Haystack Brook, Snowbird Trail forks right from the Range Trail.

The Snowbird Trail begins by following the stream and traversing seemingly near-vertical slopes. In four minutes you reach the first ladder. The descent remains continuously steep to a second ladder, elevation 3800, that ends on a brief level below sheer cliffs.

The lovely woodland trail is dramatically suspended beneath rock walls. Big steps down, zigzags, and occasional level traverses, then two very steep chutes lead to an amazingly large new ladder at 3760 feet. Just below, at another ladder, you are very aware of Haystack Brook, but you only hear it until you

Haystack from Little Haystack

descend another ladder at 3530 feet. Here you can see water tumbling over smooth rocks below and look up to the slides on Haystack above. A narrow, sometimes muddy stretch follows at 3330 feet where the descent has become quite gentle.

Now quite close to Haystack Brook, the trail crosses several small streams that have formed on Haystack's slopes. Leaving the bank of the brook, you plunge into a thick balsam stand, cross several dry washes, and contour less steeply beside the plunging brook so you are again high above it. After crossing another tiny stream, you have a glimpse of Basin above.

Around the 3100-foot level, you reach a mature evergreen forest—huge specimens of spruce and balsam. Below, lying parallel and pointing to the valley, are a number of huge logs, undoubtedly from the 1950 hurricane. The rolling trail very gradually descends to AMR lands at 2900 feet. Just beyond, in a very deep forest, a sign points left to the Warden's camp, 1.4 miles below.

Turning right, west, on the yellow and ATIS-marked Bartlett Ridge Trail, you descend slightly to a private trail intersection near Crystal Brook. Hop rocks across the brook and begin climbing again. A little brook draining the col accompanies the trail. This is a great woods with lots of cedar, but also lots of blowdown. Patches open up to reveal Nippletop peeking through the Colvin-Blake col. It is slow going with rocks, corduroy, and stairs. The grade eases at 3360 feet, and 100 feet higher the trail traverses right across the head of the draw—an opportunity to view the tremendous blowdown through this valley.

Gradually there is a forest change—young balsams fill the easing slopes and a broad valley opens up. A little stream drains the boggy swale that fills the col and even though it is level walking, you have water, roots, and boulders to navigate around for nearly ten minutes to the Haystack Trail intersection, half an hour from Panther Gorge. The 1.3-mile, 860-foot climb from the Snowbird Trail takes almost an hour.

56 Marcy from Panther Gorge

2.05 miles, 2 hours, 2100-foot vertical rise, 2 hours, yellow markers

Start as for Skylight, reaching Four Corners at 1.2 miles, 4346 feet of elevation. A right, north, turn starts you on the gradual and moderate final ascent of Marcy. Notice that you still see an occasional erratic, indicating that the glacier certainly covered everything you will see from Marcy, except perhaps the tops of the highest peaks.

You reach the top of Schofield Cobble with its views at 1.5 miles, where you are almost above tree line. This promontory was named for P. F. Schofield, a leader in the fights to create and give constitutional protection to the Forest Preserve in 1885 and 1894. He was also an active supporter of the creation of Victory Mountain Park after World War I. That park was never created, but the efforts to create it did bring a number of High Peaks summits into the Forest Preserve.

Cairns and arrows on open rock take you the rest of the way to the summit. See section 48 for more about this approach to Marcy.

57 The Panther Cirque Circuit

6.95 miles, 6 to 7 hours, 3400-foot elevation change

The cirque at the head of Panther Gorge is contained by the first, third, and fourth tallest of the High Peaks. From the Gorge, a day-hike traversing all three summits is truly spectacular. You will put it together with sections 53, 54, and 56 above, the top portion of the VanHoevenberg Trail (section 147), the upper part of the Phelps Trail (section 124), plus the the Blue Connector Trail (section 121).

Basin, Saddleback, Gothics, and Sawteeth from Pinnacle

Mileage summary of the segments: Panther Gorge Lean-to, 0 mile; Four Corners, 1.2 miles; round trip to Skylight, 1.1 miles; Marcy summit, 0.85 mile from Four Corners; blue VanHoevenberg Trail to the Phelps Trail, 0.6 mile; red Phelps Trail to Blue Connector, 0.7 mile; Blue Connector to intersection with the Range Trail below Little Haystack, 0.5 mile; Haystack summit, 0.55 mile; Haystack to Bartlett Ridge intersection, 0.75 mile; descent to Panther Gorge, 0.75 mile.

58 Pinnacle Ridge Trail
Pinnacle and Blake Peak

4 miles plus a 0.2-mile detour to Pinnacle, 3 hours, 2500-foot elevation change, ATIS trail markers

The walk along the Pinnacle Ridge (or the northern end of the Boreas Range, as this chain used to be called) is the middle segment in the great long walk from Elk Lake to the Ausable Club or vice versa, nearly 17 miles. This stretch accounts for most of the frustrating ups and downs on that ridge walk, 1000 feet or more of additional climbing added to the 2770 feet of climbing if you begin at St. Huberts, 2100 feet if you start at Elk Lake. The high point of this traverse is Colvin, at 4083 feet.

The Pinnacle Ridge Trail starts at the intersection with the Elk Lake-Panther Gorge Trail (section 52), just above Marcy Swamp. It descends 100 yards to a small brook, climbs over a low ridge, and descends to a second brook. Beyond it you wind across the hillside, with tantalizing peeks of the Range, but no real views. You cross the rocky rubble at the head of a dry gorge, glimpse the Gothics, and cross a second dry wash, all this without much change in elevation.

At 0.7 mile, twenty minutes at most, you cross a stream that drips from moss-covered ledges—it is a wild place. The pitch just beyond leads to a nice campsite to the left on the ledge, one of the few on the ridge near water. The trail now begins a gentle uphill. An opening at 2320 feet reveals the Pinnacle Ridge ahead. Just beyond, at 1.05 miles, a trail sign marks the private trail to Upper Ausable Lake. Here the Pinnacle Ridge Trail turns sharply right, southeast, and uphill.

The climb is steep, sometimes zigzagging, but relentless. Views back north reveal Marcy and Skylight. At the 2900-foot level, you wind around boulders, then cross the ridge at the 3000-foot level headed east below the ridge line. Again the trail traverses below outcrops, then zigzags back southeast to an intersection at 1.7 miles, elevation 3200 feet, a forty-minute climb and an hour and ten minutes from the Elk Lake-Panther Gorge Trail.

A scramble up a rock chute to the right leads of the crest of Pinnacle at 3362 feet. There is an occluded view of the Range from Marcy to Gothics. Cross the crest and wind gently down through a fern glen to overlook Elk Lake from a small rock perch, no more than ten feet in elevation below the crest. You can see the slides on Macomb and Hough, even the open rock on Sunrise, and Clear Pond. Niagara in the next ridge is visible, then in the distance you see Owl Pate and Bald Pate. The slides on Dix are only visible through the trees.

After sliding back down to the intersection with the Pinnacle Ridge Trail, you continue north on the ridge trail, which was cleared in 1988. It had become very overgrown and narrow—but was trimmed almost too wide. The trail climbs 150 feet to a height-of-land below the ridge of a small knob, then descends nearly 200 feet to a trail intersection at 2.25 miles. The trail left is a private one leading to Otis Ridge. The ridge trail climbs over a small hump in the ridgeline, then climbs steeply for nearly 540 feet to a sharp knob, elevation 3722 feet. A 200-foot descent brings you to an intersection at 3.05 miles with a private trail to Upper Ausable Lake. A sharp climb of nearly 300 feet in 0.3 mile leads to another knob. Descending only slightly from this one, the trail climbs 150 feet to Lookout Rock at 3935 feet, at 3.55 miles. This point is only about thirty feet below the summit of Blake, but the trail drops sharply down another 200 feet to climb again to that summit at 4 miles. The continuing trail from Blake to Colvin is described as an ascent of Colvin from the Ausable Lakes (sections 88 and 89).

The Dix Range

IN 1837, THE geologist Ebenezer Emmons named the principal peak in this jagged range after John Adams Dix, who was Governor Marcy's secretary of state and later the governor, whom Colvin urged to provide funds for the Adirondack Survey. Colvin's survey crew put the first trail up Dix Peak from Elk Lake, but it may have been climbed in the very early 1800s by the surveyor Rykert, making it the second High Peak to be climbed.

Dix is the only peak in the range with a trail. Bushwhacks and slide climbs lead to the rest—and almost every peak is scarred with a long slide. Most climbers combine the trailless summits, descending via a bushwhack or the Dix Trail. Herd paths and slide climbs leading to the herd path along the ridge are difficult, making it hard to devise loops over the southern part of the range. Strong hikers usually make a one-day circuit of the trailless peaks.

The western approaches to the Dix Range all begin from the Elk Lake Parking Area, and the restrictions detailed in the introduction to the Elk Lake Chapter apply also to the approaches to the Dix Range. The state land boundary is almost all the way to Slide Brook. Note that the new USGS does not show the tote road that serves as a part of the trail. Also note that the new metric USGS map does not show the split in Slide Brook.

Eastern approaches to the Dixes from the Boquet River Valley are described in the next chapter.

59 Dix Pond Intersection

4.3 miles, less than 2 hours, 460-foot elevation change, red markers

The intersection just past Dix Pond is only 200 feet above the trailhead near Elk Lake, but there are two small hills in between. The elevation change is not great, but if you go on to Dix, on the return, at least one of the rises seems formidable.

This trail leads to the shortest approach to Dix along a trunk trail that gives access to several great bushwhacks and slide climbs. Combining it with the 3.05 mile-climb to Dix through Hunters Pass (section 60) and a return over the Beckhorn Trail, 2.25 miles (section 61), adds up to a strenuous, 13.9-mile, more than nine-hour trip.

The trail starts through the Elk Lake Preserve on a lovely woods trail, crosses a private trail, and heads gently uphill, in ten minutes reaching a logging road. You turn left on the road. (On the return, a cairn at this intersection should direct you from the logging road to the much less obvious trail on the return, so be alert for it. The tote road continues past the footpath that leads to the parking lot, but the road is private beyond the turn.)

The Lower Range from Dix Mountain

The trail crosses a bridge over Little Sally Brook 200 yards after joining the road, which is wide and strewn with gravel and rocks. It climbs gradually to a height of land, then descends with views of Hough to the left on an otherwise dull road through second-growth forest. The going is so easy that by the time you cross Big Sally Brook, which flows through a culvert under the roadway, you have been on the trail for less than thirty-five minutes, covering 1.7 miles. Just past the brook, in a log staging clearing, watch for a cairn and an arrow pointing right, into the woods, to a very narrow route that follows a much older logging road. You cross a wet area and begin to walk on the rocks that have been placed in the trail to harden it. The slow going is nothing compared to what it was like before the hardening. In eight minutes, 0.3 mile, there is a survey marker (2290 feet) on a boulder in the trail. This marks the end of private land. The noticeably taller forest welcomes you to state land.

Split logs make a bridge over a relatively large unnamed brook, through muddy sections, and over a couple of seeps. In eight more minutes you arrive at the first branch of Slide Brook, 2.3 miles and fifty minutes from the trailhead. You can camp above the trail. Old wagon parts litter the banks of the brook. You hop rocks to cross this branch (the bridge is out) and come to the second branch, which has a two-log bridge. Immediately across the bridge there is a lean-to in a field which was an old logging site. This is a favored tenting area for those who plan to spend a few days in the Dixes. This is the point to begin the bushwhack to Macomb (section 63).

The trail leaves the field in a noble forest of big birch and maple, crosses a small stream, and heads uphill. It is rougher walking, but beautiful in this mature forest. Begin to watch for a cairn on the right side of the trail at a point where the trail angles right. This point, 0.8 mile, eighteen minutes, past Slide Brook marks the beginning of the path of section 67.

The trail starts to descend almost immediately past the cairn from a height-of-land at 2460 feet. In eight minutes you cross a small brook, then head steeply down in a rocky, rooty patch to a lean-to in a clearing at 2260 feet, beside Lillian Brook.

A high bridge crosses the brook. Beyond, the trail climbs briefly to a height-of-land from which you can see Hunters Pass and Nippletop. A steep rock chute brings you down near the swampy shores of Dix Pond. Then the trail climbs back to traverse higher up on the boulder-strewn east shore. After rough walking above the pond and below little cliffs and ledges, the trail drops to the head of the pond. Just beyond a wet meadow at elevation 2240, the site of an old logging camp, the trail arrives at Dix Pond Intersection.

60 Dix via Hunters Pass

3.05 miles from Dix Pond Intersection, 2½ hours, 2610-foot vertical rise, red markers

All of the trails up Dix have their dramatic moments, but none more than the route through Hunters Pass. The intersection 4.3 miles from Elk Lake, which is just past Dix Pond, is the beginning of this segment at 0 mile. The trail starts along East Inlet, where there are level places to camp, and quickly reaches a ford to cross to the west bank, where it begins to climb almost immediately. It is a beautiful, soft, narrow trail beside the brook.

You can glimpse a series of peaks and slides to your right as you climb. In twenty minutes the trail levels, dips slightly at the 2560-foot level, then begins to climb again. This spot at 1.2 miles is where the slide-climb on the west face of Dix begins (section 62).

With a rough climb over rocks the trail continues up beneath overhanging cliffs. Already the route is rugged and wonderful. Ten minutes past the level you cross a small brook that comes down from Nippletop. Without its water, the brook from the pass to your right is much smaller now. Three markers on a tree here at 2730 feet direct you right and up again.

More rocks than water fill the brook from Hunters Pass and moss on the rocks indicates it is the usual state. That is fortunate, because the trail now winds in and out of the rocky base of the brook. A really steep stretch all jumbled with fallen trees has great views of the slides above. Broken slabs of Nippletop's slopes fill a ferny place where you have to climb around the rocks and roots. After forty-five minutes, at about the 3100-foot level, you have your first glimpse of Elk Lake. The way ahead is more gradual, but to the right you can see the sharp cliffs above Hunters Pass on the slopes of Dix that you have yet to climb. At a small meadow slightly up on the Nippletop side of the pass, the trail turns right. This point, at 1.8 miles from the intersection (fifty minutes), has elevation 3230 feet.

The trail heads down sharply to the fallen boulders of the pass, then begins a scramble up over them. For quite a while it is a continuous scramble, where you use your hands to pull over boulders and ledges. In a series of pitches you climb the west side of a rock knob. Almost immediately, you have wonderful views of Giant, with Noonmark to its left. Some places are muddy, slippery, and steep enough that it is hard to pull yourself up them. It may take twenty minutes to climb 300 feet in elevation to the bare rock overlook, your first view back into the pass.

A forest of scraggly birches shelters the rock ledges on which the trail is routed. You turn into a narrow cleft to mount a cliff on top of which, at 3750 feet, are wonderful views of the pass and Elk Lake. Even if you no longer need your hands to climb, the way is quite steep. At 4000 feet you can see the cone of Dix ahead of you, and shortly beyond, you reach the balsam-fir layer that rings the summit. The grade eases as the trail tunnels through a dense stand of balsam. Over a stand of dead balsams, the first view of Gothics appears. At 2.6 miles and 4260 feet you reach the intersection with the blue trail from the east. Do not be surprised if the 0.8 mile, 1030-foot climb from the pass takes nearly an hour. It is that rough and there are several nice view spots.

To reach the 4840-foot (1475-meter) summit of Dix turn right on the blue trail and enjoy the unfolding views which are described in greater detail in section 76. It takes the better part of half an hour to climb the remaining 542 feet to the Colvin Bolt on the highest boulder of Dix's long rocky summit.

61 Dix via the Beckhorn Trail

2.05 miles from Dix Pond Intersection, 2 to 2½ hours, 2600-foot ascent, yellow markers

The ascent from the intersection north of Dix Pond is relatively straightforward, except for the time you will spend winding in and out of streambeds. At 6.6 miles total from the Elk Lake Trailhead, this is the shortest route to Dix and perhaps the least exciting. It is often used as a descent by those bushwhacking to Macomb and Hough and the descent permits a great loop walk up Dix via Hunters Pass or a traverse from NY 73. For those reasons, the trail is described from top to bottom.

From the Colvin Bolt near the north end of Dix's summit ridge, head south toward the Beckhorn—that prominent knob that distinguishes Dix's summit profile. It takes but ten minutes to wind across the narrow ridge to this promontory. At the end of it an unmarked but very obvious (at first) path descends to the left, east, toward Hough. The yellow trail's beginning to the west is a bit tricky. Yellow daubs on the exposed rock lead you to a difficult, tumbled chute. An alternate descent, a few feet to the south, is no less steep.

Yellow markers appear on trees, which are tall enough to show them, some

The Beckhorn

200 yards below the summit. A brief level breaks the otherwise very steep descent. Only through-the-trees views show the slides on Hough. In twenty-five minutes you have descended 550 feet from the Beckhorn. Here a slight rise in the trail takes you out to an overlook with a view north to the slides on Dix. A steep chimney follows and the taller trees reveal only tantalizing views of the slides on Hough. Another level at the 4000-foot mark, then a very gradual descent, take you out to a promontory with a restricted view of Macomb, identified by its projecting bump. The trail winds out on a narrow ridge at 3800 feet where you can appreciate how closely the shoulder of Dix, traversed by this yellow trail, clasps the cirque between it and the nearer shoulder of Hough.

Below 3800 feet, the trail is steep again and angles southwest. Birch, with balsam under, appear at 3600 feet. Alternating pitches and chutes, the trail reaches distinctly taller birch and a brook at 3100 feet, 1.1 miles but an hour and twenty to thirty minutes from the top. The brook travels briefly with the trail, then straddles it so you hop rocks right down the streambed. The stream heads off left, but the rough walking continues—a rock garden of difficult footing that lasts for ten more minutes. You feel as if you were close below Nippletop, then the trail angles southwest, then west again. The grade eases and footing is finally better. A gentle hillside traverse through a lovely rich hardwood forest lasts for twenty minutes before it drops you gently to the intersection with the red trail, 4.3 miles from Elk Lake.

Hough and Macomb from the Dix Trail

62 Dix via the West Face Slides

Slide-climb

The 1970 slides on the west side of Dix provide an almost whistle-clean, erosion-proof alternative to either the red or yellow trails from Dix Pond. Only their distance from the trailhead at Elk Lake prevents them from joining the ranks of the most popular slide hikes in the High Peaks. A wooded ridge divides the slide area into North and South sections, blocking the view of one from the other. If your goal is Dix, and you have any experience on slides, you will certainly want to consider either of these as a possible route to the summit.

The bottom of the slide is about twenty minutes up the red trail toward Hunters Pass (section 60) from Dix Pond Intersection. Follow the red trail to a level area just beyond a stretch where the trail crosses a slope dropping steeply down to the right toward the stream draining Hunters Pass. Leave the trail where it starts climbing again and descend less than a minute to the right, almost due east, through open woods to the stream. Cut directly across the stream and continue east up over an extensive rubble pile, to find the stream draining the slide at the base of steep rock slabs, about five minutes from the trail.

The elevation at the base of the slide is about 2600 feet, and you will climb to over 4700 feet before the several branches of the slide end abruptly in the fir scrub protecting the summit ridge. Only the two routes most easily followed are mentioned here, but other possibilities are visible from them for hikers who want to discover additional adventures.

The slide track eases off immediately above the initial steep slabs, curving to the right to give you a brief view of the Beckhorn high above. Your ascent is steady, with underfoot conditions varying from typically scoured streambed rocks to highway-like solid bedrock. At about 3000 feet, the top of the southernmost branch of the slide appears ahead and just beyond that there is a section of rubble evidently held back by a lodged boulder. Beyond the rubble you soon reach a steep ascent through a group of very large rocks, and arrive in five more minutes at a very definite fork in the drainage. Your elevation here is about 3200 feet (975 meters) and it is time to choose between the North and South slides.

The main slide track bears slightly right here, continuing easterly to the South Slide, and can easily be followed by keeping right in the main drainage until it finally bends up left onto the open rock face. The far right edge of the open rock slab above 4000 feet is somewhat easier to climb than any of the alternatives. Despite the twenty-minute tussle with the summit scrub above the end of the slide, ending about 150 feet toward the Beckhorn from the summit, any seasoned slide-hiker is certain to be delighted by this long scramble.

The left fork leads northeast toward the North Slide area, and slowly curves more toward the east. At about 3300 feet, the footing changes from mostly rocky to fundamental slabs, which become steeper and begin to hold moss at about 3450 feet. Remember as you climb above here that only a part of the action is at your feet. You will want to turn around frequently to watch what is unfolding behind you. Another 150 feet of climbing brings you through a narrow band of vegetation that crosses the slide track on rubble at the base of the main expanse of open rock on the slide at 3670 feet (1120 meters). The

central part of the North Slide is mossy and is kept wet by water seeping down from a tongue of vegetation that still clings to its upper half.

The best route up the main slab requires only that you stay near its right edge. The entire route is generally dry and definitely scratchy rather than slippery. A graceful escape from the slab requires a finesse to the left 60 to 80 feet below its evident top. When you reach this area, examine the thicket to the left of the slide, pick the least forbidding place you can see, and attack it. Within 20 or 30 feet, the going should get easier, and climbing straight up will bring you to a 20-foot wide chute through the scrub that will take you up most of the remaining 300 feet to the top of Dix. It is impossible to see ahead for this maneuver from slide to chute, but if you are fortunate you can execute it in under three minutes.

All good things must end, and so the chute does also, 50 feet below the summit ridge in a jumble of enormous scrub-covered rock blocks, separated by very deep cracks and holes that are hidden beneath thick fir boughs. Take your time and ten minutes or so of careful probing will bring you to the trail just seconds north of Verplanck Colvin's survey bolt.

63 Macomb

Herd path, bushwhack, and slide-climb

The naming of this peak is shrouded in mystery. It was probably not named for the Alexander Macomb who was involved in land speculation and one of the largest patents in northern New York, which is named for him. General Alexander Macomb was commander of the American forces in their great victory over the British at Plattsburgh during the War of 1812, but no one knows for certain if the peak was named for him, either.

The bushwhack up Macomb is a combination of herd path and travel along one of the slides that scar the mountain's southwest flank. The route uses the northernmost of the slides, one that was reopened in the early 1970s. The bushwhack starts along a herd path on the north side of Slide Brook, fifty minutes or more from the parking area (see section 59). Follow the path east, keeping the brook on your right. Do not recross the brook. The herd path wanders and at times may be difficult to follow as there are many criss-crossing paths near the start. If you lose the path, remember to keep the brook to your right and in sight, and there should be no problem.

After about fifteen minutes, the path swings up a steep bank, or if you are off the path and it seems as if you must cross the brook, go up the bank and begin to climb. The path follows along the top of the bank, above the brook. There are many conifers and downed trees that make following the path difficult in places. The ascent is between gentle and moderate. The biggest problem is

Part of the West Face Slide on Dix as you look toward the Beckhorn

getting around the deadfalls. The path continues to ascend, but the streambed rises more rapidly, and shortly the path and the level of the brook coincide. The brook is flowing down one of the slides filled with rock and sediment. Follow the slide upstream, still keeping near the brook.

The ascent steepens, but stay in the slide. There are piles of huge boulders. Presently there are red paint marks on the large rocks. About fifty minutes after leaving the Dix Trail, the slide that leads to the summit becomes visible. There are actually two slides; both are to your right. Do *not* take the first slide, but rather head for the second, which is 200 to 300 yards farther upstream. About an hour after leaving the Dix Trail, you arrive at the slide leading to the cliffs below the summit of Macomb. This point is about 1.1 miles from the Dix Trail.

The slide is much cleaner than it used to be, although at the beginning, where the ascent is very steep, the surface is covered with loose soil and rock. Great care is needed so as not to dislodge any rocks as you climb. After ten to fifteen minutes of careful climbing, there is much less scree on the slide and it becomes easier to negotiate the steep surface. Stop occasionally and look back on the panorama of the southern and western High Peaks.

Near the top of the slide is a huge boulder that serves as a perch for some fantastic views of the mountains. About 100 yards above the boulder are the cliffs that mark the top of the slide. It takes about forty minutes to climb the 0.6 mile up the slide to this point.

At the top of the slide there are two herd paths, which converge, though the one to the left seems to offer the most direct route. A small path turns right to ascend steeply through thick spruce and balsam scrub. Fifteen minutes from the slide you reach a blowdown and a large rock. Keep to the left. The path widens and becomes easier to follow. About twenty-five minutes after leaving the slide and nearly a 500-foot climb, the herd path intersects the main herd path from Macomb to South Dix. Turn right, south, and the summit of Macomb is less than 100 yards away.

Macomb's summit is open and offers excellent views of the surrounding peaks. There is a USGS marker giving Macomb's elevation as 4405 feet. Nearby is the Forty-sixer canister and register. Time for the climb from the trail near Slide Brook is two and a half hours.

64 Macomb—the 1947 Slide

Herd path and slide-climb

For many years this was the most popular route to Macomb, but recently it has been used much less frequently, so paths approaching its base are disappearing. There seems to be no reason for this disuse, except that the northern route,

above, is the most direct way to the summit. The slide is barely clean enough to walk, longer than the northern slide, and leads to the base of a cliff below the ridge crest.

Follow Slide Brook as above, for about fifteen minutes, no more than a 200-foot elevation gain. Or better, cross to the south side where there are also paths of sorts, or, in low water, walk right up the brook to the fork. Another brook enters from the east at this point. Follow along the north bank of this tributary until it too branches. Do not follow the branch that angles slightly southeast. If you are following herd tracks on the south side of the tributary, there is a good chance you will be drawn this way—the best herd track follows this branch away from the slide.

Stay in the main drainage for 0.7 mile to a series of slides. Avoid the first one, which angles left. The second, also angling left, appears to be growing and is passable, though it has lots of moving rubble. Continue east to a third, which forks left from the drainage. Straight ahead is a fourth slide. It is also a possible route to the summit ridge.

Encroaching brush is closing in on the third slide, but it is the way to go. It climbs about 600 vertical feet. Near the top, the second and third slides converge and lead up to the prominent cliffs at the ridgeline on the second peak south of Macomb's summit, its southernmost peak. A herd path leads around left, below cliffs to the ridgeline, then north for nearly 0.5 mile over two false summits to Macomb's summit.

65 Macomb to Dix

Herd paths along the ridgeline

MACOMB TO SOUTH DIX

The herd path from Macomb to South Dix is so distinct it might be called a trail. Follow the path north from Macomb's summit, past the junction with the small herd path from the slide. The path to South Dix makes a relatively moderate descent, down the ridge north of Macomb. You reach the col between Macomb and South Dix in about twenty minutes.

Several herd paths lead northeast out of the col toward South Dix. When they emerge from the trees, occasional cairns mark the way where it is open, and lead you up toward the wooded summit. If you miss the cairns, make your way toward the highest point on the ridge. Small trees reappear and a path is again obvious when the path enters the woods. The Forty-sixer canister containing the register is attached to a small tree, near the open ledge at the edge of the broad and scrub-covered wooded summit. It takes about twenty minutes to reach the summit from the col, forty minutes or less from Macomb. There are good views south and east only.

SOUTH DIX TO EAST DIX

The path to East Dix is relatively easy to follow, but it does swing back and forth across the ridgeline throughout its moderate descent to the Col between the peaks. At first there are occasional views toward the north, east, and south; but soon the trees block all views. Stay on the ridgeline between the two peaks. There are several branching paths, but all eventually return to the main path along the ridge. It takes almost thirty minutes of steady descent to reach the col and another thirty minutes to reach the summit of East Dix. The trail up from the col is moderately steep. Again side paths branch from the main path and some care is required to keep from straying from the easiest route. (Hikers scouting this route had to bushwhack around a hornet's nest that was in the center of the path. You may not find this impediment, but there may be others.)

You reach the tree line about five minutes below the summit of East Dix. When leaving the trees to walk out on the open rock face, be certain you know the location of the herd path, or you may spend some time bushwhacking your way along the ridge until you stumble back on it on your return. A faint opening in the trees is your only indication of it. The register is fastened to the east face of a huge boulder on the summit.

There are wonderful views to the south, east, and north. The view west is blocked by the main ridge that extends from Macomb to Dix. Plan on about two hours for the round trip from South Dix to East Dix and back. The distance is only about a total of 2 miles, but it is difficult to maintain a decent pace.

There is a move afoot today to give East Dix the name Clark, for Herb Clark, who was the Marshalls' guide and companion.

If you climb the ridge via the Macomb Slide and hike over Macomb and East and South Dix, returning via the slide, allow eight and a half to nine hours. If you go on over Hough before returning, it will take even longer.

SOUTH DIX TO HOUGH

Starting from the register at South Dix, follow the herd path west along the north edge of the summit. The first opening on the right, north, toward Hough is the start of the South Dix-Hough herd path. This may be barely an opening; but as you progress, the path widens and then descends, turning west. In about 10 minutes the path enters the col between South Dix and Pough, the next north summit in the Dix Range that is sometimes called Hogback. Hough and Pough are much more descriptive names, as well as euphonius. The col is dense with spruce and balsam and old blowdown. The path starts up over Pough, moderately at first, then steepens, drops off, and swings moderately upward. Still heading generally north, the path then goes steeply downward and enters the col between Pough and Hough. It takes about twenty-five minutes to go from one side of Pough to the other.

The herd path crosses the wet Hough-Pough Col and steeply ascends to the summit of Hough, less than 0.5 mile away. However, the path out of the Hough-Pough Col is somewhat confusing because of several blowdowns and diverse routes around them. The path leaves the col on the right side of the ridgeline. Whenever it is unclear, just make your way to the ridgeline, where you will eventually find the path, which heads generally north. It is very steep and narrow and strewn with blowdown. In several places there are short scrambles over rock faces. Even though it is only 0.5 mile to Hough's summit along the ridgeline, it takes forty minutes for this ascent.

Hough stands 4408 feet, 1344 meters tall. It has open rock facing west with great views of Elk Lake, Dix, and the western High Peaks. The names Marshall or Middle Dix were suggested for this peak; but it was named for Franklin B. Hough, "father of American forestry," member of the first legislative committee to form an Adirondack Park, but, nevertheless, one who was as interested in the growth of trees for harvest as for their preservation, a fact that has caused many to question the name.

HOUGH TO DIX

The descent from Hough to the col between it and Dix is quite steep; but the ridgeline is so narrow you have views both east and west. This descent is only 0.2 mile long, with a 390-foot drop, and it takes about fifteen minutes. The col is strewn with blowdown and it is difficult to find the continuing path. Head north, and with a bit of trial and error, you should find the ridgeline route.

Once you are on it and out of the col, the path stays on the ridgeline and is easy to follow as it ascends sometimes moderately, sometimes very steeply, making a wide arc northwest toward the Beckhorn. Depending on which side of the ridgeline has breaks in the trees, you sometimes have views to the west, sometimes to the east. The 0.8-mile, 800-foot, climb takes just over an hour. The path emerges from the cripplebush after a final scramble up the Beckhorn, just east of the yellow blazes marking the Dix Trail.

66   Hough-Pough Col to the Dix Trail

Bailout herd path and bushwhack descent from the ridgeline

This very steep descent should be considered a bad weather escape route only, as it is too steep for heavy traffic. Skirt the swamp in the col and find the stream that flows west out of the col. This is on the Pough side of the col. Remember always to keep going downhill and west, following herd paths where they exist. The brooks you follow are all tributaries of Lillian Brook and this route will eventually bring you to the marked Dix Trail. It should lead along the left side of a slide, going down. The grade levels off and skirts a fern-covered knoll. It takes about forty-five to fifty minutes to reach the knoll from the col. If you fail to follow the herd path, look for it on the west side of the clearing or fern-covered knoll, where it is quite obvious.

The herd path follows Lillian Brook as it descends moderately, crossing the brook several times as it passes through a swamp. Thirty minutes after leaving the fern-covered knoll, you reach an old tote road that crosses a muddy area and leads away from Lillian Brook. A ten- to fifteen-minute walk on the tote road brings you to the Dix Trail and the cairn that marks the start of the herd path to the Hough-Pough col.

Follow the Dix Trail left, south, toward Slide Brook. The trail is wide and level, with rocks and logs over the muddy spots. It takes about ten minutes to reach the Slide Brook Lean-to and another two minutes to reach the starting point for the trip to Macomb along Slide Brook. Remember Slide Brook has two branches at this point. It requires about an hour to hike from the cairn above Lillian Brook to the parking area.

67 Dix Trail to South Dix-Macomb Col
Herd path

Hike the 3 miles on the Dix Intersection Trail to the cairn 0.7 mile from Slide Brook as described in section 59. This cairn marks the beginning of a herd path that is relatively easy to follow to the col below South Dix, although there are occasional false paths leading off to one side or the other. These quickly peter out and it is only a matter of returning to the main path to continue the ascent.

The first part of the path is muddy with some blowdown, but it is a pleasant climb, through a forest of yellow and white birches, spruce, balsam, and some maples. Heading generally east, the path crosses several small tributaries of Lillian Brook and after about 0.8 mile, twenty minutes, it reaches the main branch of Lillian Brook. The path then follows this branch for about 0.4 mile, fifteen minutes, before swinging east, away from the brook.

Ten minutes after leaving Lillian Brook, the path crosses a small tributary and enters a swamp. It meanders through the swamp for ten minutes and emerges at the foot of a fern-covered knoll. Note that this is the same knoll and swamp described in the descent from Hough (section 66), but an ascent to the Hough-Pough Col via this route is not recommended.

The herd path to the South Dix Col has been brushed out, illegally of course, making it the obvious route out of the swamp. It swings to the right of the knoll and goes southeast toward the col. Stay to the right of the intermittent stream that flows from the knoll into the swamp. Following the herd path, it is only a thirty-five-minute, 0.5-mile climb into the col.

The total bushwhack from the cairn is 1.8 miles, an hour and fifty minutes, making this a 5-mile, less-than-three-hour trek to the ridgeline.

Headwaters of the Boquet

The Dix Range from the East

NY 73 TRAVERSES the high valley that is portal to the eastern High Peaks. To the west lies the Dix Range and numerous, small, fire-scarred mountains. The two forks of the Boquet drain the valleys between the mountains and join just west of the NY 9 intersection with NY 73. Roadside glimpses of the forks with their huge white boulders are only a small hint at what lies upstream. There is only one official trailhead along the west side of the highway, but there are numerous turnouts and two unmarked paths that lead to some of the best bushwhacks in the High Peaks. The paths make great short walks and the beginning of the two that follow the north and south banks of the North Fork can be combined into a wonderful, short loop walk.

Great patches of the area to the west were burned in 1903. Pioneering stands of birch have grown in the succeeding years to enormous size, creating an open forest with a rich ferny understory. Paper birch is a pioneer species which often reclaims land devastated by fire. It then shades, stabilizes, and enriches the soil while acting as a nursemaid tree to spruce and fir seedlings, which have more difficulty reestablishing themselves in hostile environments of the sun- and wind-desiccated mineral soil remaining after the fire. Birch trees need a lot of sunlight and are destined to disappear as stands of spruce and fir are reestablished. Despite the fact that other hardwoods are now filling in, as well as balsam and spruce, these birch woods remain the friendliest for bushwhacking in the entire High Peaks.

Most of the upper Boquet valley was acquired with 1926 Bond Act money. Much of it is trailless, but it is, nevertheless, very popular.

Mileages to trailheads and turnouts: Northway Exit 30, 0 mile; King Phillip Spring (good, safe drinking water), 0.4; NY 9, 3.4; South Fork, 3.7 (turnout 0.1 mile south of bridge, road just beyond bridge); North Fork, 4.8 (roads turn off just before and just after bridge).

68 South Fork Boquet

Path

One of the loveliest unmarked paths follows the south bank of the South Fork of the Boquet River. Just past the spaghetti intersection of NY 9 and 73, there

The Great Slide on East Dix

is a small turnout on the west side of the road. The footpath has its almost concealed beginning at this point. Just beyond on the highway, there is a bridge over the South Fork and north of it a dirt road turns left. This leads to a parking area with several camspites nearby. To the right of the parking area, a path along an old road leads up to other sites. To the left, a path leads back to the South Fork.

Set your altimeter to elevation 1160 feet. The southside path takes the route of an old road, paralleling the South Fork through second growth forests with beautiful birches. The path climbs to an escarpment above the river and stays above and back from the river for most of the way. After a forty-five-minute walk, the path returns to stream level near a bend in the river. Huge cedars line the shore. There is an obvious forest change—tall hemlocks crown a knoll at 1.8 miles, protecting a lovely campsite. This corner, where the main and south branches of the South Fork meet, was obviously never burned.

69   Elizabethtown No. 4 and Spotted Mountains
Bushwhack

This bushwhack begins at the bend where the main and south branches of the South Fork Boquet meet. Continue briefly along the south branch, headed southwest still, then cross the branch. Pick a compass course of due west and push your way through the lowland witch hobble. As you begin to climb, you find the forest opening up. As it gets steeper, about the 1600-foot level, the forest is very open with lots of tall, straight maples. At about 1840 feet you reach a white birch layer (fire again) and in another hundred feet of climbing you reach the first rock knoll, this one with no distant views, though you see the 1900-foot hill south of the South Fork with its sharp cliffs and a 2200-foot bump to the right of it. The top of Wyman is farther south. Spotted appears through the trees to the west ahead. It takes less than fifty minutes to reach this spot from the beginning of the bushwhack.

Still headed generally west, you dip down off the rock knoll and up a ridge, bearing slightly to your right. In less than fifteen minutes, at 2200 feet, you see a huge rock ahead. This 686-meter bump shown on the metric map is a monolith, rising like a Mayan temple. To scale it, find an animal path up around the south side, then climb through a cleft in the west face. Scrambling up the east side is possible, but difficult. There is a good view of Noonmark.

From here, at 2270 feet, you can see the top of Elizabethtown No. 4, so sight toward it, drop down 60 feet in elevation to a small col, and immediately pick up more open ledges that lead you toward it. Between the ledges there are great patches of blueberries and lady's-slippers with balsams pioneering this burned area. You climb pretty steadily, reaching open rock again at about 2500 feet. Now it is open all the way to the summit of Elizabethtown No. 4.

Giant and Rocky Peak Ridge above Elizabethtown No. 4 from Knob on Spotted

Charcoal stumps are dark skeletons strewn among the rocks and gravel. It is a leisurely forty minutes from the 2270 knob to the summit.

From the nub of Elizabethtown No. 4, you can already see the cirque on the east slopes of Dix with the Beckhorn thrusting south, the little nipple to the left of Hough, nicknamed Pough. Ahead you see at least one more knob on the way to Spotted. Sight toward it, your route now south of west, and drop 70 feet off No. 4 to a col. Almost immediately you see open rock patches ahead. Wind between them, picking the easiest route, to reach another knob at 2730 feet of elevation. Continue climbing to an even bigger rock knob, then push through an aldery scrub with head-high trees to another open spot at 2960 feet. You continue mostly on open rock, with patches of Labrador tea between the slabs. It is steep but easy, though it takes more than an hour to climb from Elizabethtown No. 4 to the 3440-foot level near the summit of Spotted. From here you wind slowly across the top, looking for views in all directions. The valley of the North Fork lies below to the north.

Back east you can see Lake Champlain and the mountains of Vermont. To the south lie Wyman, Niagara, Nippletop, and Hoffman. Ahead on the ridge lies Southwest Spotted, yet another knob in the chain, about thirty minutes away. You cannot yet see the summit of East Dix, only a peak that is three hundred yards northeast of it.

Return from here or from a point farther along the ridge. It is relatively easy to sight from nub to nub on the return, arcing slightly north and back to revisit them all. It takes two hours to bushwhack down from Spotted, if you follow your ascent route. Leaving the last open rock, an easterly course will take you to confluence of the South Fork's main and south branches, where it is easy to return to the path along the South Fork.

North Fork Boquet

70 North Fork Boquet—South Bank

Path, waterfall

The unmarked path along the south bank has a very obvious beginning at the camping area at the end of the turnoff road, south of the North Fork. It climbs to a shelf above the fork and passes a campsite that is below, nearer the water. Steep banks slope up to your left, but the banks on the other, north, side are even steeper, explaining the route of the path, which follows an old logging road. After less than a ten-minute walk, the path descends to stream level. Beyond this point, the path begins to climb again.

If you look carefully, you can spot a narrow path across on the north bank. This is the beginning of the waterfall path (section 71) and the route to the

Slide on East Dix (section 73). The south path starts uphill and begins to disappear. It immediately splits, with a left route heading sharply up the embankment. Stay right, close to the North Fork. The path clings to the very steep slope around a sharp bend in the stream, then begins a gradual climb. The path is much more obvious now as it ascends to the head of the North Fork flume and waterfalls. At the head of the falls there is a campsite—too close to water to be legal but a lovely spot nevertheless. The distance is shorter than the first segment, but it will take more than another fifteen minutes to reach this spot because the walking is not as easy.

The path continues beyond the campsite, climbing sharply up the gravel bank to a height with views to Elizabethtown No.4 and Spotted. There is a campsite on the top of the bank. Beyond, the path disappears and it is difficult following the stream, which is now bordered by a great alder marsh.

71 North Fork Boquet Waterfall

Path

This path has the same beginning as the South Bank, and crosses diagonally to the north bank, as section 70 indicates. Note, however, this can be a wet crossing. You can continue to the head of the waterfall and flume on the South Bank path and then cross above the waterfall; but this can be wet and dangerous as well.

The North Bank path quickly climbs to a ledge on a sort of escarpment above the stream. You are obviously following an old road again. In three minutes you hop across a small stream on a big boulder. This is the outlet of Round Pond. A hundred yards beyond, a path leads down to the flume and waterfall of the North Fork with its slides and deep pools.

The trail curves with the stream, staying at the level of the shelf above the stream. Small cliffs line the north side of the trail. As these become lower, watch for a sharp left turn in the path. The point is about seven minutes from the flume path. Someone has placed logs and brush on the the roadway that continues straight ahead. Take that route straight, staying on the shelf above the stream for about ten minutes. The roadway curves around to the right and suddenly you hear the rushing water of the North Fork. There is a spectacular waterfall down below. The path leads to a draw, then turns left to mount a rock knob, where perched above the falls is one of the most beautiful campsites you will find anywhere.

The North Fork falls sharply from the marsh below the Noonmark Intersection (section 74) to this waterfall. The path continues past the waterfall and gradually peters out; but it can be used to begin to explore for more waterfalls upstream.

72 Cranberry and Rhododendron Ponds
Bushwhacks

Three little ponds lie on the high plateau between the North and South Forks of the Boquet. Two of them are short bushwhacks from the South Bank Path of the North Fork (section 70). Both test your map and compass ability.

The ponds are shallow dishes with swampy shores, made wet with sphagnum. Thick stands of shrubs surround Cranberry, dense mats of ferns surround Rhododendron, so their more appropriate names might be Leatherleaf and Royal Fern.

Walk along the South Bank path for ten minutes until it returns to stream level, then begins to pull away. Look for the path that leads sharply up the escarpment—this is the easiest way to climb the steep 100-foot ledge that is covered with jagged rocks and dense growth. At the top, take a compass course toward southeast, going up and over several small rises, then descending through a draw beside a wet depression to Cranberry Pond. It is a twenty-minute bushwhack.

To reach Rhododendron, turn right at the top of the escarpment, following a sort of path to the southwest. After about five minutes, there is a sharp ridge ahead of you. Climb it, continue southwest along the flat area on top for 200 yards. Near its southeastern edge, turn left and head east of south through a draw and down to the pond in another ten minutes.

You might want to test your skills by heading northeast from Rhododendron to Cranberry, descending a series of steep slopes to Cranberry. Then head northwest, through a draw, and steeply down to intersect the path about 200 yards south of its beginning. *Note:* If these exercises in map and compass make you uncomfortable, do not try any of the other off-trail routes suggested in this guide until you gain a lot more experience.

73 Great Slide on East Dix
Plus side trip up the Dix Cirque
Path, bushwhack, slide-climb

Three slides slash the northern face of East Dix. Viewing them from Dix or Noonmark, the left one leads toward the col between Southwest Spotted and Dix. The two to the right are parallel and lead to points just north of the summit of East Dix. The one farthest right has been called the Great Slide, and great it is! And relatively easy! The slide is over 850 feet long with an average grade of 32 percent. Even the steep uppermost portion seems fairly mild. The only drawback is the more than 5.5-mile trek by path and bushwhack to reach the base of the slide. Start early and plan on a long day, a nine-to ten-hour trek. An altimeter is really helpful on this trip. Because the lower part of the slide can be very slick in wet times, plan your trip after a dry spell.

The secret to finding this route lies in deciphering the many branches and tributaries of the Boquet River. To aid this task, one which is as complicated as describing the veins on a leaf, some of the branches are given identifying names.

Start by following the paths along the south and north banks of the North Fork of the Boquet (sections 70 and 71) as if you were headed to the North Fork Waterfall. In half an hour you reach a sharp left turn, where the waterfall path goes straight. Turn left, following the path steeply down the embankment to valley level and make a reasonable rock-hop crossing of the North Fork. The path continues southwest in a cedar, birch, and maple valley. In five minutes you descend to cross a small tributary that flows from the west. Follow it briefly, then climb a knoll. At the top there is a faint path to the left. It leads 200 yards upslope and down steeply to Lilypad Pond, the third teacup in the ridge between the forks of the Boquet.

The path continues south up over the watershed between the forks, reaching a height-of-land in another seven minutes—there is a view of Dix through the trees here at 1570 feet elevation. The route continues level, then climbs again, to an open camping area with more views—Elizabethtown No. 4, the nub of East Dix, and the long shoulder of Dix. Water is fifty feet below.

From a high point just beyond, you glimpse the Beckhorn on Dix. The course is rolling and slightly obscure because of dead beech and new growth. Except for stream crossings, this is the only obscure part of the path. Thirty minutes after crossing the tributary, you hear the South Fork. On the return, a lone boulder in the woods used to be the only way to know when to head away from the South Fork. Today the path is pretty clear in both directions.

You continue close to the South Fork, which is on your left, and pass an old clearing and campsite. In five minutes you begin to climb—openings let you view the rocks on the way to Spotted and Elizabethtown No. 4, for you are now quite close to that ridge. You continue a gradual uphill; jagged boulders lie between you and the stream. There is a lovely waterfall with a pool beneath at about 1900 feet elevation.

Almost forty minutes after reaching the South Fork, the path leads to a campsite, elevation 2035 feet, beside the Dix Branch of the South Fork. The campsite is too close to the stream to be legal, but otherwise it is a lovely spot. Ledges above to the right may provide a flat area for camping. The South Fork has actually split just downstream from the campsite, out of sight from the path, and there is a major flume on the South Fork downstream from the split.

[If you are camped nearby in warm weather, you will not want to miss exploring upstream as well. A path follows the south side of the Dix Branch less than 300 yards to a quarter-mile stretch of open slabs, along which there is a choice of pools, small flumes, and pothole tubs. There are no paths above the slabs. The Dix Branch drains the great east cirque on Dix and the cirque does provide a graceful route to the summit of Dix. The steep slide that opens up

Looking down the Great Slide on East Dix

just below the Beckhorn is a delightful attraction that abandons you in the thick cripplebush of the extremely steep upper reaches of the cirque, and other possible approaches are worse. (Without the cripplebush, this would be rock climbing!) You can reach Dix by leaving the Dix Branch within 0.7 mile above the slabs, bushwhacking southwest to a ridge crest 500 to 600 feet above the stream. Follow the ridge generally west to west-southwest to the Hough-Dix ridge and herd path (section 66). Bushwhacking through the Dix Branch drainage varies from reasonable to fabulous, rivaling that to be found in Railroad Notch. If you are looking for viewpoints, wind your way up the northwest to the open ridge there at 3400 feet.]

To continue on to the Great Slide on East Dix, cross the Dix Branch in front of the campsite and climb over the ridge that separates it from the South Fork, which drains the entire Dix Range from Hough around to East Dix. The path now follows the South Fork very closely, and in ten minutes reaches a wonderful, cool, crystal-clear swimming pool with a rock slide above.

The path gets much rougher. The valley becomes very narrow, finally forcing you out into the stream to rock-hop for a bit. Boulders choke the valley. You are forced into the stream a second time and here at 2280 feet the going gets sticky. The path crosses to an island in the stream, then back, and finally to the southwest bank. Continue up with the South Fork on your right. The path reaches another illegal campsite where there is a mud slide on the opposite bank. Again the stream splits and the path winds through mud to the south side of both. Shortly beyond, at 2320 feet, the stream splits again. The left branch is a major tributary that drains the slide coming from the col between Southwest Spotted and East Dix. The moss-covered slabs are the beginning of the slide, which is not especially open or clean.

You cross this stream and continue with the South Fork on your right along one of several paths that line the steep slopes. One leads steeply up, then back to stream level again. You cross several seeps, but the path becomes clear along the South Fork again. You already notice rubble in the stream from the wash on East Dix. The valley opens up a bit at 2520 feet. The herd path skirts to the left of an area of rubble that marks the spot where, if you were headed to the Hough-Dix col, you would continue in the stream. The rubble actually conceals the entry of the Hough Branch into the South Fork.

There are actually three branches here, but by keeping a stream on your right after you pass the rubble, you are following a branch headed toward East Dix. At 2760 feet you can see Hough and Pough ahead on the right side of an opening in the forest. The path angles south and finally, at 2860 feet, as the birch become distinctly shorter, you reach a cairn and the beginning of the slides. A hundred feet beyond, a cairn marks the turn left to the first slide—the Zipper—which starts and ends lower, is a more exposed and slightly steeper climb than the Great Slide, and lacks the latter's easy escape route through the summit scrub and cliffs.

Continue on for a hundred yards—half on open rock, half on a path to the bottom of the Great Slide at 3100 feet. There are two discontinuities, with trees closing in slide patches that are about 150 feet long, then it is all open. Already you can see the nub of rock near the summit of East Dix as well as Hough and Giant. You can sense the deep valley you have been following.

As you progress up the slide, Noonmark peeps up, then South Dix, which appears even lower than Pough. The climbing is great sport. At 3800 feet you are below sharp cliffs. Go up through a cut on the left side, then angle back right. Head up some more and at the 3840-foot level you are just below vertical rocks. To the right of them, a herd path leads up another hundred feet. Walk back left to the top of the slide at 3990 feet. Another 20 feet of climbing and a 100-yard walk along the ridge takes you west to the split boulder on the summit.

This is one slide you can walk back down, and that may be the easiest way. If you are disinclined to tackle the direct descent, there is a good bushwhack route to the base of the slide. Find the herd path descending west from the summit toward South Dix (section 65). As it reaches its low point, 300 feet below the saddle, turn right, crossing to the north side of the saddle, and then bear around left until you are descending north, keeping the drop-off on your right. An assortment of animal trails angles down in the same direction, all steering clear of the steeper upper portion of the slide. The forest along the descending ridge is fairly open, but there are a few low cliffs along the way. The drop-off on the right will eventually diminish, and the ridge will vanish as you merge with the slide track at about 3000 feet. Then watch for two small cairns to guide you back onto the herd path descending on its east side.

Fire-scarred summit of Spotted

74 Round Pond and Noonmark Intersection

2.3 miles to the intersection, 1¹/₃ hours, 740-foot elevation change, blue markers

The trailhead for Round Pond, Dix Mountain, and the southern approaches to Noonmark and Round mountains is 3 miles north of the spaghetti intersection of NY 9 and 73. There is a small parking area 90 yards to the north. It is often full on weekends, but people somehow manage to pull their cars off the pavement to park parallel to the highway. Watch out—the shoulders drop off sharply!

Blue markers take you past the registration booth steeply up a traverse of the face of the mountain on a narrow trail, which gradually pulls away from the road. The grade moderates, then steepens again through a draw in a lovely birch glade until a height-of-land. A 40-foot descent in elevation brings you past a huge boulder and down to the shore of Round Pond, which is 170 feet above the highway and 0.5 mile from it—a fifteen-minute walk. There are No Camping signs by the boulder. From the shore, you can just see East Dix peeping over the hills across the pond.

The trail turns right and begins to circle the north shore of the pond. Paths lead to a good campsite up to the right. Another 0.5 mile and fifteen minutes takes you to the western shore, where the trail turns right, away from a marshy area, and heads generally west along an inlet stream. You climb moderately, then steeply up the side of the valley, which drops sharply to your left. The tall maple trees suggest that this draw escaped the fires. You cross several small seeps, then gradually level out about twenty-five minutes from the shore of the pond, back in the birch and balsam stands. A slight descent follows, then a three-log bridge over a sluggish stream, stringers over the mud, and a second slippery bridge. In twenty minutes more you see a marsh out left—it surrounds the North Fork of the Boquet. Angling right, away from a second marsh, the trail descends to cross a stream toward a four-way intersection at 2.3 miles, an hour and twenty minutes from the highway, and 740 feet above it.

Signs indicate the trail straight ahead to Noonmark is not maintained by DEC. It is only another mile, but the nearly 1300 feet left to climb will give you a taste of what the higher peaks are like (see section 75).

75 Noonmark via Round Pond
The Felix Adler Trail
3.3 miles, 2¼ to 2½ hours, 2000-foot vertical rise, blue and ATIS markers

The ascent of Noonmark from Noonmark Intersection is a continually steep climb over a relatively smooth trail that is in places worn to bedrock. The mile-long, 1260-foot portion from the junction is maintained by ATIS and takes about an hour. It is known as the Felix Adler Trail, after the founder of the Ethical Culture Society, who also inspired the formation of ATIS after a fatiguing climb on Noonmark.

From the junction, climb moderately, cross a short level, and head up a steep chute. In ten minutes the trail heads up through a draw in a rock wall; there are paths both left and right over the rock, but the scramble through the draw is the easiest way. In another five minutes, watch for a cairn. At about the 2700-foot level, where the trail draws close to the base of a steeply sloping rock outcrop, it appears as if a path continued straight. The cairn marks the point where the trail makes an acute turn to the left, climbing up the rock.

Stands of huge birch follow as the trail makes a winding traverse along exposed bedrock. There are few markers, the trail is narrow, and the climb is steep for thirty minutes, until at the 3450-foot level, stairs take you to a ridge of the mountain. Dix appears through the trees. After climbing a rock slide, there is a little overlook with a great view of the Dixes and Hunters Pass. The trail has now moderated and the cover opens up. Look down to the marshes near the intersection—they do seem directly beneath the summit! Ahead you see Marcy, close to Haystack. The slides on Basin and Gothics and the jagged teeth of the Great Range appear.

A rock cube sits atop the summit. To its left is the beginning of the Stimson Trail to St. Huberts (section 80).

76 Dix via Round Pond

6.85 miles, 9 hours round trip, 3200-foot ascent, blue markers

It takes a fairly strong hiker to make this nearly 14-mile round-trip in nine hours, so you may want to camp part way in to shorten the hike. Several opportunities are noted. Otherwise allow about five hours for the climb, four for the descent.

The trip begins as for Round Pond and continues to the Noonmark Intersection at 2.3 miles (section 74) after climbing only 740 feet. Take the left fork, shortly crossing a small stream. The trail is on a level shelf above the North Fork of the Boquet, which is off to the left at first. In ten minutes you are beside it in a felicitous glade with large birch that surround the Fork. You soon pass a campsite, though it is too close to water. In less than ten minutes more you reach a broad oxbow in the stream over which you can see Spotted, Elizabethtown No. 4, and the shoulder of East Dix.

In another few minutes the trail pulls away from the oxbow and starts gently uphill into a balsam thicket. There is a balsam and spruce bog out to your left. As you cross a dry wash, there is a large beaver meadow out to your left. A three-log bridge takes you over one stream, then you jog south with stringers in a wet area. Less than twenty minutes from the oxbow, you reach the north branch, called Gravestone Brook, which has lots of beaver dams flooding upstream. Cross on the slippery bridge and turn left to walk briefly along the side of the area flooded by beavers, then turn uphill slightly again. Shortly you hear the North Fork and descend to its banks. In a hundred yards or so you cross the outlet of Dial Pond near its confluence with the North Fork, which is here about twenty feet wide and quite rocky. Huge white birch surround the stream. You cross several small drainages and reach a campsite. The Boquet River Lean-to is just ahead. It takes only seven minutes to walk between Dial Pond Outlet and the lean-to, which is at 4.2 miles and 2360 feet, and an hour from Noonmark Intersection.

The trail crosses the North Fork diagonally in front of the lean-to and climbs some stairs to another campsite on the right. Another campsite is ahead to the left, down between the trail and the Fork, which splits just upstream from the lean-to.

Pause to enjoy the forest—this is one of the noblest stands of white birch in the mountains and it continues along the next half mile of trail. Adding to the pleasures are the deep water bars that keep this trail dry. The trail is remarkably level, then rises slightly to return to the North Fork near a lovely series of cascades and flumes beneath moss-covered walls.

Still climbing only slightly, the trail is occasionally rocky but still good as it pulls away from the North Fork. In fifteen minutes you hear water again. The birch forest with its ferny understory is spectacular. The climbing now becomes a bit more serious and you cross a couple of seeps and small brooks. A tributary of the North Fork is below the trail to the north. Shortly you see it emerging from a mossy cut of vertical rock, which you cross, then you cross two more small streams. Fifty minutes past the lean-to at elevation 3180 feet you reach a small meadow made by the rubble at the bottom of Dix's North Slide. Turn sharply left just before the meadow and walk upstream along the slide for 200 feet, then head out across the slide on a narrow shelf.

This slide was widened and extended in 1985. It branches shortly above the crossing. Both parts are enormously wide. If you want to climb, note that as you head up, the one to your left is the dirtier, but the right-hand one is pretty clean if you follow its left side. There is a lot of water coursing down it, though, and it can be very slippery. In wet weather, you are apt to slip just crossing the slide, even if you use the shelf. However, if it is not too wet and slippery and you want to try it, go ahead, but remember that it will not lead you to the summit. The North Slides end below the shoulder of Dix, a horrible half mile or so from the trail to the summit. Consider this just a slide for sport and return to this spot.

From the shelf you use to cross the slide, you see huge birch trees tumbled below at the bottom of the slide and this sort of tangle even surrounds the trail as it starts up across the slide. The next 0.7 mile and 1050 feet of climbing is really a scramble and it can take an hour. Blowdowns mark the beginning of this stretch, then rooty staircases, water in the trail, and cliffs to the right (at one point there is a deep hole leading into them, to a cave perhaps?). Even the muddy handholds are greasy! There are great views across to the North Slide and occasional glimpses, behind, of Giant. Gradually the grade eases, the birches are shorter, and the trail moderates along a narrow ridgeline on bare but dry slabs. Gothics and the Wolf Jaws, Big Slide and Nippletop appear through the trees. At 4300 feet there is a good view of Big Slide over the Wolf Jaws Col. Soon you reach the intersection with the Hunters Pass Trail (section 60).

You have 542 feet left to go in 0.45 mile and it can take a half hour. It is still steep, over bare rock, leading to an opening with views of Elk Lake, Boreas Mountain, and the end of the Pinnacle Ridge with the North River Mountains above it. To the west of Nippletop you see Allen, with Santanoni on the horizon. Moving around to your right you see Redfield, Skylight just peeping up, Haystack, Basin, then Saddleback and a wonderful view of Pyramid, which from this angle appears quite distinct from Gothics. Outlooks as you climb reveal Whiteface. Dial Pond sits in a saucer on a line between you and Noonmark. The scramble continues—you have to pull up and over a couple of vertical outcrops. At tree line you find mountain blueberry and Labrador tea. Shortly thereafter, you can see a false summit. You descend from its knob to walk on open rock across Dix's long, thin summit ridge. Finally you can see Marcy—its cone lies between Haystack and Little Haystack. Look on the highest rock for the bolt placed there by Colvin in 1872.

Returning the way you climbed takes twenty minutes to the intersection, almost another hour to reach the bottom of the slide. It's forty-five minutes more to the lean-to, another forty-five minutes to the intersection below Noonmark, and an hour and ten minutes to reach the trailhead on NY 73.

Adirondack Mountain Reserve

ST. HUBERTS IS the name of the tiny settlement where the Ausable River turns north toward Keene Valley. Nineteenth-century mountain climbers stayed there when they explored the beautiful fault valley of the Ausable Lakes to the west. St. Huberts is also the name of the ornate inn built on the grounds of the private club which owns that valley.

In the early nineteenth century, Thomas Armstrong acquired all of Township 48 of the Totten and Crossfield Patent. The 28,626-acre tract included the summit of Mount Marcy and the Upper Range—that chain of jagged peaks from Haystack to Wolf Jaws, the Ausable Lakes, and Colvin, Nippletop, Dial, and Noonmark mountains. Armstrong sold this tract in 1887 to a group of men who wished to build summer homes in the Ausable Valley and to preserve the peaks surrounding it. That year they built a stage road from St. Huberts to the Lower Ausable Lake; a stage ran along it twice a day. They founded the Adirondack Mountain Reserve—also known as the Ausable Club. Their members numbered statesmen, artists, and philosophers, many chronicled in AMR's centennial publication *Up the Lake Road*.

A group from AMR founded the Adirondack Trail Improvement Society (ATIS) to build and maintain trails on its land. AMR owned the northern slopes of the Great Range and Marcy until 1921. There had been a public effort to raise funds to acquire these slopes to create a World War I memorial to be known as Victory Mountain Park. Only a small part of the necessary funds were raised through public donations, so the state provided the rest. The name Victory Mountain Park quickly faded from use.

However, ATIS trails from the south remained closed to the public until 1978, when the state acquired all or parts of eleven of the forty-six peaks. This 9000-acre purchase followed earlier ones in 1922, 1925, and 1932 and brought the state's holdings in Township 48 to 18,215 acres. As important as the acquisition was an easement that limited development on the Ausable Lakes and granted public access over the Lake Road and along trunk trails to state land.

ATIS still maintains many miles of trails on state land that lead to the Great Range and south to Pinnacle Ridge, as well as all the AMR trails. A few trails, principally those from the Upper Lake, are restricted to club members, but the public can walk the rest. No camping, straying from the trails, dogs, or fires are permitted and all of the buildings on the Ausable Club grounds, as well as the waters of the two Ausable Lakes, are off-limits except to members and their guests.

The main route into the heart of AMR's 7000 acres of mountains, lakes, streams, and waterfalls—and the main access route to the many trails originating on AMR land—is the Lake Road, which begins at the Ausable Club's St. Huberts Inn and ends by the boathouse at the foot of Lower Ausable Lake. The road parallels the East Branch of the Ausable River, but from no point along it is the river visible. Many hikers, who use the Lake Road as a quick way to reach High Peaks trailheads, do not know what they are missing when they walk (or ride the bus) along that road.

The East Branch from the Lower Lake to the inn is a varied, beautiful, and powerful stream. If you are not trying to make time on your way to the interior, or if you want a wonderful, lowland loop walk, there are two trails that are nearly always within sight or hearing of the river. This guide takes you to the Lower Lake on the West River Trail and back on the East River Trail.

Those who are intent on reaching more distant trailheads may still want to walk the road. Mileages are given below. Note that most signs on the interior give mileages to St. Huberts, the inn, not the parking area on the side of NY 73.

Mileages on the Lake Road from the Public Parking Area on NY 73

0.1 mile - Weston Trail
0.4 mile - Stimson Trail to Noonmark, Dix Trail
0.7 mile - Intersection with members' entrance road in front of the inn, left turn by tennis courts is the Lake Road
0.9 mile - Gatehouse and trail to bridge and West River Trail
0.95 mile - The gate
1.35 miles - Ladies Mile to the right and trail to bridge at base of Cathedral Rocks Trail
1.65 miles - Henry Goddard Leach Trail to Bear Den
1.85 miles - Trail right to Canyon Bridge and west end of Cathedral Rocks Trail
2.15 miles - Trail right to Beaver Meadows Bridge, followed by road bridge over Gill Brook and the trail left along the Flume just beyond
2.35 miles - Flume Trail rejoins the road
2.7 miles - Gill Brook Trail to the left
3.45 miles - Bypass Trail to the left
4.1 miles - Height-of-land, trail left to Indian Head; just downhill to the right is the trail to the bridge, the West River, Gothics, and Sawteeth trails
4.2 miles - The boathouse on Lower Ausable Lake and the end of the road

(One and a half hours is considered good time for walking in either direction along the road between the Upper Lake and the parking area.)

In July and August, the Ausable Club has provided a bus from the inn to the boathouse on the Lower Lake, primarily for members and guests. Crowding in 1988 led to changes in procedures. The bus will now pick up non-members at the gate on the Lake Road for the trip to the Lower Lake trailheads and at the hilltop east of the boathouse for the return. Members and guests will have first choice of seats, which are limited to 22 with 8 standees. All non-members must pay a $3.00 one-way fare, exact change only, on entering the bus. Tickets for non-members are not available in the inn as in the past, and the inn is off-limits to non-members. Bus schedules will be posted; in the past they have left the inn at 9:00, 9:30, 10:00, 11:00, 1:00, 2:00, 2:30, 3:30, 4:15, and 5:15. The return from the Lower Lake leaves at 9:15, 9:45, 10:30, noon, 1:30, 2:15, 3:15, 4:00, 4:45, and 5:30. Note especially the hour of the last bus and the fact that the buses are invariably on time. There is a chance an additional early morning hikers' bus will be added, perhaps at 8:30. Without the bus, many interior trails become too long for all but the strongest hikers. Trails from the AMR are the most beautiful in the High Peaks, and although they will always be open to the public, the bus ride certainly enhances their pleasure.

77 West River Trail

3.8 miles, 1²/₃ to 2 hours, 500-foot elevation change, ATIS markers

Turn right at the watchman's hut on Lake Road, 300 yards southwest of the inn. Descend gently on a driveway and then on the trail itself to the river. There the trail turns left and runs along the river's east bank briefly before crossing on a log bridge just above a very large pool.

Across the bridge, there is a junction at 0.15 mile. The trail to the right is the William A. White Trail to Lower Wolf Jaw and the Great Range (section 94), with connections to Snow Mountain and Rooster Comb. The West River Trail to the left was first blazed in 1899. Follow it upstream at easy grades, sometimes close by the river's bank or along side channels, sometimes veering away from water. At 0.6 mile, fifteen minutes, you reach a cross trail; the way left goes over a bridge to connect with the East River Trail and the Lake Road. The lower end of the Cathedral Rocks and Bear Run Loop (section 92) is to the right.

Continuing straight, the West River Trail arrives at the mouth of Pyramid Brook in another ten minutes, then passes close to a huge hemlock twelve feet in circumference, off to the right. At 1.1 miles, it crosses Pyramid Brook and almost immediately joins the upper end of the Cathedral Rocks and Bear Run Loop, thirty minutes.

The trail now climbs at easy to moderate grades with some pitches. In another ten minutes, there is a view of Noonmark's summit cone, south through the trees, and after this the grades are easy. Another pitch is followed by a level walk, with the river far below but very noisy. Views through the trees reveal mountains to the south. At 1.7 miles, just short of an hour, you come to a fenced overlook. This is a great place for an extended break. The river, perhaps two hundred feet below, comes churning straight at you over a staircase of cascades with the southern ranges as backdrop.

From here, after a moderately steep upward pitch, the trail, with relatively easy ups and downs, passes a view through the trees toward Giant Mountain, at 1.9 miles, and reaches Wedge Brook, which flows in a little gorge of its own. Angling right, the trail follows up the left rim of this ravine at moderate grades and crosses the brook on a bridge between two waterfalls at just over 2 miles, and a little over an hour. This is another nice spot and a good place for a short break. Immediately beyond is the junction with the Wedge Brook Trail to Lower Wolf Jaw (section 93), which forks right and uphill.

The West River Trail now descends and in a couple of minutes is directly over the river at the mouth of a long series of flumes. Following the brink of the flumes, you enjoy many views down into the turbulent water. After seventy minutes, the trail crosses a very small tributary. Follow it a few yards to your left to the river's edge (BE CAREFUL!) for a stunning view of a waterfall that is not very high—twenty-five feet—but nevertheless very impressive because a great deal of water is shot out of a very narrow space above it.

Another minute of moderate climbing along the trail brings you to a view down to the falls; and shortly there is a view back to the falls from upstream. Above the flumes, the trail flattens out and follows the river closely as it rolls in a wide and bouldery bed. After an hour and twenty minutes, you reach Beaver Meadows Falls, 2.75 miles. This 60-foot bridal veil cascade is considered by many people to be one of the prettiest falls in the High Peaks. A long break here is practically mandatory.

Immediately after crossing the brook below the falls (no bridge), the West River Trail comes to an intersection. The right fork heading up the ladder is the Beaver Meadows Falls Trail to Gothics (section 96) and leads also to the beginning of the Lost Lookout Trail (section 79). To the left, the trail crosses the river on a log bridge to connect with the East River Trail and the Lake Road. The large, blue-green, plastic pipeline in the river transfers water to Gill Brook to augment the Ausable Club's supply.

Beyond this point, the West River Trail goes through the Beaver Meadows—an extensive area of flatwater, sloughs, wet meadows, and alder thickets—skirts the base of a cliff at 3.2 miles, and at 3.75 miles is joined by the upper end of the Lost Lookout Trail coming in from the right. A minute later, the trail bridges Rainbow Creek; and immediately comes to another

Colvin and Lower Ausable Lake from Lost Lookout

junction and the long log bridge that takes it across the river just below the dam at the foot of the Lower Lake. The trail straight ahead leads to Sawteeth, Gothics, and Rainbow Falls (sections 97, 95, and 79).

Before crossing to the East River Trail, go a few seconds out of your way and continue straight to a small, grassy area above the dam for an excellent view across the lake toward Indian Head, Fish Hawk Cliffs, and Mount Colvin.

78 East River Trail

3.3 miles, 1½ to 2 hours, 500-foot elevation change, ATIS markers

If you have just come from the West River Trail across the bridge below the Lower Lake dam, you are standing at a T intersection with the East River Trail. A right turn takes you in 0.15 mile to the boathouse and the end of the Lake Road. Turn left.

The East River Trail stays close to the river for a minute and then bears right along a side channel and enters a boulder field. It weaves its way among the rocks along the base of cliffs for five minutes or so and then comes close to the river again. In ten minutes, the trail starts to cross a lovely meadowy area (part of the Beaver Meadows); and five minutes later it begins to follow the shore of a slough. Three minutes later, from the mouth of the slough, there is a very fine view back toward Sawteeth. Seven minutes more brings you to the end of the Beaver Meadows where there is an old wooden dam and just beyond, short of 1 mile, the East River Trail joins the connector to the Beaver Meadows Brook Trail to Gothics. (A left turn leads to the bridge over the river near Beaver Meadows Falls.)

Continue straight, with little elevation change, and at 1.1 miles, the Gothics Trail forks right, heading to the Lake Road. Five minutes later, just over half an hour, the East River Trail arrives at the head of the flumes and the beginning of the canyon. In two minutes there is a great view of the waterfall. You are very close to it.

Gradually now, the river drops farther and farther below the trail. After forty minutes, you pass the mouth of the flumes and begin a series of ragged ups and downs over broken ground as the trail traverses a very steep slope, keeping just below the rim of the canyon. There is an overlook into the canyon at nearly 1.7 miles. After forty-five minutes, you begin a gradual descent along the rim or just behind it; and, at 2.4 miles, fifty minutes, there is a view of Giant Mountain, followed by a moderately steep descent which lasts about a minute. The grade briefly returns to easy and there are views of Wolf Jaws through the trees to the left, and then the descent steepens again as the trail steadily drops to the level of the river, though at some distance back from it.

You cross a tote road at 2.7 miles, nearly seventy minutes. A left turn on it would take you to Canyon Bridge, while a right would lead to the Lake Road

Beaver Meadows Falls

about 1 mile from the gate. Continuing straight, the East River Trail descends gently, coming up along the side of Gill Brook, following its bank to a bridge at 2.8 miles, just above the brook's confluence with the river. This is a very scenic spot, and not a place to pass in a hurry.

The trail goes over a hump via two routes, one marked steep, the other easy, with the steep route closer to the river. You reach a complex junction at 3.15 miles, after nearly an hour and twenty minutes, where a left turn would take you across a bridge to the West River Trail and the lower end of the Cathedral Rocks–Bear Run Loop. Just beyond this, there is a connector trail forking right to the Lake Road. Another trail, connecting with Ladies Mile, follows the river, while the East River Trail veers away from the river at about a 45° angle to terminate at the Lake Road at 3.3 miles, 0.3 mile short of the watchman's hut and the beginning of the West River Trail.

You can also return via the Ladies Mile Trail, which is a modest loop in the flatlands along the lower part of the Ausable River. The segment nearest the river ends near the gate.

79 Lost Lookout and Rainbow Falls

2.1 miles detours from the West River Trail, 1½ to 2 hours, 375-foot elevation change, ATIS markers

The Lost Lookout Trail can be walked as a high-road alternative to the Beaver Meadows section of the West River Trail, or combined with it to make a loop trip from the Lower Lake dam. The main attraction of the trail is Lost Lookout itself, a pair of ledges high on a shoulder of Armstrong Mountain. The trail begins at Beaver Meadows Falls and coincides for its first 0.3 mile with the Beaver Meadows Brook Trail to Gothics.

From the base of the falls, the trail ascends a sixteen-rung ladder and then climbs very steeply. In two minutes an obscure, unmarked spur path breaks away to the right leading to the top of the falls. As the trail moderates, after five minutes, there is another short side trail leading right to the brook at a lovely pool situated between the bottom of a flume and the top of the series of cascades that precedes the falls. There is a view of Noonmark and Bear Den Mountains from the brook.

Now the trail ascends at easy grades to a junction at 0.3 mile; straight ahead leads to Gothics (section 96). Turn left and you begin to ascend, crossing a wet area at fifteen minutes, continuing to climb moderately as views begin to open up to the left across the valley and behind you toward Lower Wolf Jaw. Then the grade rounds off, and you reach the first ledge of Lost Lookout at 0.6 mile, less than twenty minutes.

The view from this ledge ranges from a shoulder of Rocky Peak Ridge to a shoulder of Sawteeth and includes Noonmark, Bear Den, Dial, and Nippletop;

but the real gem of this scene is the lower end of Lower Ausable Lake, with the river spilling out of it and Indian Head, Fish Hawk Cliffs, and Mount Colvin towering above it. You will definitely want to spend some time here.

Beyond the first ledge, the trail runs on the level for a minute and then drops steeply for another minute to the second ledge at 0.7 mile. From here, the prospect is not as sweeping as from the higher vantage point, but there is a fuller view of Sawteeth and glimpses of the river meandering through Beaver Meadows.

Now, after some initial ups and downs, the trail drops moderately to cross a small stream, immediately recrosses it, and follows its bank on a gentle descent. The trail then veers to the left, drops moderately, and crosses the stream a third time at just short of half an hour. In another minute, you cross a fair-sized stream, then another, and for the next eight minutes, the trail barely loses altitude until it arrives at Rainbow Falls overlook at 1.5 miles.

The overlook is a nice one, but the view of the falls is somewhat obstructed by trees. The temptation here is to scramble down from the trail to the edge of the gorge so the trees will not be in the way. Please do not do this. If you fall, you won't see anything.

From the overlook, the trail descends, sometimes steeply, to the West River Trail at 1.65 miles, nearly forty-five minutes. Turn right on it and follow it across Rainbow Brook to the junction at the bridge at 1.7 miles.

To get to Rainbow Falls, continue straight ahead. In quick succession, you pass the dam, a view across the Lower Lake, and the beginning of the Scenic Trail to Sawteeth (section 97), which breaks away to the left. Then a mostly easy climb brings you to a junction in 200 yards, five minutes from the bridge. The Alfred E. Weld Trail to Gothics (section 95) is a left turn here. Turn right toward the falls. The grades are easy, but the going gets tricky as the trail runs along the brook. This is no place to wear shorts—horse nettles thickly line the trail.

A pipeline comes from a large pool, and beyond it, the trail winds up through a jumble of always wet boulders, treacherous footing, and ends just below the falls at 0.2 mile, fifteen minutes from the dam.

Rainbow Falls is a splendid sight—a 150-foot unbroken plunge into a narrow gorge. The area near the base of the falls is almost always drenched by spray and is home to a number of moisture-loving plants, including stately turtle-head.

80 Noonmark via the Stimson Trail

2.65 miles, 2½ hours, 2277-foot vertical rise, ATIS markers

Noonmark has a great trail from the north. It was named for Henry L. Stimson, an AMR member who was secretary of state under President Hoover and secretary of war from 1940 to 1945. He was also a great mountaineer who pioneered some very exciting climbs in Glacier National Park.

Though a lesser summit compared with its neighbors, Noonmark has an incomparable view. There is no better introduction to the Dixes, the Ausable Valley, and the Great Range. And, if you have never climbed one of the tall peaks and are wondering if you are up to it, you can climb Noonmark via the Stimson Trail, descend by the Adler Trail (section 75), climb Round, and descend via the Weston Trail (section 81) for a 7.65-mile loop from the parking area that ascends a total of nearly 3000 feet, enough to give you a taste for the big climbs.

Head west from the AMR parking lot, passing the Weston Trail in 100 yards. The road climbs, and at 0.4 mile you are near a corner of the golf course. Here a driveway forks left; the trail follows it uphill past several cottages and through a bent-birch arch at the end of the road. The trail continues uphill along a hemlock ridge, across several intermittent streams. You can hear Icy Brook in the ravine below to your left. The trail crosses to state land, and at 0.55 mile from the road, fifteen minutes, you reach a fork in the trail.

[Straight ahead is the beginning of the Old Dix Trail that climbs a total of 1100 feet from St. Huberts to a valley between Noonmark and Round mountains. It crosses several small streams and reaches a wet height-of-land just over 1 mile from this intersection. It then descends over 0.6 mile to the Noonmark Intersection. It is slightly shorter than the Round Pond approach to the Dix Trail, but its greater climb and wet footing make it much less desirable. The Round Mountain Traverse of section 81 uses the southern end of this connector. You can use it also to complete a loop over either Noonmark or Round mountains.]

The Stimson Trail is a right fork that begins to climb immediately through birch and hemlock stands. There is only a little erosion on this trail, which has been well cared for. At the 2050-foot level, you make a sharp turn to the right. Switchbacks follow; on one you have a view back toward Giant. The forest changes to birch with spruce at the 2350-foot level. Now a very narrow route, the trail winds around outcrops, to the first real overlook at the 2430-foot level. Beyond, the trail goes around to the right of the ledge, through a spruce thicket.

Shortly you are on open rock again. As you angle left, you glimpse the narrow triangular summit ahead. From a rock ledge at the 2840-foot level, you can already see the top of the peaks of the Range; 50 yards beyond, there is a view of Round, Giant, and Rocky Peak Ridge. Up through a steep chute and you have another view of the Range, this time with Saddleback and Basin in the cleft between Sawteeth and Gothics. Bear Den is in the foreground, with Dial and Nippletop beyond.

Again the trail winds up through rocks. Around 3200 feet there is a wonderful stretch with views every few feet. In clefts in the rock you can see alpine plants. Peer around the rock faces for views of the slides on Dix,

Hunters Pass, Nippletop, and Colvin. At 3360 feet, you angle left, east, below the crest, then scramble up, past a sign pointing back to St. Huberts, using your hands to pull around the small cliffs that ring the summit. Just below the summit, look back to the rock face of Big Slide. One more pitch puts you beside the squarish rock on the summit.

To descend via the Adler Trail (section 75), head across the rock to the trail sign. Views of the Dixes dominate the beginning of that trail as Giant dominates the Stimson Trail.

81 Round Mountain Traverse
Descent via the Weston Trail
1.3 miles from Noonmark Intersection, 1 hour, 800-foot climb; 2.3 miles Weston Trail, 2 hours, 1820-foot descent, ATIS markers

Let's assume you want to climb Noonmark and Round on the same day. From Noonmark you descend 1 mile to Noonmark Intersection and take a left turn on the Old Dix Trail. Mileage begins from this intersection. This leads uphill beside a small stream that sports a chain of beaver dams starting in 0.1 mile. The trail may be flooded; the valley is filled with dead snags. You climb to a ledge above the flow, descend to cross a very wet place, then cross the stream, all the time continuing up through the narrowing valley.

The valley levels off and fifteen minutes from the intersection, at just over 0.6 mile, a trail sign alerts you to the Round Mountain Trail that angles back right. (If you continue straight ahead, you reach the AMR Parking Area in forty minutes.) Heading right to Round, you only climb a minute or so before you realize how steep the slopes of Noonmark are across the valley. You traverse to the right as the forest has become definitely scrubbier. Climb over a knob, drop into a draw—a cleft with ledges on both sides. (If you are descending Round, there is an arrow at the streambed, pointing you right and uphill.) This is a magical sort of walled valley; and all too soon, you climb steeply out of it. Cross an open ledge and angle left into the woods. This spot is not well marked, so you may have to search for the trail.

The trail zigzags through the woods again, then a cairn points you right across open rock where, at 2800 feet, there is a wonderful view of Dix. Lady's-slippers clump beneath the balsams. You make a level traverse to the northeast, climb again, head through a cleft, and turn right. Now you look through Hunters Pass. All these contortions have been on the southwest face of Round. Finally, you reach open rock and cairns lead you across slabs with views of the top. Cairns angle you back left and are a bit confusing as you cross a small glen. A cairn and a sign at the ridgeline points you left to the Weston Trail. The summit, at almost 3100 feet, is 100 yards to the right.

Allow forty-five minutes for the 0.7-mile, 700-foot climb to the summit, partly because there are several points where you have to search about for the trail. Clearing will shorten this time, however.

Map lichens turn Round Mountain's rock green. This spot seems nestled between Noonmark and Giant, but it still has pretty good views of the Range Trail.

Your descent is via the trail named for S. Burns Weston, member of the Ethical Culture Society and father of artist Harold Weston. Head north from the summit, signs pointing you over a rocky gulch for a level but not easy traverse on open rock. You need the cairns to direct you into the woods, for you head east as you leave the open rock. The trail is narrow as it drops down into birch and balsam, steeply, with pitches at first, then a traverse through a lovely birch glen. Most of the way is now on open rock with cairns pointing you down seemingly paved sidewalks. At 2900 feet you walk right to an overlook toward the lower cliffs on Giant.

The trail continues moderately down, much of the time on open rock, in tall stands of balsam, cedar, and birch that cut off all views. At 2300 feet, about 0.8 mile from the summit, you walk out on a rocky nose, where you can see the cairns that point you right into the woods below the nose. Immediately you angle left to another slide, then head down a very steep chute into woods. From the next stretch of open rock, you can see the arm of Giant and Hopkins. You can also hear the highway, even though you are way above it, with a deep cleft between you and the slopes that border it.

The trail winds along the cleft, then turns away to cross a stream whose base is like a moss-covered sidewalk. Across the stream, you make a gentle traverse through much taller trees. The trail actually climbs slightly, as it returns to the edge of the steep slopes. Continuing along the edge beneath lovely hemlock and spruce, the trail drops over a rock face into a cleft, 1.7 miles from the summit. (Headed up Round on this trail, you would find this a surprisingly steep climb up a chute over this enormous rock face.)

The traverse, almost level again, continues with a small rise. Then you wind through a hemlock forest so dense that there is no growth underneath, and no foot tread visible in the needle carpets. You continue along the lip, now circling around to the west, contouring, passing a notable hemlock at the 1500-foot elevation, just as the bottom of the deep valley to your right becomes visible. The way is steep and slippery down the hemlock escarpment as the trail zigzags back and forth. The trail descends stairs cut into a fallen tree. You reach the property boundary, and shortly cross a wet area to emerge on the road, 100 yards east of the parking area.

Fairy Ladder Falls

82 Gill Brook Trail

5.4 miles to Colvin Intersection, 3 hours, 1920-foot elevation change, ATIS markers

Make this trail your first walk on the east side of the Ausable fault, walking in early spring when the leaves are just bursting. Choose a day after a rain when the whole world is washed to crystal sparkles and the streams are full to overflowing.

The length of the one-way trip reflects the fact the bus does not run in spring. If you choose to add the bushwhack (section 84) to Fairy Ladder Falls, you will add an hour to the walk. You have several options for the return: the shortcut route, which does not shorten the mileage but is considerably easier to walk, or a trek over Fish Hawk Cliffs and Indian Head with another choice of descent routes (sections 85 and 86).

Half your walk is along the Lake Road. From the visitors' parking area walk 0.7 mile to the inn, 0.25 to the gate, 0.7 to the Henry Goddard Leach Trail turnoff, and another 0.5 to the bridge over Gill Brook. Shortly beyond, at 2.15 miles, there is a right fork—a bypass—leading close to the flume on Gill Brook. This trail rejoins the road in 0.2 mile and you certainly want to make the side trip to view this dark, hemlock-covered flume.

The next intersection, a left turn at 2.7 miles, is the beginning of the official Gill Brook Trail. Unless you pause at the flume, this walk takes an hour.

Gill Brook Trail, 0 mile, follows the brook quite closely, occasionally winding away briefly, but always returning to let you enjoy the numerous waterfalls. It is all a joyous cascade, but the first real falls are in under 0.5 mile, about a fifteen-minute walk (the trail is much slower going than the road). Another falls tumbles below the cedars that overhang the brook. In twenty minutes you reach a V-shaped falls sheltered in a little gorge where rock walls create a beautiful deep glen. One of these falls was named Artist's Falls, though which one is unclear. Upstream a bit, water chutes down a lovely slide, sparkling the rock surface to make another falls. Above it there are a number of fallen trees, a wild scene of destruction.

The trail pulls away from the brook briefly before returning to yet another falls. Climbing moderately beside the brook you reach a long, narrow chute that pours over square ledges, another picture stop for sure. Upstream a lovely slide, then another falls over square rocks, before the trail pulls away from Gill Brook. Finally, at 1.3 miles, you reach an intersection, which is not very obvious in this direction because the Bypass Trail makes an acute angle back right.

You will spend more than an hour on this part of Gill Brook Trail unless you are heading to some distant spot—or unless you are walking the trail in summer, when the brook is nearly dry, in which case you will wonder what all the fuss is about. The Bypass Trail (section 83) is one possible return route.

One hundred yards beyond the intersection with the Bypass Trail, you reach a second intersection marked Indian Head either way. The way right, a second possible return route, is described in section 85. Stay left or straight and immediately cross a tributary of Gill Brook. You are at the AMR boundary, so camping is permitted, and there is a campsite here, though it is too close to water. The cliffs on Dial are visible through the trees.

The trail starts steeply through an area with lots of trailwork and stairs and blowdown and climbs to a ridge way above Gill Brook. Fifteen minutes and 0.5 mile later, at 1.8 miles you reach a third intersection and possible return route. It leads right to Fish Hawk Cliffs and Indian Head (section 86). Continue straight ahead climbing moderately again. The trail levels briefly, then resumes the climb, reaching a third intersection in another 0.8 mile. The Colvin Trail (section 87) starts steeply up to your right and Elk Pass is ahead to the left (section 89). The crown jewel in a day hike along Gill Brook is the bushwhack of section 84.

83 Bypass Trail

0.65 mile, 20 minutes, 410-foot elevation change, ATIS markers

If you are making a loop along Gill Brook, the shortest descent is via this Bypass Trail, which intersects the Lake Road 0.75 mile south of the Gill Brook trailhead. Even though it is slightly longer, this route takes less than twenty minutes to the road and ten minutes back to the Gill Brook Trailhead.

If you are headed from St. Huberts to Colvin, Blake, Nippletop, or the Pinnacle Ridge, this trail's relatively gentle ascent with good foot tread is only 0.2 mile longer, but much easier and faster than the Gill Brook Trail, which ought to be savored.

84 Fairy Ladder Falls

Bushwhack

Fairy Ladder Falls was discovered and named by Colvin in 1873. Having been marooned by darkness on the way down from the summit of Dix, his survey party next day moved their camp up the east side of Nippletop to the summit, then down into Elk Pass where they found the falls in the upper reaches of Gill Brook. After camping overnight at the falls, they climbed the peak now called Colvin, dashed back down into Elk Pass, broke camp at dusk, and picked their way down the valley to a late evening supper at present-day St. Huberts.

Heroics of Colvin proportion are not required to reach the falls, but the dense terrain between the trail and the falls, a distance of less than 0.25 mile, is a half hour bushwhack, and it really gives you a flavor for the difficulty of the work Colvin and his men had to do to complete the Adirondack Survey.

At the point the Colvin Trail forks right from the Gill Brook Trail, there is a faint path leading left. It may be the remnants of an old route to the falls, but it is so choked with blowdown as to be impossible. The best route to the falls is the shortest one (several were attempted for this description). Continue toward Elk Pass beyond the Colvin Intersection for about 200 yards. The trail climbs some more, then levels off. Turn left, southeast, at a right angle to the trail, and bushwhack downhill through sticky spruce, over ledges, around cliffs, letting your ears be your guide, for in high water you can hear the falls from the trail. You can also see it from several ledges along the way. There is one twelve- to fifteen-foot cliff to avoid—go left. You descend to a feeder stream that drains the north side of Elk Pass. Cross it and head over a small but dense balsam- and spruce-covered knoll. It is horrible, but still the shortest way. You should emerge from it on Gill Brook just below the falls. For the return, head northwest, uphill beyond the feeder stream, again taking the shortest route.

The spray and foam and rainbows gilding the ninety-foot stairs that forms the falls are compensation for the rough trip. In high water, the stairs are draped by lace, surely a fairy ladder. Note that in summer the falls are almost dry and it is not too difficult to rock-hop upstream to reach the falls from points downstream. Then, as an alternative to fighting the severe tangle between the Elk Pass tributary and the Fairy Ladder, it may be preferable to follow the tributary a short distance down to the junction with the main Gill Brook, and walk up it to the falls.

85 Indian Head Loop

2.1-mile loop from the Lake Road, 1½ hours, 700-foot vertical rise, ATIS markers

The distance assumes a ride on the bus. Add 4.2 miles in and 3.45 miles out for a total of 9.75 miles round trip without it.

At the top of the rise just before you reach the boathouse on Lower Ausable Lake, a trail heads south and begins to climb steeply. In 100 yards, right above the boathouse, there is a nice overlook with views toward Sawteeth. Beyond, the trail begins a series of zigzags. You can appreciate how the trail was rerouted about fifteen years ago to provide nice grades and traverses on this steep mountainside. Even with them, you are climbing pretty steeply. Ten minutes from the road a sign points right: "Gothics Window—117 feet" on a short detour that you should make.

The trail continues fairly steeply, but with nice traverses. You end a long zig to the left below small cliffs then zag back right beneath more cliffs up to your left. Already there are glimpses back through the trees to Gothics. A series of quick zigzags leads to a ladder, more quick switchbacks and a second ladder,

Wolf Jaws from Indian Head

followed by a level traverse beneath a lovely cliff. Then you climb again, moderately, for another five minutes to reach a four-way intersection at 0.8 mile after a thirty-minute, nearly 700-foot climb.

Turn right for 100 feet, descending to the top of the Indian's head and the most wonderful views down the Ausable Lakes. Snowy and Vanderwhacker mountains mark the skyline beyond the deep cut of the lakes. The precipitous slopes of Colvin and Sawteeth clasp the Lower Lake.

Returning to the intersection, go straight through it, up slightly to the top of a ridge and across it on a relatively level walk. From a height-of-land, there is a view of the Wolf Jaws. Shortly beyond a sign points left to a side trail that leads 50 yards to an overlook with views from a rocky promontory to Giant and Rocky Peak Ridge over Noonmark. The trail turns right beyond the intersection with the outlook path and starts steeply down, then moderates to reach the Gill Brook Trail 0.6 mile from Indian Head. Turn left, then left again in 100 yards for the Bypass Trail, which leads 0.65 mile back to the road.

86 Fish Hawk Cliffs

2.65-mile loop from the Lake Road

This loop adds only 0.55 mile and a second great overlook of the Ausable Lakes, the Great Range, and the face on Indian Head to the loop of section 85. Needless to say, you can choose many other combinations of these trails.

From the intersection near Indian Head, head south, directly downhill, for a steep 160-foot drop to a col. Traverse in deep woods in the col, not far from a pool known as Wizard's Wash-bowl, and climb slightly to the top of Fish Hawk Cliffs, 0.25 mile and eight minutes from Indian Head. Slides make identifying slashes on the peaks of the Range from Sawteeth past Gothics. A lower ledge offers the best view of Indian Head, but be careful near the cliff tops.

Behind the ledges on top of Fish Hawk Cliffs, the trail, freshly widened, heads down slightly, then levels below the crest of a hill to the edge of state land. Cross a small stream and descend slightly to the Gill Brook Trail in 0.45 mile, ten minutes. Turn left for 0.5 mile to the junction with the Indian Head Trail and the Bypass, which is 100 yards farther along.

87 Colvin

1 mile, 1 hour from the Gill Brook Trail, 885-foot vertical rise, ATIS markers

Colvin's 4085-foot summit was surveyed in 1896 by Colvin, who placed bolt number 289 in the rock between the three eyebolts that held the original transit.

The point the trail leaves the Gill Brook to Elk Pass Trail (section 82) is well marked; but the trail takes off up to the right over such a steep incline that at first you wonder if the trail really goes that way at all. The trail continues moderately with some steep pitches around some large cliffs, but without views. The moderate ascent continues through conifers to within 150 feet of the summit, where the trail becomes steep again.

The 360° view is unobstructed. This is a great place from which to study the slide on Nippletop if you plan to try that bushwhack. Nippletop hides views of Dix, but you can see Giant through the Ausable Valley, both Ausable Lakes, Wolf Jaws, Gothics, Sawteeth, Saddleback, Basin, Haystack, and Marcy.

The total distance from the St. Huberts Parking Area is 6.4 miles, with 2788 feet of climbing, via the Bypass and Gill Brook trails (sections 82 and 83), making it a long round trip. With a bus ride, the climb to Colvin from the Ausable Club Road is almost 3 miles long with 2180 feet of climbing, short enough that most people go on to Blake (section 88).

88 Colvin to Blake Peak

1.35 miles, 1⅓ hours, descent 690 feet, ascent 590 feet, ATIS markers

Named for Mills Blake, Verplanck Colvin's longtime friend and associate in the Adirondack Survey, this peak is the first one south of Colvin. Headed just west of south from Colvin's summit, the ridge trail to Blake Peak passes an outcrop and makes a moderate descent for 0.5 mile with some ups among the downs along the long, thin shoulder of Colvin that begins the trail to Pinnacle Ridge. Then, the trail descends steeply for 0.3 mile, dropping 400 feet to a col and the intersection with the trail from the Carry Trail (section 99).

Almost immediately, the ridge trail to Blake starts climbing steeply, then levels, and remains moderate with steep pitches. In 1988 there were no trail markers, but water has eroded the trail down to bedrock, so it is easy to follow. Near the wooded summit, the ascent moderates. This summit misses the magic 4000 feet by about 20 feet, though its summit is a magnet for those who are touring the Forty-six. Just beyond the summit, there is a good view of Elk Lake and points southwest. The trail drops a few feet, and then comes out on an open outcrop about 50 yards beyond the summit. This point has a view that makes the trip worthwhile.

There is only one more good view among the many tantalizing glimpses between Blake and the side trail to Pinnacle (section 58). You may want to continue to it, descending steeply for about 220 feet of elevation to a col, then ascending to a lower shoulder of Blake, which overlooks Upper Ausable Lake.

Blake is 7.75 miles from the St. Huberts Parking Area via Colvin, and 4 miles via the Pinnacle Ridge Trail from the Elk Lake-Panther Gorge Trail, which it intersects 5.4 miles from the Elk Lake Trailhead.

89 Elk Pass and Nippletop

1.6 miles from Colvin Intersection on Gill Brook Trail, 1½ hours, 1440-foot vertical rise from intersection, ATIS markers

To climb to Nippletop's peaky summit through Elk Pass requires a 14-mile round trip and a 3200-foot vertical ascent without the bus, a 7.1-mile round trip with it.

The upper portion of the trail winds through forest stands along the upper reaches of Gill Brook, Elk Pass, and the slopes of Nippletop that have never been logged.

From the Colvin Intersection, the trail that has been following Gill Brook climbs, levels off, and even descends slightly, giving you a view across to Nippletop. Another steep pitch follows, putting the trail way up on the Colvin side of the valley. The trail continues level, then descends slightly, angling toward the valley and reaching Elk Pass at the first of three beaver ponds, 0.5 mile and nearly twenty minutes from the intersection. This pond holds a mirror to the cliffs on Colvin's flanks. There is a second pool just beyond on the left, then the trail cuts through the bog that fills this gentle, open, and very wet pass. Colvin gave one of these ponds the apt name Lycopodium. The trail makes a hairpin turn on somewhat dry ground, turning back left around

The Upper Great Range from the Nippletop Trail

the pond to a sign that says Nippletop is 1.1 miles away. It is also nearly 1300 feet up, and that makes it quite a climb!

The beauty of the climb is the unfolding of views back to the Range Trail as elevation increases. In five minutes you already see Wolf Jaws and Gothics peeking up over the Colvin Ridge. A long traverse left ends with a climb over a rock ledge out to a birch and balsam ridge at 3660 feet. At the end of a very steep section that follows you can see Basin over the Sawteeth. A scramble follows and you need your hands to pull up a couple of the steep pitches. Then a shoulder of Giant appears over a shoulder of Dial. The slides and cirque on Basin appear. Marcy's emergence above the steep valley between Haystack and Little Haystack is another good excuse to rest and enjoy the view.

The trail moderates and becomes prettier in a balsam and cedar stand with lovely ferns and sorrel, but the climbing resumes and you can spot Whiteface between the two knobs of Upper Wolf Jaws. Still higher, your perspective separates Pyramid from Gothics proper. A more moderate stretch ends at an intersection in a col on the ridgeline at 4530 feet, 0.2 mile north of Nippletop's summit. A left turn leads to the Dials and Bear Den (section 91). Turn right toward the summit along the narrow ridge with views out to both sides—the north face slides on Dix seem very close. You descend a bit, then climb up the nipple, where views to the south and west greet you. The Pinnacle Ridge stretches out with the Great Range behind and to the right. Elk Lake is to the left with Boreas Mountain and the North River Mountains behind.

90 Nippletop Slide

Slide-climb for experts

The slide on Nippletop parallels the trail to the summit from Elk Pass and ends within 150 feet of the ridgeline at a path that leads 150 yards north to the summit. The slide is twenty times as wide as it was twenty years ago and it is still growing. There is some rubble along part of its mile-long span, but much of it is fairly clean. With a vertical rise of over 1500 feet over a horizontal distance of 0.85 mile, the slide has an average slope of 33 percent.

Getting to the bottom of the slide is no mean feat because of the bog that fills Elk Pass. Bushwhack southwest from the hairpin turn on the Nippletop Trail down about 400 feet in elevation to the base of the slide. It will take you six or eight minutes to maneuver around the bogs in Elk Pass, but the drainage opens up, with views of Elk Lake appearing in twenty minutes. Resist any temptation to cut across the steep slopes of Nippletop to the slide track—they are dense!

The slide ascends to the ridge in two major sweeps, the upper one rising steeply enough near the top that you will definitely be climbing with hands and feet, and not just walking up. Handholds are plentiful where needed, however, so that you need not take to the brush early. Exit to the right at the top to find a path left to the summit.

91 Nippletop via North and South Dial and Bear Den

Henry Goddard Leach Trail

7.45 miles, 4-hour descent, 3210-foot elevation change, ATIS markers

This route was named for Henry Goddard Leach, AMR member who edited *The Forum* from 1923 to 1940. It is quite popular to climb to Nippletop and return over the Dials and Bear Den via this trail, a loop of 14.65 miles. Taking the bus to the Bypass Trail shortens the loop to 11.25 miles, still a full day hike. There are advantages to making the loop in a clockwise direction, but since most people climb Nippletop first, the return is described from south to north, descending Nippletop.

Head north from Nippletop's summit to the intersection in the col and continue north along the ridgeline, which remains quite narrow, but without views. The trail goes through a couple of S curves, descending very gradually at first. Here, as recently as twenty-five years ago, the balsams were shorter than the average hiker, so there were views. A pitch down the north side of the ridge follows. From a low point at 4260 feet, you go up, then down again. The trail opens up in a blowdown area—the end of a fir wave. It is a wonderful, soft trail, cushioned by needles, easy to walk. Past a second blowdown area, where the trail has dropped down under 4100 feet, there is a distinct forest change, with the balsam now quite tall. The ridge is wider and carpeted with ferns beneath the balsam. The descent continues with a glimpse at 3860 feet through Wolf Jaws Col (how deep it looks!) to Big Slide. A gradual climb leads up to the 4070-foot summit of South Dial, a wooded hummock so undistinguished you probably won't know you have reached it, even if it is the official Forty-sixer Dial peak. It is 1.55 miles and fifty minutes from Nippletop.

After a steep descent of 200 feet, the trail starts up again. You pass another opening that reveals Big Slide through the Wolf Jaws Col and climb almost as high again as South Dial to reach the summit of North Dial at 2.05 miles, twenty minutes more. There is a wonderful ledge to the left, on top of the cliffs that face Dial's northern slopes. To the right of Colvin is Allen. Going on around to the right you see Skylight, Haystack, Marcy above Little Haystack, then Basin, with Sawteeth in front and Saddleback just above the slide on Saddleback, then Gothics, Armstrong, Upper Wolf Jaws, Big Slide, Lower Wolf Jaws, the whole Porter Ridge where Cascade is the open rock at its western end, Whiteface over Porter Ridge, Cobble Mountain, and the Sentinels. Best of all is the tremendous drop off to the valley below from this tiny perch. Dial is a very old mountain name, though perhaps it was applied first to Nippletop.

If the distance given to St. Huberts means to the gate, the sign here really belongs on South Dial; it is 5.4 miles from here to the visitor's parking area.

Dix from Nippletop

North of North Dial a long, steady descent begins—easy enough to suggest that climbing in the other direction is equally nice. The trail remains narrow and lovely through balsam and birch, with thick stands of sorrel and mosses beneath. In twenty minutes you reach two patches of birch blowdown. Five minutes later you reach a low point, 3300 feet, down 700 feet already, then climb a small knoll with an opening and more blowdown. Past the col beneath the knoll, the trail starts up a steep pitch, then angles left on a level traverse. Views back reveal Dial's long ridge. Climbing gently, the trail reaches a cairn 1.3 miles, forty-five minutes, from Dial. This little rise in the ridge is Bear Den, elevation 3400 feet, 1036 meters.

A path continues straight beyond Bear Den's wooded summit, but the trail turns sharply right to continue descending. Openings reveal the rocky peak of Noonmark with Giant to the left of it. A steep pitch down and a gentler descent in a beautiful birch glade lead to a low point on the ridgeline, 2880 feet. The original trail from St. Huberts to Dix passed through this col headed for Gravestone Brook. Barely visible now and only near the col, it is nevertheless an easy bushwhack to the Dix Trail (section 76) from here and vice versa. It is also a good place to begin a bushwhack arcing south around the western slopes of Bear Den, looking for the caves that may have inspired this little mountain's name.

You climb out of this col heading north then northwest through a cleft between small cliffs. Just as you think you have emerged on high ground from the draw, you turn right and continue up, zigzagging back, headed to the left of Dix, which shows through the trees. After turning back left, you finally reach a height-of-land, elevation 3150 feet, where a path forks left to an overlook featuring the slide on Dix. A second ledge below reveals the jagged ridgeline of Sawteeth and behind it Pyramid, Gothics, then Armstrong with its precipitous northern profile. Behind to the west lie Marcy, Little Haystack, and Allen with the Cobble as well as the Dial-Bear Den ridge you have just descended.

(If you wanted to bushwhack along the ridgeline to nearby Noonmark, you would leave the knoll here and head east-northeast. That route is remarkably easy until you reach the 300-foot summit cone.)

The trail still has a 1.65-mile descent of 1670 feet elevation to get off the ridgeline. It starts down north of the intersection with the path, but still climbs one more bump where there used to be a lookout—you'll wish for a shortcut here. Angle right into a draw, descend, circle around a spruce knoll, and finally begin a steep descent. You zigzag around and beneath a cliff and, twenty-five minutes from the lookout, reach the AMR boundary. Tall maples, then a layer of mostly beech, and finally the hemlock, which shelter the deep draw beside a stream, mark progress on your steep descent. A truly magnificent stand of hemlock shrouds the lower reaches of the trail, which ends after nearly an hour at a point 0.7 mile from the gate.

Note that except for the stream near the road, there is no water along this route.

92 Cathedral Rocks and Bear Run

2.1-mile loop with 0.5-mile detours, 2 hours, 890-foot vertical rise, ATIS markers

A pair of loops and a dead-end probe some very interesting terrain high above the lower section of the West River Trail. The logical starting point is at 0.6 mile on the West River Trail, opposite the lowest bridge linking the West and East River trails.

Turn right onto the Cathedral Rocks Trail (or continue straight ahead if you cross the bridge). The trail dips slightly, crosses a small brook, and climbs at easy grades along its left bank. In five minutes, the trail flattens out in an area of seeps and a little wet meadow where, if you look carefully, you will find rattlesnake orchids.

Beyond the meadow, the trail climbs again, and crosses a dry streambed in twelve minutes. You skirt the first ledges and cliffs shortly thereafter, then the trail passes through a sort of notch before climbing more steeply to the base of a fairly high cliff (twenty-five minutes). There the trail bears left and runs along a wide shelf at mostly easy grades between a major drop to the left and minor cliffs to the right. You cross a small stream, probably dry in summer, and if you follow it to the base of the cliff, you can see a number of places where dikes of dark, fine-grained diabase cut the coarse, lighter, anorthosite country rock.

At 0.8 mile, over thirty minutes, the high cliffs to the right are called Cathedral Rocks. Just beyond, the trail forks. The left fork is the Bear Run Bypass. You can make a shorter loop by going this way, as it reconnects with the main Cathedral Rocks–Bear Run Trail in 0.25 mile, reducing the walk by 0.3 mile. It is steep at each end (down, then up) with a fairly easy going middle. Walking time is twelve minutes. However, the main attractions of this bypass are very near either end. Less than 100 yards along the bypass from this intersection, there is an excellent view of Giant and Noonmark mountains, Roaring Brook Falls, and the Ausable Club Golf Course.

After detouring for this view, return to the main trail to the right and follow it uphill, along a stream bed, at moderately steep grades, crossing onto state land and then arriving at a junction at the bottom of a really impressive cliff at just over 1 mile, forty minutes. There is a large, deep pool here, very dark, with steep sides merging into the vertical foot of the cliff.

Bear Run is a detour to the right marked by a sign reading "don't miss." It is to be taken seriously. The path winds upward along the base of the cliff past another, smaller pool and into a corner from which it seems the trail must go downhill to escape. Instead, the trail goes up, up through a long, very deep, very steep, narrow, vertical-walled and tunnel-like passageway—actually an eroded dike—finally emerging after passing under a big chockstone. Then it turns sharp right and descends briefly to a ledge with a view from Giant to

Sawteeth. The distance is about 300 yards and it only takes a few minutes to get there—but what a few minutes! As the sign says: "don't miss."

Back at the junction by the big pool, proceed west, following the base of the big cliff again upward until you leave the cliffs behind at a height-of-land. You descend at moderate grades to another overlook toward the southeast at nearly 1.3 miles. After this, the trail drops very steeply as it enters and makes its way down through the gorge of Pyramid Brook. This is a very picturesque area, with the stream sliding over smooth, wide shelves and plunging through boulder-choked ravines and narrow flumes.

At 1.35 miles you reach the other end of the bypass trail. You will be well-rewarded to wander just a short way left down this trail to a set of high and curiously broken-up cliffs, which are much more cathedral-like than those so named.

Back on the main trail, you continue descending steeply, passing two small, slick-rock waterfalls, after which the trail begins to flatten out and crosses Pyramid Brook to a junction at 1.55 miles. Either right or left will bring you to the West River Trail. A right turn takes you there in under 0.2 mile to a point near the Canyon Bridge, which is farther upstream than if you turn left.

The left turn reaches the West River Trail in 210 yards, at a point that is a fifteen-minute, 0.45 mile walk back to the lower end of the trail.

93 Lower Wolf Jaw
The Wedge Brook Trail
2.15 plus about 3 miles, 3½ hours, 2860-foot vertical rise from Ausable River, ATIS markers

Of the five great trails that climb to the Range from the Ausable Valley, the Wedge Brook Trail to Lower Wolf Jaw is relatively easy. You can combine any pair of trails with a walk along the Range to make satisfying loops. This is described as an ascent, and descending via this route needs little additional information. The easiest route to combine with it is the William A. White Trail (section 94). Using this trail to lead to the Range and on to Upper Wolf Jaws and Armstrong (section 118) involves two real scrambles on rock faces. In that loop you probably would return with the descent to Beaver Meadows Falls (section 96).

You can reach the intersection of the Wedge Brook Trail with the West River Trail by two different routes. One is a longer but easier 3.1-mile trek made up of a walk along the road to the gate and, just under a mile later, to the 0.45-mile connector that crosses Canyon Bridge to the West Side Trail at the western end of the Cathedral Rocks Trail. The other heads across the Ausable just short of the gate to the West River Trail (section 77). Continue west on it to the western end of the Cathedral Rock Trail at 2.25 miles. Both approaches combine for the last 0.75-mile walk on the West Side Trail, high above the Ausable to the beginning of the Wedge Brook Trail. The latter approach, 3 miles total, takes a little longer than the former.

Wedge Brook tumbles to the Ausable River through a series of small waterfalls, one of which drops into a pool right beside the West Side Trail at elevation 1870 feet, just a few feet east of the fork to Wolf Jaws. At first the trail is close enough to the brook so you can enjoy its rock slides and chutes, but at 2100 feet elevation, the trail turns west, away from the brook. You wind uphill through a very disturbed forest with many beech among the maples. The strangest aspect of this disturbed forest, however, is this forest floor—rampant with horse nettles.

Leaving the AMR at 2280 feet, 0.35 mile, the trail continues gently uphill, crossing a dry wash. There are several glades of horse nettles. From one opening you can glimpse ahead to the cliffs on Lower Wolf Jaw. A wet meadow filled with jewelweed, the ubiquitous nettles, and a huge boulder marks the end of the gentle ascent, at 2750 feet, 1.15 miles. Allow fifty minutes for this part of the climb. Now you are right below the Wolf Jaw's cliffs and the trees are already much smaller.

The ascent is very steep now—at 2870 feet you are right beside a moss-covered slide. The trail angles even closer to the cliff face as it climbs through a ferny draw. Watch for the spectacular and rare Braun's Holly Fern, *Polystichum braunii*, right beside the trail. Finally, at the 3360-foot level, in a very steep section, a curious sign—"End Denettling"—announces the last of that prickly scourge. Moss-covered cliffs loom above and the trail zigzags across the steep slopes to an intersection at 3540 feet and 1.45 miles, twenty minutes from the last meadow.

This intersection is the east angle of a nearly equilateral triangle. The way left, the base of the triangle, leads 0.3 mile, with little more climbing, to Wolf Jaws Col and an intersection with the Range Trail, where a left turn leads to Johns Brook Valley (section 117), and a second left turn, almost immediately, takes you to Upper Wolf Jaw (section 118). At this first intersection, a right turn on the Range Trail leads you toward Lower Wolf Jaw, where the first steep segment is a 0.25-mile climb to an intersection at the northern angle of the triangle.

If you turn right at the east angle, the first intersection, toward Lower Wolf Jaw, you find a narrow trail angling below little cliffs. It climbs, then is almost level at 3730 feet as it angles north to the intersection with the Range Trail, the north angle of the triangle.

Heading north, a right turn, from this intersection leads 0.3 mile to the summit of Lower Wolf Jaw. As you start zigzagging up the narrow ridge, there is a nice view of Nippletop, Colvin and Blake, and the ridge leading up to Gothics, with Sawteeth beyond it. Scrambling now through shorter balsam, you reach another good view, a level traverse, and another scramble that levels off near of the summit. A path left leads to a view with Haystack,

Marcy, MacIntyre, Saddleback, and Basin now visible. The last 440-foot climb takes more than fifteen minutes. Just to the east of the view spot, you reach a guideboard with mileages on the summit, which has no view.

94 William A. White Trail
Lower Wolf Jaw
4.45 miles, 3½ hours, 2860-foot vertical rise, ATIS markers

This trail to Lower Wolf Jaw was named for William A. White, who was an avid mountain climber, one of the founders of AMR, and the first president of ATIS (1897–1927). The trail begins near the gate and climbs to Lower Wolf Jaw by way of three intimate overlooks of the Ausable Valley and the cut between Giant and Round mountains. With the exception of a couple of pitches, it provides a relatively easy climb to Wolf Jaws; but the trail is here described as a descent. As part of a day trip it is a toss-up whether making a clockwise loop (starting with the Wedge Brook Trail and ending with this one) is better than a counterclockwise trip. Some lower portions of the trail have been logged and are not too pleasant, but the overlooks are certainly nice.

Northeast of the summit of Lower Wolf Jaw, paths branch from the trail to overlooks as the trail crosses the narrow ridgeline. After a level or slightly descending stretch, the trail, here part of the Range Trail, drops precipitously for over 250 feet in a very short space. It is rough going down! Leveling out in a col on the narrow ridgeline, the trail passes a camping spot to the left. Heading up again, the trail traverses below a cliff and reaches an opening with a view across Dial to Dix. You scramble up a cliff to the north side of the ridge, which overlooks Big Slide and Yard. A little more scrambling brings you to a point on the northern edge. What a steep drop to Johns Brook Valley! The view of the valley with Porter and Cascade beyond is wonderful, though mostly bracketed by trees. The top of the narrow summit ridge of Lower Wolf Jaws' second knob at 0.55 mile (twenty minutes) is without views, but as you start to descend northeast of it, you see the rock face of Rooster Comb, and the Hurricane and Jay ranges.

The trail climbs slightly, then begins a long, gentle downgrade, passing a camping spot to the right on the way. With steep drops on both sides, the ridge walk is very pleasant. You descend into stands of large birch dotting ferny glades. Level traverses or gentle descents are punctuated by a few steep chutes. Thirty minutes suffices for the 0.85-mile descent to an intersection in a col, elevation 3160 feet.

The Range Trail continues left toward Hedgehog and Rooster Comb (section 104). Turn right to commence a long, side-hill traverse, descending gently, then more steeply, but hardly ever at a moderate grade. Hedgehog shows a distinctly furry, flat back in views from this stretch. The forest of tall birch with good-sized spruce is especially nice—it has an open understory. Steep slopes to your left end as you head uphill in a little draw at about the 2640-foot level. A short pitch down and a level lead out to a balsam and spruce knoll at 2600 feet. This point, at 2.4 miles, is 1 mile below the intersection with the Range Trail. From this vantage you see Giant and the northern slides on Dix. Nippletop appears a little higher than the Blake-Colvin Ridge.

You descend only 100 feet in 0.2 mile to a second overlook, this one with a wonderful view of Giant, Noonmark, and Round. A third overlook is a bit beyond. The trail now zigzags down through patches of brambles to steep hemlock-covered slopes. At 3 miles, a side trail leads 50 feet to an overlook right above the Ausable Club. Below this overlook, the trail descends very steeply through the hemlocks to continue below a cliff wall, which is up to your left. A very wet place forces you close to the wall. Raspberries and thimbleberries crowd the trail.

At 3.4 miles, 1800 feet, you reach an intersection. St. Hubert's is straight ahead; Rooster Comb (section 103) is a left turn. The trail is now on a logging road and there are views of Giant looming above. Giant appears to be looking over his shoulder at you when you reach a second field, a log staging area. The road now descends to a sign for a spring at 1600 feet. At about 1500 feet, 3.8 miles, where the road angles left, the W. A. White Trail angles right for a traverse to the west and a gradual descent to the level of the river. In ten minutes more, 0.5 mile, you reach the river. Cross it and head up to the east for a brief walk beside a lovely trout pool. Turn right for 100 yards to the road, reaching it at the old guard house, within sight of the gate that is to your right. Turn left for the parking area.

95 Gothics via Pyramid
Alfred E. Weld Trail
2.65 miles, 3 hours, 2900-foot elevation change, ATIS markers

The most spectacular trail to ascend the Range from AMR is the trail to Gothics via Pyramid. The trail starts from the Lower Lake, heads back up the road and down to the bridge over the Ausable River, where it heads north and almost immediately forks, with the left fork leading to Sawteeth (section 97). Going straight ahead, the trail forks again with the right fork heading to Rainbow Falls (section 79). This time go left on the Alfred E. Weld Trail, which was only built in 1966.

After climbing quickly to the top of Rainbow Falls, the trail continues moderately, zigzagging through stands of dying beech with many deadfalls. At elevation 2360 feet, just under 0.5 mile and fifteen minutes, you cross a brook where two small side streams come together; one comes from the Rifle Notch near the summit of Sawteeth. Openings yield views of the Dials and Bear Den. You reach the edge of AMR property at 2630 feet and shortly beyond have a view of the slides of Gothics. The forest is definitely nicer with an open understory; Cascade Brook, which drains the eastern slides on Gothics, is way below on your right.

A relatively level traverse follows, then a pleasant climb beneath handsome boulders in an area frequently cleared out by small avalanches of ice and snow. After an hour's walk, at the end of a second traverse at about 3100 feet and 1.3 miles, you cross a feeder stream that comes from the saddle near the intersection of the Weld Trail with the Range Trail. You briefly follow this brook northeast, then leave this last source of water.

You can see the slides on Sawteeth on the west side of the valley. That brook curves back east, so the trail crosses it once more, though it is little more than a chain of moss-covered rocks, pretty in this great stretch of woods. Just beyond, the trail levels and shortly you reach a trail intersection, 1.75 miles, elevation 3657 feet—an hour and thirty minutes and nearly 1700 feet above the Lower Lake.

(The way left leads 0.5 mile to Sawteeth. That trail starts moderately, but zigzags through some very steep pitches before finishing the 656-foot, forty-minute climb to the Sawteeth Summit.)

Gothics is to the right. The trail is briefly on the ridgeline, then it begins a steep climb with several pitches. Dial and Nippletop appear. You go straight up a steep, smooth rock face, zigging right to 3950 feet, then zagging back left. At 4100 feet, Giant and Rocky Peak Ridge appear. More zigzags and then you can see the boathouse on the Lower Lake as well as Indian Head and Fish Hawk Cliffs. Nippletop's slide appears; Dix is behind Nippletop. You are past the steepest part.

The trail levels off and bends right at 4480 feet. To the south you can now see Boreas and Vanderwhacker, with Texas Ridge and Hoffman behind the Pinnacle Ridge. As the trail levels off, a path to the left leads to the pyramid on Pyramid, elevation 4595 feet. The 940-foot, 0.6-mile climb from the intersection may take fifty minutes.

The great, soaring slides of both the east and west arms of Gothics are awe-inspiring. From this vantage they really do seem to curve like gothic arches above the valleys far below. Even if this spectacle is the most striking in the High Peaks, do not forget to survey the panorama to the south and west. Above Boreas you can see Gore and Crane, then Snowy to the left of the North River Mountains and Allen in front of them. Skylight just peeps over between Haystack and Little Haystack, then brooding Marcy, Basin with its knobs, and a great view of its rock slides. Further right you see Colden, with its backside (south) slides, then MacIntyre, and Wright with its slide.

In spite of the lofty vista, the descent from Pyramid toward Gothics may suggest a scramble on an elephant's trunk, for surely from this view, Gothics is the head, the slides are the ears, while the Pyramid ridge is the trunk. You descend about 140 feet, then head up, briefly through scrubby balsams, to the Gothics' rocky ridge. You reach an intersection with the Range Trail (section 118) and turn right to reach the true summit in 0.3 mile, elevation 4735 feet (1443 meters), a twenty-minute walk. The last bit along the ridge reveals the Johns Brook Valley and the Porter Ridge. You look across Big Slide to Whiteface and Lake Placid is to the west of Yard. Beyond Lake Placid you see McKenzie and Moose. The Sentinels are tucked between Cascade and White-face, with Lyon Mountain on the skyline over Cascade. To the right you can pick out Ebenezer and Rattlesnake.

Johns Brook Valley is much wider and more gentle than that of the Ausable. At its head you can see Tabletop below Wright, Phelps with open rocks is on the right side of the long ridge, and over Phelps you can see Street and Nye with Ampersand beyond. Emmons lies between Colden and Iroquois, and Panther is the only part of the Santanoni Ridge that is not hidden. To the northeast are Saddleback in the Jay Range, Lake Champlain, and Hurricane with its tower. The top of Jay is visible over Armstrong, which is the next bump in the Range to the east. Colvin Bolt 287 was placed on this summit in 1876.

96 Gothics and Armstrong to Beaver Meadows Falls

3.75 miles to West Side Trail, 3 hours, 3526-foot descent from Gothics, plus 150-foot ascent of Armstrong, ATIS markers

An absolutely wonderful trail climbs from the Ausable River near Beaver Meadows Falls to the col between Gothics and Armstrong. On the other hand, because it is so exciting to emerge from the woods on the climb of Pyramid to the magnificent vista of Gothics, that is undoubtedly the best way to climb that peak. So, no matter how good the trail to the Armstrong-Gothics Col, it may be best to enjoy it while you are descending from Gothics, thus making a loop that is unquestionably my favorite in the High Peaks.

This trail appears on the 1902 map, when it was the only one leading from the Ausable Valley to the Range. The present trail still essentially follows that original route.

Instead of descending directly from Gothics, you can add a detour to Armstrong, a peak named for the original owner of Township 48, which encompasses a good part of your view from Gothics. Heading to Armstrong from Gothics on the Range Trail, you at first make an easy descent on open rock that makes you feel as if you were walking on the edge of the world. Watch carefully as the trail makes a sharp right turn down ever steeper slopes, for as it turns, a path straight ahead leads to a hole in the rocks. The trail traverses back right, descends a chute, ending in the woods. Again the trail

The view from Gothics of Haystack, Skylight, and Marcy over Basin and Saddleback

splits because the ledges are too tall for some; the northern fork is the shallower and the routes rejoin in 60 feet. The trail levels out in the dead balsam that fill the col.

In fifteen minutes you descend nearly 400 feet and 0.45 mile to the Armstrong-Gothics Col and the intersection with the Beaver Meadows Trail, to which you will return after a brief detour to Armstrong. Take the left fork, which is the continuing Range Trail, and immediately climb up a little knob to bare rock. Chutes and ledges lead up to a flat place on top of the ridge with views of Armstrong ahead. A brief descent and you start up again. A narrow ramp angles up an outcrop and shortly the trail is beneath a rock wall. The trail goes right around it—then up it, where a path forks left to a ledge on top of Armstrong's northern cliffs. This point has elevation 4428 feet (1350 meters) and is fifteen minutes and 0.45 mile from the col.

The view from Armstrong is edgewise along the sheer northern slopes of the Range. One of the most prominent features to the west from this perspective is the steep point that rises near the head of Johns Brook Valley. Point Balk was named for Dr. Robert Balk, a geologist who first studied the origins of the Adirondack dome or shield.

When you return to the intersection in the col, take the left fork, headed toward St. Huberts. The trail begins by doubling back below the knob, climbing slightly on a trail that is so narrow and precarious that it feels as if it were about to join the slide for a precipitous trip into the valley below. Steep slopes above convince you that it is wise that the trail makes this hairpin turn, wrapping around the knob on its way back from Armstrong. As it is, the trail now climbs a couple of ladders. There is a wonderful view of the rock and slides below. Shortly after a third ladder, the trail drops behind an outcrop, so you no longer are on the exposed southwestern side of the shoulder that thrusts toward the Ausable Lakes.

As you cross over the shoulder you see the slides on Armstrong. You descend, round another rock outcrop, and level off to a beautiful birch-woods traverse. The northern side of the shoulder is very steep with rich moss coverings on its cliffs. The trail cuts right across them and reaches a balancing rock at about 4020 feet, 0.45 mile from the col. This huge boulder with trees on top is like a big jaw ready to snap.

After a brief level, the descent alternates between gentle traverses and chutes, some of them through steep crevices. For a time the trail parallels the Range Trail from Armstrong to Upper Wolf Jaw, heading northeast, but except for glimpses of Wolf Jaws, which appears quite close, there are no more views. The route is fairly steep and obvious, even as it crosses several dry washes that drain to the left. The forest becomes taller and more majestic and the grade and walking easier as you head out on a little nose, paralleling a draw.

The trail turns south of east, reaches the AMR boundary at just short of 2 miles. The intersection to Lost Lookout is at nearly 2.2 miles. Shortly beyond, hear the stream in the deep valley below. Finally, at 2.4 miles you are close to the stream at a point where it slips over smooth slabs. The trail plunges down the hemlock banks that shelter the stream, which now plummets over Beaver Meadows Falls. A sixteen-rung ladder takes you down the last few feet of near-vertical slope. The West River Trail is right ahead between you and the old Beaver Meadows on the Ausable. The bridge to the East River Trail is just below the old beaver dam. Cross the bridge, turn left, then angle right for the last 0.5 mile to the road, which you intersect 1.75 miles from the gate.

This 2.4-mile, 2400-foot descent from the col to Beaver Meadow Falls takes almost two hours.

97 Sawteeth via the Scenic Trail

3.2 miles, 3 or more hours, 2180-foot vertical rise, 2700-foot elevation change, ATIS markers

The trail over the jagged points of Sawteeth is a challenging walk, enhanced by a series of views (some numbered) of the Ausable Lakes. Each vista is spectacular. The easiest—and it is not really easy—way to enjoy this walk is to combine it with a descent to the col between Sawteeth and Gothics and return via the trail of section 95. This 5.45-mile loop is a great hike, long enough even with a bus ride at either end. Without the bus, the 13.65-mile day is more than strenuous. Whether climbing via the Scenic Trail and making the loop in a clockwise direction is better than the reverse is a matter of question. This is a hard enough climb that descending becomes difficult, and the vistas offer plenty of reasons to pause on the way up.

[A longer, even more challenging hike combines this route with the descent to the Upper Lake (section 98), the Carry Trail (section 99), an ascent of Colvin from the Upper Lake (section 101), and a descent via the Colvin Trail (section 87). This hike has 4280 feet of climbing and is 11.9 miles long, even with the bus. And even with the bus—you have to rush to catch the last one back—it is a very hard day. You also have to make better times for the segments than the estimates given.]

From the boathouse at Lower Ausable Lake, walk back up the road to the ATIS marked trail that descends to the bridge over the dam and turns sharply left. The trail follows the northwest shore of the lake. The trail to Gothics via Pyramid branches right in 50 yards. The Scenic Trail undulates along the shoreline, sometimes twenty to thirty feet above it, sometimes right beside it. Indian Head's craggy, overhanging face looms above; views of the steep slopes of the Ausable fault are wonderful. You climb over and around large boulders, slowing your progress so that it may take a half hour to traverse the 0.7 mile from the boathouse where the trail leaves the shoreline and begins its steep ascent up the mountain. As the trail turns north from the lake it ascends steeply, with occasional level traverses in switchbacks. At 1.1 miles, after 0.4 mile of steady climbing, there is a small overlook with a nice view of the valley and the ridge to the south. A much better view is just 100 yards up the trail where an open outcrop is labeled Number 1. From it you see the entire Lower Lake, some of the Upper Lake, and the Colvin-Pinnacle Ridge. After ascending another 120 yards, there is a path to the left leading a short distance to another outcrop and view Number 2.

Climbing now moderately to steeply with views through the trees, the trail passes several tall cliffs and comes out to a large unlabeled outcrop (Number 3), 1.6 miles from the boathouse at 2800 feet. This overlooks all of both lakes, as well as the mountains to the south.

The upward course continues and at 2.1 miles, nearly 3600 feet, the trail levels off at the top of one of the teeth. A fourth outcrop, called Lookout Rock, perches above cliffs that appear to rise straight from the lake, 1600 feet below. From this vantage you see Giant, Rocky Peak Ridge, Noonmark, Dial, Nippletop, and the Colvin-Pinnacle Ridge above the two lakes. Through the trees to the north you can see Gothics, as well as the sheer sides of the next tooth. After descending for a short distance, the trail climbs in a nearly dry streambed. After several yards in the streambed, the gradient again becomes very steep as the trail starts up over the next tooth. The climbing is increasingly difficult as the trail passes over boulders and ascends a log ladder placed against an open cliff that affords excellent views to the south.

The ascent moderates as the trail reaches the top of the tooth, this one a summit over 4100 feet in elevation. After descending the back of this tooth to a col, the trail immediately starts climbing moderately up over a smaller tooth.

Lower Ausable Lake and Sawteeth Cliffs from Fish Hawk Cliffs

The trail descends from this tooth into a col called Rifle Notch and then makes one last steep ascent toward the summit. At 3.1 miles you reach an intersection with the trail to the Upper Lake (section 98), which is to the left. The summit is a large boulder about 100 feet to the north of the junction. Continuing straight on the trail to a second knob at 3.2 miles, you can now look northeast to the slides on Pyramid and Gothics. The Marshalls considered this view toward the Range the best single view in the High Peaks.

Continue north, descending steeply 656 feet in 0.5 mile to the intersection with the Alfred E. Weld Trail (section 95), for the shortest return to the Upper Lake.

98 Sawteeth to Upper Ausable Lake

2.8 miles, 2 hours, 1830-foot descent, ATIS markers

The trail from Sawteeth to the Upper Ausable Lake branches west about 100 feet south of the true summit. It ascends slightly and then begins a moderate descent along one of Sawteeth's gentler shoulders. The trail is in good condition and there are occasional views of Saddleback, Basin, and Marcy through the trees.

After 0.8 mile of steady, moderate descent, with only a few steep pitches, the trail angles left, south, descends into a mixed hardwood forest, and 150 yards after entering the hardwood forest crosses a branch of Shanty Brook at 1 mile. This is the first possible camping spot after leaving the Lower Lake via the Scenic Trail—all other places are too steep and without water; below, all spots are on the posted AMR lands.

After crossing the brook the trail descends gently, crosses the AMR boundary at about 2800 feet, and 0.3 mile beyond the brook comes to the upper junction of the Tammy Stowe Loop. This loop is nearly a mile long, 0.6 mile longer than the main trail, and was named in memory of a resident of the Upper Lake. It passes two man-made lookouts. From a point near the upper part of this loop there are excellent views of the Range and from the lower part there are views of the Ausable Valley.

The main trail now drops at a moderate rate and at 1.7 miles meets the lower end of Tammy Stowe Loop. The trail is now more gentle, with occasional moderate descents. At 2.6 miles the trail crosses Shanty Brook and 50 yards beyond the brook, the ATIS trail to Haystack via Bartlett Ridge branches to the right. It leads up 785 feet in elevation in 1.2 miles through private lands to intersect the trails of section 55.

Remember that not only is no camping permitted on AMR property, you cannot leave the trail on these posted lands without permission. The Warden's Camp is 0.2 mile below Shanty Brook, near the intersection with the Carry Trail.

99 Carry Trail and Tote Road

1 mile, 20 to 30 minutes, level, ATIS markers

Two trails, parallel to each other, connect the Warden's Camp at the Upper Ausable Lake with the Colvin Trail at the Lower Ausable Lake. The lower trail is the Carry and is a footpath that follows the outlet of the Upper Lake. This trail crosses wet spots and small tributaries on footbridges. About halfway along it, there is a spring where fresh water is available.

The tote road runs above the Carry and is wider and above most of the wet areas. The wooden bridges over tributaries are capable of carrying motor vehicles. These two routes converge just before the start of the Colvin Trail near the inlet to the Lower Ausable Lake.

100 Upper Ausable Lake to the Snowbird Trail

1.5 miles, 1½ hours, 800-foot elevation change, ATIS markers

This trail leads from the Upper Lake to the intersection of the Snowbird Trail and the Haystack Trail that goes via Bartlett Ridge (sections 55 and 54). Its entire length is on AMR land so you cannot camp along it or stray from it. Unless you are a member of AMR or are ambitious enough to carry a pack over Sawteeth or Colvin to the Upper Lake, you will probably not find this route very useful for exploring the interior of the eastern High Peaks.

The trail leaves the Warden's Camp and forks left from the Sawteeth Trail at 0.15 mile. It climbs at a moderate grade with an occasional steep pitch. A private trail forks left at 1.2 miles. The intersection at 1.5 miles is just short of state land on the Snowbird Trail, the right fork at the intersection. You can find level campsites north along that trail and a few small streams with water within the first 0.5 mile of the intersection.

101 Head of Lower Lake to Colvin-Blake Col

1.1 miles, 1½ hours, 1400-foot vertical rise to the col, ATIS markers

This trail begins near the inlet of Lower Ausable Lake, shortly after the Carry Trail and the tote road converge. The many posted signs telling that the trail passes through private property remind you that it is imperative to remain on the trail until you reach state land.

A footbridge takes the trail over the inlet. Across it, the trail turns left and begins a moderate ascent along the brook that flows from the Colvin-Blake Col. After about 0.2 mile of moderate ascent, the trail crosses to the right, east, bank and becomes very steep. The trail is very rocky. About 0.5 mile from the inlet, elevation 2690 feet, 820 meters, the trail reaches state land and recrosses the stream. There are some camping spots in this vicinity and this may be the last good source of water until you are back at either Gill or Virginia brooks.

The grade moderates; at 0.6 mile you cross a small tributary, but in summer it is apt to be dry. Beyond this crossing, the gradient steepens again and remains steep until 0.9 mile. The last 0.2 mile is a moderate climb through thick conifers to the col, which is small and contains many blowdowns and rocks, but no good camping spots. In the col, your route intersects the trail connecting Colvin and Blake in the col.

From the col it is 0.85 mile and a 690-foot climb to Colvin's summit, a trek that requires about forty-five minutes (see also section 88). The first 0.3 mile is steep, rising 400 feet before moderating as the trail climbs over several small shoulders of Colvin. Moderate ups and downs continue for 0.5 mile to an open outcrop to the left with good views north. The final ascent brings you to unobstructed views in all directions, with an excellent view of the slides on Nippletop.

Return to St. Huberts via the Colvin, Gill Brook, and Bypass trails (sections 87, 82, and 83).

Keene Valley

KEENE VALLEY'S UNUSUAL mountain beauty has attracted artists and mountain climbers almost from the time it was first settled. Soaring mountains rise from the narrow valley and views from here reveal the interior of the High Peaks. Little used yet charming trails begin at roads in the valley. Johns Brook flows through the settlement to join the Ausable River and trails along the brook lead to the Great Range and Marcy. The brook was probably named for a John Gibbs, who farmed in Keene Valley as early as 1794.

Orson "Old Mountain" Phelps, who guided at Tahawus, moved to Keene Flats (the original name of the valley settlement) after the death of David Henderson. He set up a guide service to rival that of Tahawus, making Keene Valley the principal entrance to the mountains. From 1849 to 1869 he led a growing number of mountain climbers, who included the author Charles Dudley Warner, Reverend Joseph Twichell, and Dr. Horace Bushnell. Scenic spots, like Bushnell Falls, were named for these avid climbers, many of whom were clergymen.

A dozen guides or more worked out of the valley, each with his own woodsy character and humorous turn of phrase, but none as well known as Phelps, who was the subject of one of Warner's books.

The valley's beauty attracted almost two dozen artists in the second half of the last century, some of them world famous, like A. H. Wyant, who sketched the Wolf Jaws from Noonmark, and many amateurs, who filled sketch books with lovely pen and ink drawings.

Valley farms became guest houses and summer residences sprang up in the valley and high on the slopes surrounding it.

The High Peaks Trailhead is called the Garden—it once was a garden—and it is 1.6 miles from NY 73 along Johns Brook and Interbrook Roads from the center of Keene Valley. Parking is limited to about 55 to 60 cars, a figure which is reached on almost every summer weekend. *There is no parking anywhere along the narrow road approaching the Garden and illegally parked cars may be towed away.* If you are staying at one of the new and excellent bed and breakfasts in Keene Valley or at one of the traditional inns there, you may be able to arrange transportation to the trailhead.

Although the parking area is regularly checked by rangers, there have been numerous incidents over the years of theft from parked automobiles. Do not leave valuables in your car.

Indian Head from Fish Hawk Cliffs

102 Snow Mountain and the Deer Brook Gorge

3.5 miles, 2½ hours, 1280-foot elevation change

Snow Mountain is the lowest of the foothills of the Great Range. Even so, the top of this little mountain is 1360 feet above the floor of Keene Valley. The south side of the mountain is very steep and is cut by a gorge through which Deer Brook flows after dropping about 75 feet over a two-stage waterfall.

A number of trails serve the Snow Mountain area. The Deer Brook Trail is the main route up the mountain. It splits into two trails for part of its length, one side following driveways and tote roads, while the other, the gorge trail, follows Deer Brook through the gorge. There is also the Snow Mountain Connector Trail, which links the Flume Brook or Sachs Trail to Rooster Comb with the William A. White Trail to Lower Wolf Jaw (section 94). The Deer Brook Trail coincides with this connector for 0.15 mile. Another connector, the Deer Brook Cut-off, joins the upper end of the gorge trail with the Snow Mountain Connecter, near its White Trail terminus. Finally, there is a short spur trail leading from the Deer Brook Trail to the falls. The following walk describes a double loop taking the better part of all these short trails.

Deer Brook Trail starts from the southbound lane of NY 73, 1.9 miles south of the High Peaks trail signs in Keene Valley. A sign marks the trailhead, but it is parallel with the highway and so not easily visible. Just south of the trailhead, the road crosses a steel-sided bridge over the Ausable. If you park along the roadside 0.1 mile north of the bridge, you should not have any trouble finding the trail.

Deer Brook Trail begins by climbing at an easy grade along Deer Brook. In two minutes it arrives at a driveway. The main trail turns left onto it, while the gorge trail continues straight ahead. If you turn left, the climb continues easy to moderate, curving right above a house and past a view of Noonmark at nearly 0.3 mile. At a sharp right turn just beyond, the trail continues straight, off the driveway and onto an old tote road. At this point, there is a small parking area or turnout to the left, beyond which there is a rock knob in the trees.

Along the tote road, the trail starts out on the level, but soon begins to ascend, with Deer Brook far below to the right. At a cross junction at 0.65 mile, right is the upper end of the gorge trail, left is the lower end of the cut-off. Go straight, and soon the tumbling brook comes into view as the grade eases. At 0.8 mile, twenty-five minutes, you arrive at another junction where the Deer Brook Trail goes straight ahead across a bridge, below which are beautiful, slick-rock cascades and a deep, pot-hole pool. A three-minute walk to the left will take you to the base of Deer Brook Falls—do make the detour.

Returning to the bridge, cross to the other side and continue your climb of Snow Mountain on moderate grades, paralleling a tributary of Deer Brook, which is below to the left in a little gorge of its own.

At 1.3 miles, fifty-five minutes, the grade eases considerably as the Deer Brook Trail joins the Snow Mountain Connector, which comes in from the left. The two trails run together almost level now for about three minutes through a very fine, open hardwood forest in the high valley between Snow and Hedgehog.

At 1.45 miles, just past a huge erratic surrounded by birches, the Connector breaks away to the left, leading gently down 0.35 mile to the Sachs Trail at a point 1.25 miles above NY 73 and almost 0.45 mile below the Rooster Comb-Hedgehog junction (section 103).

Turning right and continuing on the Deer Brook Trail, the grade is at first easy; but, following a sharp right turn, it becomes steep as the route ascends Snow's summit cone to a ledge at 1.6 miles, where there is a good view of Hedgehog, Rooster Comb, Porter, and Little Porter. The climb is still steep immediately above this ledge, but moderates as you gain altitude. A second ledge at 1.7 miles gives excellent views of Rooster Comb cliffs, good views of Big Slide and the Brothers behind Rooster Comb, and a very nice view north down the Ausable Valley beyond the village of Keene Valley. Slightly above this, there is a west-facing ledge; and just above and to the east of that, is the summit—2360 feet in elevation, 1.7 miles, and an hour and ten minutes from the start.

If you are here in late July or early August, you find the delicate wild *Campanula*, called harebells, with its nodding, violet-blue, bell-shaped blossoms. If you are here in July, the blueberry season, you can have a feast.

The finest prospect from Snow Mountain is from a steep rock slope just below the summit to the south. There is an inspiring view of Giant to the east-southeast, framed by Green to the east and Chapel Pond Pass to the southeast. The rocky summit of Hopkins is north of Green. The odd couple of Round and Noonmark dominates the view to the south. Dix, Dial, and Nippletop form a serrated wall to the south-southwest; but the distant views to the west are completely blocked by the obese humps of Hedgehog and the lanky south-easterly ridge of Lower Wolf Jaw.

For the return trip, retrace your steps, turning left at the first junction until you get to a second, where the Deer Brook Trail and the Snow Mountain Connector, having joined at the first junction, separate again. The signs at this intersection read: "1.0 mile Rooster Comb" (behind you via Connector); "1.3 miles Route 73" (left via Deer Brook Trail); "1.75 miles St. Huberts" (straight ahead via Connector and W. A. White Trail). Go straight.

You cross a tributary of Deer Brook twelve minutes below the summit of Snow. You cross Deer Brook itself seven minutes later, at 0.85 mile, by the upper end of a shallow flume. The trail now winds around a bouldery area at the base of ledges. The grade, which has been easy to moderate, now becomes moderately steep in places as you descend off state land into a lumbered area, reaching the top of an old logging road after twenty-five minutes. The trail follows this road, which levels out just before reaching a trail junction at 1.1 miles. Straight ahead here leads to the William A. White Trail (section 94) in 125 yards.

Turn left onto the Deer Brook Cut-off. The descent is sometimes steep, sometimes easy, but mostly moderate. The cross junction with the Deer Brook main and Gorge trails is at 1.3 miles, thirty minutes. Continue straight through this junction onto the Gorge Trail. The next half mile is so scenic that it could be considered a goal in itself, quite the equal of Snow Mountain summit, though, of course, very different in character. The trail descends very steeply to Deer Brook and immediately crosses it. This is the first of six crossings. None have bridges. Some are a bit obscure—especially the fourth one down. All of them could be dangerous during periods of high water. If the conditions make you feel uncomfortable, try it another time.

There is a cave in an inside corner at the base of the cliffs above the first crossing. Between the last two crossings, there is a wonderful array of huge boulders. There are flumes and falls and deep, emerald pools. There are places where the trail is nearly level, and there are steep scrambles over the rocks. Practically the entire north side of the gorge is lined with vertical cliffs. You could spend hours here, especially with a camera or sketchbook, but it is only a twenty-five-minute walk.

Not far above the mouth of the gorge, you start to see waterlines, which supply the houses below. Leave the gorge, with the stream to your left, pass a house, cross the driveway, rejoining the main trail at 1.8 miles, and arrive at NY 73 0.1 mile farther, at just short of an hour.

103   Rooster Comb

3.65 miles, 2 hours, 1720-foot elevation change, ADK markers

This craggy little peak is a buttress of Hedgehog Mountain, which is, in turn, a buttress of Lower Wolf Jaw at the eastern end of the Great Range. The top ledges of the high cliffs just below the summit offer superb views to the south and west.

There are two trails to Rooster Comb. One, the Sachs or Flume Brook Trail, is so superior to the other, the Interbrook or Village Trail, that the latter is not recommended except as a descent route when making a loop trip. Further complicating the descent route is the fact there is no parking along Interbrook Road.

The Sachs trail begins on a private drive 0.75 mile south of the High Peaks Trails sign in Keene Valley. There is no sign or marker indicating the trailhead; but the driveway is just north of a small red fire hydrant by the southbound lane of the highway. The driveway forks in 0.1 mile, and a sign points right to Rooster Comb. The route begins climbing at easy to moderate grades, past a house on the right as the driveway swings left. Then at 0.35 mile, eight minutes, where the driveway curves back to the right, the trail breaks away to the left.

Follow this trail up a moderately steep grade for a couple of minutes to the rim of the flume of Flume Brook—also called Rushing Brook. Though not large, this is an impressive formation, because you are standing on the brink of its vertical north wall.

The main trail veers away to the right almost immediately after reaching the flume. It is poorly marked and tricky to follow in an open hemlock forest where you could walk unimpeded in any direction. You might want to follow a path along the rim of the flume up to a small waterfall, then make a 90° right turn and bushwhack a short way back up to intersect the main trail. It is still rather vague, so be careful not to overshoot it.

Now you climb more steeply until you cross onto state land, fifteen minutes from the start, after which the grade rounds off to mostly easy, with a few moderate pitches. After eight minutes more, the grade increases markedly as the trail climbs through an impressive grove of hemlocks. It continues moderately steep, with some breaks, until it levels off well up the north slope of Flume Brook ravine. After you have been on the trail for thirty minutes, it ascends again, then levels off once more. This level stretch, too, is brief, before the trail resumes an easy to moderate climb and begins to parallel the left bank of a tributary of Flume Brook. Things start to get interesting again here. Two huge erratics are on the right at the top of a moderate pitch and at 1.25 miles, almost forty minutes, the ATIS Snow Mountain Connector Trail splits off to the left. Soon the Sachs Trail is running right in the bed of the tributary. Then it pops out, and the grade eases in a beautiful stand of paper birch, after which it ascends gently in a fine hardwood forest, still following the tributary.

In fifty minutes, at nearly 1.7 miles, you reach an intersection where a left turn will take you to Hedgehog and Wolf Jaws. Turn right. Now comes the best part of the trip. From the junction, the trail becomes steeper and steeper as it winds its way through a garden of boulders to the base of a cliff where it turns hard right, and then, almost immediately, back left. The route is up an extremely steep chute with the cliff to your left and a series of ledges to your right. It takes five minutes to reach the top of the chute.

The trail now turns sharp left, and although the grade eases somewhat as the trail zigzags up over ledgey ground toward Rooster Comb's crest. Shortly, there is a view south toward Giant and Round Mountain. A minute later, there is a much wider view encompassing everything from Hopkins to Hedgehog. Two minutes more, and the grade eases as the trail reaches the ridge top.

A junction at the 2762-foot summit of the mountain comes at 1.9 miles, one hour. There is no view from this point, but a left turn takes you 75 yards to the

brink of the Rooster Comb Cliffs, a crescent of crags 250 feet high, topped by a half acre of open rock with a view that will make you want to jump and shout. With a bit of walking around you can see from the Jay Range all the way clockwise around to Porter Mountain.

Especially nice are the views of Hurricane Mountain above Keene Valley to the northeast, Giant and Chapel Pond Pass to the southeast, with the Green Mountains of Vermont visible through the pass, where, with good light, you can see deep into the pass to the water of Chapel Pond. Lower Wolf Jaw and Mount Marcy, with the top of Basin between them, lie to the southwest. Much of Johns Brook Valley lies before you with the Big Slide homocline dominating its north side.

To make a loop walk, return to the summit junction and bear left. Descend for only two minutes to an overlook of Johns Brook Valley and Porter Mountain. Just beyond, at 2 miles, you come to a view north and northeast down the valley of the Ausable. This is at the top of a very steep, fairly long descent on bare rock. Below, the grade eases a little, then there is a slight break, a steeper pitch down, and another break at 2.15 miles where the trail crosses a dry wash and goes over a slight rise. Following this, steep sections gradually diminish. Twenty-five minutes from the top, you reach a streambed on your left, where you turn sharply right. At 2.8 miles, you cross another streambed on planks. For the next ten minutes, the trail follows ancient logging roads at relatively easy grades; but the going is made less than pleasant by severe erosion.

This all ends when the trail turns left onto a private drive, crosses a bridge, and arrives in a field where many roads come together at 3.2 miles, thirty-five minutes from the top. Turn right and reach another multiple junction in four minutes. Turn right again to a gentle descent past driveways coming in from both sides as you enter a more populated area. You reach the pavement of Interbrook Road just below the Johns Brook Bridge at 3.65 miles, 1.75 miles and forty-five minutes from the top. A half-hour stroll through the village will return you to the head of the Sachs Trail and your car.

104 Hedgehog (loop)

1.5-mile segment of the Range Trail from the Flume Trail to the William A. White Trail, 1 hour, 995-foot elevation change

If you are climbing Hedgehog for the view, you are making a mistake. There isn't any view—at least not from the main summit; and what can be seen from other places along the trail is really not reason enough for your toil. Most people climb Hedgehog not so much because it is there as because it is in the

Giant from Rooster Comb

way. If you are a purist, and you want to hike the Great Range from the beginning, you have to go over Hedgehog; and if you are an ultrapurist, you will do it first, going over Rooster Comb via the Interbrook Trail (section 103).

But what if you are not interested in hiking the whole Range? What if you are just curious and looking for a good day's exercise? Then climb Hedgehog simply for climbing.

The best approach is via the Flume Brook or Sachs Trail (section 103) to Rooster Comb. You can go up and back the same way, making a ten-minute detour to the summit of Rooster Comb for its spectacular view on the way down; or, you can make a long, 0.8-mile, loop trip going over Hedgehog, descending out of the col between it and Lower Wolf Jaw via the William A. White Trail (section 94), then returning to the Sachs Trail on the Snow Mountain Connector Trail.

Beginning at the junction nearly 1.7 miles up the Sachs Trail (0.25 mile below Rooster Comb summit), turn left. You start out on an easy grade but very soon hit a moderately steep pitch as the trail climbs out of the saddle between Hedgehog and Rooster Comb.

Climbing moderately, the trail approaches a long ledge that runs upward to the right. The trail turns right and climbs along the base of the ledges. Fifteen minutes from the intersection, the trail turns left at the upper end of the ledges and begins a steep climb that gradually rounds off, drops slightly, then circles around a steeply sloping shoulder of the mountain, allowing through-the-trees glimpses over the Johns Brook Valley toward Porter, the Brothers, and Big Slide.

After another slight dip, the trail now becomes quite steep as the trail ascends a ledgey section, then levels off at the north summit, elevation 3280 feet, of Hedgehog at 0.7 mile, less than thirty minutes.

It takes about a minute to walk across the summit to a campsite with a firepit on the west rim. The firepit is more like a fire hazard—just a hole in the duff. The trail descends for 0.25 mile to the col between Hedgehog's two summits, ten more minutes, where a small intermittent brook crosses the trail. Immediately after this, you ascend an eroded, muddy trail at moderately steep grades that ease before a final, short, steep pitch to the main summit at 1.1 miles, elevation 3388 feet, for a total ascent from the beginning of the Sachs Trail of 2330 feet over a distance of nearly 2.8 miles.

The summit is covered with a heavy cloak of spruce and fir which gives the mountain a spiney profile and may have something to do with its peculiar name (Colvin named it). There is no view. Only a crumbling, barely legible sign on a dead spruce confirms you are on Hedgehog.

The continuing route is a 250-foot descent over 0.3 mile to a wet draw with a small stream, the headwaters of Deer Brook. Across the brook is the intersection with the William A. White Trail.

105 Little Porter

1.95 miles, 1½ hours, 1310-foot vertical rise, ADK markers

Climbing Little Porter and returning via the same route is an excellent short hike. Continuing on to Porter and returning (section 106) makes a good day's outing. Even better is the two-car loop returning over Blueberry (section 107). That's 8.4 miles of great hiking.

The trail begins from Interbrook Road, 0.2 mile short of its end at the Garden parking area, but you have to park in the Garden lot as there is no parking *anywhere* along the road. The trail begins on a road on private land with an easement to permit public travel. Take the marked right fork and reach a lovely two-log bridge over Slide Brook, 0.25 mile from the road, 0.45 mile from the Garden. The trail first climbs then levels through a stand of very big, old hemlocks, climbs again to a knoll, then angles right where an old roadway angles left beside a small stream. Pitches, the first beside a huge boulder, alternate with levels as the forest changes to beech and maple.

At 1.1 miles, twenty-five minutes from the Garden because the walking has been easy, you reach a property line and a log shed where an arrow directs you left, up beside the shed, and onto a tote road for 20 feet, then right away from it onto a narrow path and steeply up.

The next 0.35 mile is much slower and steeper. You angle left with rock outcrops up to your right, then back right again. As you wind uphill, watch for the rattlesake fern, *Botrychium virginianum*. The slopes are even steeper as you angle left with cliffs ahead before you turn to follow a rocky valley beneath the cliffs. You angle left again to cross an abandoned road at just over 1.45 miles. There is a shanty—Hi View Camp—to your left.

The trail is steep again, zigzagging left up a rock scramble, then out to a small overlook—your first view of the valley beneath and Giant behind. After descending this rock knob, you climb to a road at 1.7 miles. Cross it and head left, up behind the house with the spectacular view. You are now on the ridgeline of Little Porter. The next 0.25 mile to the summit is a spectacular walk along the narrow ridge between outcrops. Views include the cliffs on the arm of Porter, the Porter Ridge, and the sweep of Johns Brook Valley. Little Porter is the last outcrop along the trail at 2875 feet.

106 Porter from Little Porter

2.1 miles, 1½ hours, 1280-foot elevation change, ADK markers

Crossing the last rock ledge on the summit of Little Porter, the trail heads north and drops down into a swale in an open birch forest. After crossing an

Little Porter view to Big Slide

intermittent stream, the trail begins a gradual uphill, angling northwest. Several paths diverge in the wet marshes surrounding Porter Brook. You make a sharp right at 0.35 mile to cross the brook and turn west-northwest up its valley. In five minutes you descend slightly to cross the brook again, this time as it flows from a little gorge.

The beautiful birch glade continues, now with spruce emerging. Underfoot are lovely stands of woodferns and bunchberry. Crossing another knoll, you descend slightly again, continuing through the picturesque valley. Thirty minutes from Little Porter, you begin to traverse gradually up, zigzagging more steeply, until cliffs appear ahead. The trail enters a jumbled valley—a small draw that leads below the cliffs and up past them to a meadow at the 3280-foot level. Sparse birch make this look like an orchard, with mountain elderberry, mountain ash, and many woodferns beneath the twisted, white trunks. It is an extraordinary place.

A short but steep descent follows; there is a change to a deep-woods understory of sorrel, clintonia, and goldthread. The trail rolls up and down as it makes a side-hill traverse, slowly gaining elevation. Just past a steep little glen with cliffs up to your right, at the 3500-foot point, a scramble begins. You are climbing to the ridgeline at a fair rate now. Again the forest is reminiscent of an orchard as the grade eases. You traverse northwest, then climb to the intersection with the trail from Blueberry to Porter at 3920 feet, 1.65 miles, and an hour and twenty minutes from Little Porter.

Turn left, west, for the lovely ridgeline walk, gently rising with teasing views through the trees. The first real opening reveals Pitchoff, Cascade, the Sentinels, and Whiteface. A second overlook reveals the cluster of MacIntyre summits and the volcano-like cone of Colden. A last pitch brings you to the summit at 4067 feet (1240 meters), ten minutes from the col. This west-facing rock promontory adds Marcy to the view. It looms above the Panther Gorge cut. To the northwest, the McKenzie Range leads up to Whiteface. Below, you see South Meadow and Railroad Notch and across this deep valley spread the Wolf Jaws, Gothics, Saddleback and Basin, Haystack behind Big Slide, then Marcy.

If you can arrange a second car you can make a through trip including Cascade Mountain and down to the Cascade Lakes (sections 126 and 127), or over Blueberry as in the next section.

107 Porter to Keene Valley via Blueberry

4.55 miles, 3½ hours, 3080-foot descent (plus a half dozen small ascents for a total of 300 feet), ADK markers

Because logging has so disturbed the slopes of Blueberry, the pleasures of a climb to it from the Keene Valley Airport have diminished. If you can arrange two cars, the best walk is up Porter by way of Little Porter (sections 105 and 106) and a descent from Porter along this trail. Therefore this route is described west to east. The terminus is at a field opposite the Keene Valley Highway Department at the north end of Airport Road, 2 miles north of the High Peaks sign for Johns Brook Valley. There is a small parking area right off NY 73. The trail begins along a tote road to the west behind piles of gravel. Descend from Porter along the ridge to the col at 0.45 mile where the trail to Johns Brook forks right, south. Continue straight along the ridge, descending, then climbing to a lovely view toward the Sentinels and Whiteface. Climb to a rocky bluff with a view of Porter and Cascade and the cirque between them. Cross the narrow ridge to another outlook, then continue walking in a stunted forest without views, but nevertheless great walking on the ridge. A rock scramble leads to another overlook back to Porter, then up to a narrow crest with outcrops. The trail continues to undulate, then rises to a 3780-foot knob. The view is similar to that from Porter itself, except due west, which is blocked by Porter and Cascade. All of Pitchoff is now visible.

The trail continues level across this knob, with views toward Giant, then descends steeply into a saddle, and climbs again to a 3775-foot (1151-meter) knob, 1.45 miles and nearly an hour from the summit. After gently descending along open rock interspersed with patches of crunchy lichens, the trail begins a very steep descent in a balsam forest. The trail seems to plunge below a ridge line that is faced with round-topped, smooth cliffs. Dry at first, this section picks up a seep in a crevice, then crosses it. After twenty minutes and a 550-foot descent, the trail moderates, but becomes much wetter as it passes huge, moss-covered boulders, which have slumped off the cliffs above. The ridge of cliff tops begins to taper down as well. You turn right for a pitch down and away from the cliffs, then make an S curve down, and angle back left beneath a fifteen-foot boulder, one more jagged piece that has fallen from above.

The trail descends nearly 775 feet to a col at 3000 feet. A sharp wall rises to the north of this enchanted balsam glen that is rich with ferns. As you climb to open rock beyond it you can see the whole ridge of Porter spread out behind you with the rock knob of the cliff-topped shoulder to the right. The trail climbs another 100 feet to a cairn on open rock and from here on, cairns point to an even higher knob at 2.15 miles. This western summit of Blueberry, at 3050 feet (930 meters), is a broad, flat, rocky field with a huge boulder in the middle. There are great views to Giant and Keene Valley as well as to Hurricane and Jay to the north.

Leaving the rock to descend into the woods, guided by orange daubs, you pass a lot of blueberries. An opening in the woods reveals the slide on East Dix and that ridge down to Spotted. Emerging at the top of a slide, stay along its top, guided again by cairns, and go back into the woods from the upper corner. Again you descend slightly, then climb again on a gentle traverse with intermittent views of the Dial-Bear Den Ridge, and East Dix around to Dix and Nippletop. The trail leads around, then up and over a knoll—Blueberry

East—at 2.55 miles and over 2920 feet (890 meters) in elevation. From here you can see Airport road, 1900 feet below and a good hour and a half away.

Red dots lead you across open rock, bordered with meadowsweet, and back into the woods. The trail crosses to the north side of the ridgeline to another overlook, then reaches a rounded and precipitous slide that takes you down into the woods. Openings with views of the Dixes follow. Leaving the birch, to enter a stand of maples, marks the 2500-foot level. Oak, popple, and pine follow as the trail is alternately gravelly or over rock slabs. The steep descent continues until at about 2000 feet the woods becomes deeper and there are stands of gay wings, *polygala*. You continue zigzagging steeply until you reach a draw and cross the head of it turning down between ledges and cliffs over smooth rock to cross a stream at 3.35 miles. Here, at 1750 feet, in the pretty little hemlock glen, the trail turns left to follow the stream on its right bank, traversing level at first. The stream drops away quickly and soon you reach the edge of the logged lands. If you can remember what it was like twenty years ago, you will want to weep. Even if you cannot remember, you may want to weep. But keep you eyes on your boots and pretend it is the dead of night.

The trail now follows a logging road steeply downhill for a half hour. A skid road forks back uphill to your right (the spot would be confusing if you were headed up to Blueberry, except that your choices after leaving the stream are all to the right as you ascend). The trail goes over a knoll and reaches the stream at 3.95 miles. Cross the stream to a cairn and cross the logging road on the far side to another road that leads left into a red pine plantation. This road now leads over a knoll and down through a grove of hemlock to a T at 4.35 miles. Turn right and downhill to the field and your waiting car.

If you choose to climb Porter from this direction, note that the dirt road heads out the west side of the field hidden behind piles of gravel, marked only by a small green sign reading "Porter." Turn left, 100 yards into the woods, and for the rest of the trail it is easy to reverse the description.

108 Northside Johns Brook Trail

3.6 miles, 1½ hours (with a day pack), 790-foot elevation change, yellow markers

The Garden is the major trailhead for several Keene Valley trails as well as many interior routes (see the next chapter "The Range from Johns Brook Valley"). Two major trails connect the Garden with Johns Brook Lodge, which is run by the Adirondack Mountain Club. They offer bunks and meals in season, a few private lean-tos, and rough cabins for winter camping. Perhaps the best way to get acquainted with this access is to make a loop, water level permitting, over both routes, with a side trip to Short Job for a view of Johns Brook Valley. Use a 0.5-mile portion of the blue Ore Bed Brook Trail to join them.

The Northside or Johns Brook Trail is above Johns Brook with no brook views. It rolls gently most of the way as it ascends first to the Interior Ranger Station at 3.1 miles, then Johns Brook Lodge.

The trail leaves the Garden and ascends rapidly for a short distance, then levels off and continues the rolling ascent. The valley is covered with a deep, rich, acid-tolerant woods consisting of yellow and paper birch, beech, maple, basswood, and hemlock, with many wildflowers underfoot. Numerous erratics of various sizes, dropped by glacial retreat, fill the valley.

The trail is wide and the trees form a shaded canopy. After 0.5 mile, ten minutes from the Garden, you reach a trail junction. The Southside Trail (section 111) branches to cross Johns Brook. This trail is poorly marked and there is no bridge over Johns Brook. The guideboard points the way along the yellow Northside Trail to the Ranger Station and the Lodge. Continuing this way, just short of 1 mile, you reach a footbridge over Bear Brook. The Bear Brook Lean-to is in a small clearing to the left side of the trail across the bridge.

As you travel along the trail, you can still see the swaths that were cut for the telephone poles for the line to the Ranger Station some time ago; the never-used poles are still scattered along the trail. After twenty-five minutes, at 1.3 miles, you reach Deer Brook Lean-to. It sits on a knoll overlooking the brook.

Beyond, the trail descends sharply and crosses the two branches of Deer Brook on sturdy wooden bridges. The climb out of the valley of Deer Brook is equally sharp. Then the rolling course continues. At approximately 1.5 miles, thirty minutes from the Garden, a huge erratic stands to the right side of the trail. Beside it is one of the largest popple trees you may ever see. The trail skirts a second erratic 100 yards farther along. This one marks the midway spot between the Rangers Station and the Garden.

After nearly forty minutes, at 1.75 miles, notice the two huge erratics to the left of the trail that have large saplings growing from them. At 2 miles, about fifty minutes from the Garden, you cross a wide, shallow, usually dry stream, called Dry Brook (to the amazement of those who wade across it after a summer downpour). The trail crosses several more small streams and at 2.5 miles, an hour from the Garden, enters an open forest with very little underbrush. Another three minutes brings a view of Lower Wolf Jaws and part of the Range Trail. Another minute of walking brings you to a fork in the trail. Stay right, with the yellow markers, as the trail left is along a wet area and is not much shorter. The way right ascends a small hill and then descends to the trail junction at the Ranger Station, 3.1 miles.

Stop at the Ranger Station and cross the clearing to the east side of the building. At the end of the clearing there is a suspension bridge over Johns Brook. Here the brook has cut a small gorge into the anorthosite and there are waterfalls and deep pools visible from the bridge. You will cross this bridge to the Southside, Wolf Jaw Brook, and Ore Bed Brook trails. It serves also as the highwater crossing for those starting along the trails from Johns Brook Lodge.

Heading to Johns Brook Lodge, the yellow Northside Trail now bridges Slide Mountain Brook, immediately passes the trail to Big Slide (section 114), and is almost level to the bridge over Black Brook. Grace Camp is nearby and several ADK lean-tos follow. Just beyond is Johns Brook Lodge and on the far side of it you find a huge guideboard and four-way intersection. Open fields once surrounded the lodge, which was built at the site of the Mel Hathaway farm, but forest now hides views of the slopes above.

109 Woodsfall Trail

1.1-mile connector to the Wolf Jaws Trail, 40 minutes, 375-foot elevation change, ADK markers

Heading south across Johns Brook from the guidepost beside the lodge, this trail is the major low-water connector to the Wolf Jaws and Ore Bed Brook trails from Johns Brook Lodge. After crossing Johns Brook on stones, the trail zigzags up the far bank, crosses two small ridges, fords Ore Bed Brook at 0.25 mile, climbs log stairs, and, at 0.3 mile, arrives at a five-way intersection. The way right and left is the blue-marked Ore Bed Brook Trail. Ahead and left is the Short Job Trail (section 110). Ahead, right, the continuing Woodsfall Trail begins a gentle climb and crosses several small streams before reaching a height-of-land at 0.8 mile. It now continues relatively level toward its intersection with the Wolf Jaws Trail (section 117) near the Wolf Jaws Lean-to, 1.1 miles from the Ranger Station.

110 Short Job Loop

0.8-mile loop, 45 minutes, 525-foot elevation change, ADK markers

A quick trip to Short Job for its views is a fillip on the loop between the Northside and Southside Trails. If Johns Brook is low enough to rock-hop, head south from the Lodge, across the brook on the blue-marked Woodsfall Trail, and wind for just over 0.3 mile along it to the five-way intersection (section 109).

Ahead and left is the 0.4-mile trail to Short Job. It takes twenty minutes to climb, less to descend. There are several outlooks from cliff tops, across the knob and a bit below it. You do have to walk about to enjoy them all—the view down Johns Brook Valley, the spectacular panorama of the Range from Wolf Jaws west to a corner of Haystack, with Marcy in the distance, and to the north, Yard and Big Slide. This is a small gem, the equal of Owls Head and Mount Jo.

If the brook is not low enough to ford, you can make this climb by returning on the yellow-marked Northside Trail to the Ranger Station, cross, and walk back to the five-way intersection along the blue-marked Ore Bed Brook Trail.

111 Southside Johns Brook Trail

3.1 miles, 1½ hours, 600-foot elevation change, ADK markers

The Southside Trail is described west to east as it descends from the suspension bridge at Johns Brook, near the Ranger Station. Keep in mind that there is no bridge over Johns Brook at the crossing just above the Garden and this lower crossing may be difficult if you have a heavy pack or in times of high water. Perhaps if you plan to return this way, you should check out the water level at the bridge on Johns Brook Road.

Across the suspension bridge by the Ranger Station, the Ore Bed Brook Trail (section 119) forks right. (If you are making the loop along both Johns Brook trails with the side trip to Short Job, you will reach this point by walking east for 0.5 mile along that blue-marked trail.)

The Southside Trail follows an old tote road full of small rocks and gravel. After five minutes, 0.25 mile, the Wolf Jaws Trail (section 117) forks right and a guide board indicates that it is 2.85 miles to the Garden. A wide truck bridge crosses Wolf Jaw Brook 0.1 mile farther along, where that brook is quite pretty, with large white anorthosite boulders and a series of small waterfalls.

Muddy sections follow well-drained sections. After fifteen minutes, the trail swings close to Johns Brook, giving excellent views of the huge boulders, rushing water, and potholes in bedrock. The trail crosses Bennies Brook—little water here—and after twenty-five minutes, a mile from the suspension bridge, the trail branches to the left, away from the tote road.

Two minutes later, at 1.15 miles, the trail crosses Rock Cut Brook, so named because this shallow stream comes out of a dike. At this point there is a small cliff in front of you. Look to the right; there should be a red ADK marker. Climb the small cliff and then pick up the trail to the left. The foot tread is evident here. The trail comes out on a lookout over Johns Brook where there are large waterfalls and some potholes. The trail swings right over some steps and then it goes down, over rocks and small boulders, with Johns Brook on the left, and the base of a cliff on the right. After about 100 yards, the trail moves up out of the dry riverbed and parallels the bank of the brook.

Thirty-five minutes from the suspension bridge, at 1.6 miles, the trail moves away from the brook and rejoins the tote road. The trail snakes back and forth, coming close to the stream, and then farther away. After forty minutes, there is a wet place in the trail and few markers to guide you as the trail branches around the wet place, then rejoins. At 2.15 miles, you cross Rooster Comb Brook. After fifty minutes, you see an ADK marker that indicates a branch to the left. Follow it, passing a large pile of erratics covered with moss and trees.

Three more minutes of walking brings you to a sign that indicates the direction to the Garden. The trail now is foot-worn and marked with red ADK disks. Another two minutes brings you to a second sign at 2.25 miles and an arrow for the Garden. Follow the path down a short, steep embankment, and as soon as it levels off, make a sharp turn to the right. Follow the path to water's edge. Look across Johns Brook to a huge boulder near the shore. Next to the boulder stands a large paper birch with an ADK marker. Cross on the rocks, coming out near these two landmarks. The trail on the opposite shore is well-defined.

Follow it until you reach a steep ascent where you may see an old ADK marker embedded on a large hemlock tree. Climb the first ascent, picking up other markers. The trail comes to another ascent of a ridge that appears to be an esker. Its top is relatively flat. Follow along the top of the esker until another short, steep ascent is reached. This brings you to the yellow Northside Trail, 2.6 miles and an hour and ten minutes from the suspension bridge. Here a right turn takes you, in 0.5 mile and ten minutes, back to the Garden.

If you are using this route to ascend Johns Brook Valley, allow more time, and watch for problems between the point where the Southside Trail leaves the Northside Trail, and Johns Brook crossing. Here you need to pay careful attention to stay on the proper route.

112 The Brothers

5.2 miles round trip, 4 hours, 2200-foot vertical ascent, ADK markers

The Brothers are a series of prominences on a long ridge. For nearly half its distance, the trail over them clings to the very edge of the steep northern slopes of Johns Brook Valley. Views begin after only a half-hour climb and unfold to include Keene Valley, Hurricane and Giant mountains, and the Great Range from Hedgehog to Basin. A walk to the Brothers and back makes a great, short, day hike, but the view spots are so lovely, four hours just will not suffice for the trip. This route can be combined with a hike on to Big Slide (section 113), as part of a loop with several choices for the return via Johns Brook Valley.

The trail begins at the Garden parking area to the right of the Northside Trail and starts right up through a lovely forest of hemlocks. Excellent waterbar construction combined with the help of nature on these generally dry slopes make this trail a delight to walk. In fifteen minutes you climb over 200 feet to a very pretty hemlock knoll and descend to cross a small stream. A long traverse on the side of a hardwood hill ends beneath a small rock cliff. Go right around it—already there is a tremendous drop off to your left. Continue steeply up, and at the 2100 foot level, you go right around then up another small cliff. You climb over 600 feet in a half hour to this spot with its views of Giant.

The trail continues steeply beyond this point on open rock and shortly you pass a nice erratic and reach the first real overlook. The trail is atop a thin ridge, climbing to another small outcrop at the 2400-foot level where you again go right to climb around and up a small cliff. The bypass right has views of Hurricane; the trail up the cliffs leads to a ledge then back into the woods where the routes meet and continue up the ridgeline. Bracken and lichens, saxifrage and birch all attest to the fire which once cleared these slopes.

There is a very nice overlook at the 2560-foot level; now you begin to see from Gothics to Armstrong, a deep col, then Saddleback and Basin, and a second deep col. Beyond, the trail stays on the ridge with views as you climb steeply again. You duck into the woods, then out to the edge again—big cliffs are now up to your right. Another picture stop is followed by a series of good-sized steps. There are cliffs both right and left as you reach a real scramble up through a cleft in a small cliff at the 2880-foot level. More great views greet you above in an open rock patch which also opens to the north—Porter and its cliffs and the Jay Range beyond Keene. An absolutely wonderful walk on open rock follows. Near here is a "fat man's misery" squeeze-through shortcut route to delight the young—hard to spot going up, obvious going down. You pass a neat overhanging rock in a small spruce swale and continue on the narrow ridge to the summit of First Brother 1.5 miles, an hour and twenty minutes from the start, and a climb of nearly 1480 feet.

A relatively level traverse follows, with a drop of no more than 20 feet, then a scramble here where you can again go right to make climbing easier. On top you can appreciate the deep cirque bordered by Gothics and Saddleback, also the deep cirque between this point and the Third Brother. The trail ducks into the woods to a beautiful overlook toward Porter and back to First Brother. Bare rock ledges at the edge of the cliffs are as smooth as sidewalks as you continue to Second Brother at 1.75 miles. You know this bump is Second Brother because there is a small sign on its summit at the point the trail leads into the woods. You are at 3160 feet (962 meters) now.

The trail remains on the ridge with views ahead to Third Brother, then drops 20 feet into a swale. Go just west of north from here to the best view down into Railroad Notch. The trail begins to climb again, without views, but the beautiful birch forest compensates. Ferns create a lovely open understory—lady fern and three *Dryopteris* species—spinulose, intermediate, and mountain. For twenty-five minutes you will be climbing in the woods, then at 3700 feet you emerge to a great view of the slides on peaks of the Great Range. You can see Big Slide over the top of intervening slopes. Soon you are on the summit of Third Brother at 3720 feet (1134 meters). Good views of Noonmark and Round add to those of the promontories below, as well as views of Dix between the summits of Lower Wolf Jaw.

The Upper Range beyond Big Slide

113　From Brothers to Big Slide

1.4 miles, 1 hour, 607-foot vertical rise, ADK markers

This segment of trail is slow going because of trail conditions and the very steep, nearly 0.3-mile scramble just before the summit of Big Slide. It contrasts with the Brothers Trail in that it is nearly all in the woods without views, but the summit of Big Slide is one of the great ones. A round trip over the Brothers to Big Slide and back to the Garden (8 miles) is a fine day excursion. Several loops using sections 114 and 115 can vary the return.

From the Third Brother at 3720 feet, the trail turns right into the woods to a No Camping sign and several paths leading in search of camping spots. The trail angles left toward Big Slide's summit and is noticeably wetter. After five minutes you pass an overhanging rock to the left of the trail, protection of sorts. You descend to a low point of the wooded ridge, walk on several series of log stringers, and descend some more along the north side of the ridge. The woods are now balsam and spruce with sorrel and sphagnum beneath. The trail is very wet and muddy as it crosses the low point at 3600 feet, then rises very slightly. You cross a mossy stream in a balsam and spruce bog then climb some more on a rooty, muddy section of trail. Usnea, a form of lichen sometimes called old man's beard, drapes in hairy garlands from the balsams. You climb moderately for ten more minutes to a three-way intersection at 1.1 miles, forty minutes from the Third Brother, elevation 3800 feet (1160 meters).

The trail left (section 114) leads to Johns Brook Valley. You turn right and immediately begin to scramble up 150 feet in elevation. The next 50-foot gain seems almost vertical until you walk left on a narrow path to see the edge of Big Slide's cliff. What a view! It extends from Giant to Basin and includes the slides on Dix and, of course, the cliff right beside you.

The trail continues the very steep scramble—and five more minutes puts you on the summit, elevation 4215 feet (1285 meters). You can see all around, from Porter above the marshes of Railroad Notch around to the Jay Range, pieces of Lake Champlain, Hurricane and Green mountains, Giant, to the slides on Dix over the Dial Bear Den ridge. Finally you have a view to the west of south of Haystack and Little Haystack, then the deep col at the head of Panther Gorge leading up to Marcy, Colden, MacIntyre, and Wright. The view clockwise from Giant includes Round, Noonmark, Lower Wolf Jaw, Dix, Upper Wolf Jaw, Macomb, Armstrong, Gothics, Saddleback, Basin, and Haystack. The whole Johns Brook Valley is spread beneath your cliff-top perch.

The mountain has experienced two major slides; one in about 1830 swept down the west face into John Brooks Valley, the other north toward South Meadow about 1856. Either one might have prompted local people to name the mountain.

114 Johns Brook Valley to Big Slide

2.4 miles, 2 to 2½ hours, 1968-foot vertical rise, red ADK markers

Descending via this very direct route allows you to make a 9.6-mile loop from the Garden over the Brothers and Big Slide and end with the Northside Trail. It is also a nice climb from the valley and is easy enough to follow in either direction. Thus the trail is described as an ascent.

The trail starts 0.1 mile west of the Ranger Station, just to the west side of Slide Mountain Brook. It follows up along the brook with its lovely waterfalls, then crosses to the east in 0.2 mile, only to recross shortly beyond, and cross again to the east. The brook flows over a big slide. As the trail pulls away from the stream, look back to the slides across the valley on Gothics; this is the only good distant view from this trail.

Shortly beyond, elevation 2450 feet (750 meters), the trail again crosses to the west. It goes back to the east at 2680 feet. In less than ten minutes, there is a sharp left, then a right. The stream opens up to huge rock shelves. You walk up the slides in a small gorge. A stream with nice cascades enters from the west. Shortly beyond there is an opening, clearly marked No Camping.

You rock-hop to cross to the west—there are steep cliffs up to your right. At 2750 feet, under 1 mile, you cross over the branch of Slide Brook. From here on it is a steep, rocky climb through thick birch and balsam stands for over 1 mile to the intersection with the Big Slide-Brothers Trail. The last 0.3-mile scramble to the summit is described in section 113. Do not miss the side path to the edge of the cliff.

If you descend via this route, the section from the intersection to the first stream crossing is straightforward—steep and rocky. The many stream crossings are marked and not really confusing—just slow, because there is so much to see.

115 Big Slide over Yard to Johns Brook Valley

3.85 miles, 2 hours, 1180-foot descent, ADK markers to Klondike Trail, which is marked with red

This may not be the most exciting of trails, but it is fairly easy to walk, except for the last part along the Klondike Trail and even that may change, as much-needed trail work is being done there.

The trail turns into the woods from Big Slide's summit to a number of herd paths. The trail is the one to the left and it makes a very gentle descent in a balsam woods. Although the ridgeline slopes steeply off to your right, there are no views. The trail becomes almost level. After twenty-five minutes you

From Gothics to Marcy beyond Third Brother and Big Slide from the Porter-Blueberry Ridge

glimpse the summit of Yard ahead through an opening created by a patch of dead balsams. Dense ferns and grasses choke the trail here. You descend a bit, cross to the north side of the ridge, then wind up through a fairly thick balsam stand to a three-way intersection, 1.3 miles from Big Slide. Yard's summit at 4008 feet (1222 meters) is a wooded hummock 30 yards to the left.

The descent from Yard begins to the right of the intersection where it seems you walk out to the edge of the world—the valley of Klondike Notch lies so steeply below you. All the nearby slopes seem covered with dead balsams. Gothics' western slides appear very close and there is a nice view of Haystack and Marcy.

The trail angles right along the edge, then turns to descend sharply. Two overhanging rocks constrict the trail, which is lined with mountain maple and raspberries. After leveling briefly, the trail resumes the steep descent, now on bare rock. It zigs north, then zags back south below the cliffs you were on top of moments before. It continues across a beautiful rock ledge, then squeezes between two boulders to come out on a short level again. You are traversing south with a steep drop to your right. A second set of cliffs appears to your left, then the way becomes so steep you zigzag again. Below the next cliff, you cross a rubbly wash and traverse on the level below beautiful mossy cliffs that lead to a horizontally jointed rock that rises above like ancient temple walls. The very narrow trail stays nearly level, bringing you just below an even taller jointed ledge—another temple—with a god-like sculpture broken from the end to stand peering into the bottom of the valley below.

The trail now descends steeply again, traversing back and forth to a level in a spruce and balsam bog followed by one more short descent to intersect the Klondike trail. The intersection is ten minutes below the temple ledges, fifty minutes, but only 1.25 miles, from Yard's summit—and 974 feet below it.

Turn left for the forty-minute, 1.3-mile descent to Johns Brook Lodge along

the south end of the Klondike Trail (section 130). It is wide and grassy and follows an old tote road, descending gently with a few slightly steeper stretches. The forest, which now includes big yellow and white birch along with the spruce and balsam, grows taller. There are a few level, muddy places, then after nearly twenty-five minutes you reach White Brook, where the mud begins in earnest. The trail is close to the brook, across stringers not quite long enough to span the mud. In ten minutes the valley has become much narrower and you turn to cross the brook on a two-log bridge. Turning left into a field, the trail ends in 100 yards at a huge sign pole in front of Johns Brook Lodge.

116 Railroad Notch

Bushwhack

At one time there was a trail from Keene Valley to South Meadow and the present trail to the Brothers uses the first part of the old route. The South Meadow Trail passed through Railroad Notch between Porter and Big Slide. (Klondike Notch, between Big Slide/Yard and Tabletop/Phelps, has at times been erroneously referred to as Railroad Notch, but newspaper accounts of a railroad proposed and surveyed in the 1880s, as uncovered by Tony Goodwin, show that the lower-altitude pass between Porter and Big Slide is the true Railroad Notch.)

Beaver activity may have contributed to the abandonment of the South Meadow Trail, although as far back as the early '30s, guides referred to it as the "abandoned trail." Of the four ponds shown on the 1979 metric map, the westernmost is dramatically visible from the huge boulder that lies athwart the trail connecting Cascade and Porter. Today Railroad Notch is strictly bushwhack territory, requiring careful attention to map and compass.

One approach is to follow the Porter Trail up beyond Little Porter and watch for a prominent split rock just west of the trail. From this point, a level bushwhack due west takes you to the easternmost of the four ponds. This area is subject to ongoing alteration by beavers. A faint path may be visible along the north side of the four ponds. At times, long grass hides pitfalls between the rocks.

An approach from the west, favored by Vern Lamb and others from Lake Placid, follows high on the north bank of South Meadow Brook. The original trail, which ultimately connected with the Klondike Notch Trail not far from South Meadow, used the south bank of the brook.

A third approach, probably the most interesting historically, is to start up the Brothers Trail from the Garden. Just before the trail dips left to cross Juliet Brook, look for a carved arrow high on a tree to your left. At this point a bushwhack at 300° magnetic follows a ridge paralleling Juliet Brook. After some initial floundering through brush and downed small trees, the route begins to look like a faint path with some evidence of axe-blazes.

Near an interesting lumpy rock, your compass course would begin to take you up the side of the Brothers. At this point, head across the little valley on your right. As you approach Slide Brook, watch for a line of yellow paint-blazes, a state land boundary. Follow this line to your left. After a steep scramble you should come to a yellow-topped pipe, marking the southwest corner of Lot 90. Here the yellow blazes turn north and cross Slide Brook. If you continue west from the pipe, you may see a few more axe-blazes before they and the path peter out. Approximating your original compass direction will take you across the main branch of Slide Brook that comes from Third Brother.

After your cross this brook, your compass will take you steeply up into the flat-topped pass, where you may come out at the western pond, which has a head-high, sturdy, tangled dam ringing the south side. Amazingly huge trunks have been dragged for a distance; the pond has a fascinating landscape of thick moss on rounded boulders amidst dead trees. Its next-east neighbor is a somber black pond with a mud dam. The next and longest of the ponds shown on the 1979 map was, in 1980, only a broad meadow with an abandoned beaver house near each end, and a view of the top of Giant. In 1984, it was a pond again.

Since beaver activity is generally restricted to the north side of the notch along the base of the steep slope up to the long Porter Ridge, you can walk southwest to south from the ponds, through narrow bands of softwoods, and out into a wide-open forest of mostly birch and ferns. This lets you enjoy the spectacular birch and ferns that continue all along the steep slopes coming down from Big Slide. A course southeasterly along the base of these slopes soon leads to Slide Brook, across which a fairly steep, more southerly route will take you up 300 feet through open woods to the trail near Second Brother.

You may also choose to return by heading east to the Porter Trail to descend via the Little Porter Trail.

The Range
from Johns Brook Valley

THE GREAT RANGE is a series of jagged peaks that rises between the depths of the Ausable and Johns Brook valleys. The Great Range Trail, or just plain Range Trail, is a continuous route that climbs over every one of those peaks from Keene Valley to Haystack. Four trails climb to the Great Range from Upper Johns Brook Valley. Loops using pairs of them offer a number of ways to explore the Range. You could even pair these routes with treks over the Range to the Ausable Valley, using one of the six trails from that valley. This guide does not describe the Great Range as one route, because most people have to break it into segments. Segments of the Range Trail east of Lower Wolf Jaw are given in earlier chapters.

The closer trails are to Mount Marcy (sometimes called the end of the Range Trail, with Haystack viewed as a spur), the more dense the network becomes, with many of the direct routes comprising parts of several variously named or colored trails. This chapter arranges these segments as simply as possible.

As an organizational convenience, this guide breaks the four Johns Brook Valley Trails into three loops, each divided into two sections. The first loop is a combination of the section up Wolf Jaw Brook, with a spur to Lower Wolf Jaw; the Middle Range Trail, which traverses Upper Wolf Jaw, Armstrong, and Gothics; and a descent along the Ore Bed Brook Trail, which is sometimes known as the ADK Range Trail. You can climb the Ore Bed Trail to make the second loop, where the upper part is the Upper Range Trail from Gothics-Saddleback Col over Saddleback and Basin to Haystack. The descent combines one of two segments to connect the Range to the Phelps Trail, either the Blue Connector or the Shorey Short Cut. The third loop combines an ascent via the Hopkins Trail to Marcy and back via the Phelps Trail.

The Upper Range Trail, which is sometimes called the DEC Range Trail, is described heading west; there are some really steep and rough places along it, so you may want to hike it in a reverse direction. Both Ore Bed and Hopkins are nice climbs; Phelps is best for a descent from the Range; but there are no clear choices here, just limitless possibilities. With the segments described in the Keene Valley and Ausable chapters, the description of the Upper Range Trail completes the description of the whole Range Trail, a route that covers 10.65 miles and climbs 7775 feet in elevation, while rising 3921 feet from Keene Valley to the summit of Haystack.

The trails to the Range start from Upper Johns Brook Valley where there are a number of lean-tos and campsites as well as ADK's Johns Brook Lodge and its cluster of camps and lean-tos, which provide public accommodation for a fee.

There is a manned Ranger Station in case you have a problem. Obviously, you can walk these loops as day hikes from the Garden, but the additional 6 miles or more limits those who can explore the Upper Range or Marcy this way.

117 Lower Wolf Jaw via Wolf Jaw Brook and Col

2.6 miles, 2 hours, 1970-foot vertical rise, red and ATIS markers

Start along the Southside Trail where it crosses the suspension bridge, 0 mile, near the Ranger Station. Seventy-five yards from the bridge, a blue trail forks right. Turn left on the Southside Trail for 0.25 mile, five minutes, to the Wolf Jaws Trail, where a guideboard directs you to turn right.

The red Wolf Jaws Trail swings up over a rubble of rocks and is poorly drained, but after five minutes of walking, the trail becomes wider, smoother, and drier. It is not steep, but climbs steadily for 2 miles in which it gains 1400 feet to the Wolf Jaws Notch.

Wolf Jaw Brook flows along to the east, left of the trail as you ascend. You see or hear it for most of the climb to the col. After a mile, thirty-five minutes from the suspension bridge, you reach the trail junction with the Woodsfall Trail (section 109). This trail, also marked by red ADK markers, leads back to Johns Brook Lodge in 1.1 miles, first intersecting the Ore Bed Brook Trail before reaching the Lodge. In low water, this is an alternate starting route for those staying at or near the Lodge. Just past the trail junction, on the left of the trail to the col, is the Wolf Jaws Lean-to, at a point nearly halfway between the suspension bridge and the col.

The trail continues to ascend, becoming somewhat steeper than the first mile, but the climb is still relatively easy. Less than fifteen minutes past the lean-to, you have your first glimpse of Lower Wolf Jaw up close and it looks very rugged and wild. The trail crosses several small tributaries of the main stream. The areas between the tributaries is like crossing a series of fingers, and each small ascent is followed by a small descent. Beyond these, you cross a small swamp and ten minutes from your first glimpse of Lower Wolf Jaw, you see part of Upper Wolf Jaw for the first time.

The trail steepens as it approaches the col, and after an hour and twenty minutes, 2 miles from the suspension bridge, you reach the col, elevation 3500 feet. The col is relatively thick with lichen-encrusted balsam and paper birch. There are many blowdowns and it is quite swampy in spots. An official yellow sign designates a camping area in a drier part of the col. The Range Trail to the right leads to Upper Wolf Jaw and eventually joins the Ore Bed Brook Trail in the Gothics Col (sections 118 and 119).

The trail to Lower Wolf Jaw leads across the col, crosses a swampy area, passes another trail junction, where an ATIS trail leads to St. Huberts (section

93). Beyond this junction, the Range Trail with ATIS markers begins the climb up Lower Wolf Jaw. The way is very steep with few level spots between the long, sharp ascents. Ten minutes from col, at 0.25 mile, you reach the junction with the Wedge Brook ATIS Trail to St. Huberts (section 93).

The Lower Wolf Jaw Trail becomes even steeper, and you have occasional views of Upper Wolf Jaw and the Range if you stop and turn around. After thirty-five minutes, 0.5 mile from the col, and 660 feet above it, you reach the summit. Magnificent views of the Range, Slide, and other mountains in the Johns Brook area greet you. If you walk east, past the large outcrop that marks the summit, you can see Giant of the Valley through the trees.

118 Middle Range Trail

3.3 miles, 3¹/₃ hours, 1817-foot ascent, 1309-foot descent, red markers

This portion of the Range Trail begins at the intersection with the Wolf Jaw Brook Trail (section 117) and ends at the intersection with the Ore Bed Brook Trail (section 119). It traverses Upper Wolf Jaw, Armstrong, and Gothics.

To some people, the Wolf Jaws are a series of knobs that resemble teeth in a strong jaw that grips the heights above both the Johns Brook Valley and the Ausable Lakes. If that is so, then Upper Wolf Jaw is certainly an incisor. At the intersection in the col, 2 miles above the suspension bridge on Johns Brook, the Range Trail heads southwest out of the col on a moderate grade that quickly steepens. Soon you find yourself climbing steeply over the rock outcrops of Upper Wolf Jaw, where the trail snakes back and forth as it ascends. There are many open areas that provide excellent views of Lower Wolf Jaw, Cascade, Porter, and the surrounding region.

The mountain is covered with relatively small balsam fir and spruce that frame your views toward the Johns Brook Valley. You reach the first tooth at 0.5 mile, thirty minutes and 560 feet from the col (it is steep). Here there is an excellent view of the area around the Ausable Lakes and also of the Gothics. The trail, which is very muddy, follows along the ridge, then drops down nearly 100 feet and follows another ridge to begin the ascent of the second and higher tooth. The distance between these two teeth is about 0.4 mile, and the ascent of the second (250 feet) is very steep, but relatively short, requiring about five minutes of hard climbing. Moderate grades follow, then the trail levels off as it swings off toward the summit, about 1 mile and fifty minutes from the Wolf Jaw Col. The trail to the summit branches right, north, from the main trail. It is about 150 feet from the main trail to the rock outcrop of the 4201-foot (1281-meter) summit from which there are many fine views in all directions.

UPPER WOLF JAW TO ARMSTRONG

The next summit on the Range Trail, 0.8 mile away, is Armstrong, at 4400 feet (1342 meters). From Upper Wolf Jaw, the red trail drops very quickly toward the Wolf Jaw-Armstrong Col. It then levels off with a gradual descent for about 100 yards, followed by a steep descent of another 200 yards. It takes about ten minutes to cover the 0.2 mile, 280-foot descent to this col, which is filled with dead trees and stubs broken by wind and snow. The trail swings sharply up, moderates as it passes a large erratic, then curves left up and over an outcrop, and comes to the base of a cliff. Marked now with ADK red disks, the trail skirts right along the base of the cliff then cuts back left, west, and passes up over this small rock knob. The trail continues along the face of the ledges until it approaches a view of the Ausable Lakes. Then the trail turns back right until it reaches the top of the knob and levels off. It stays relatively level until the ascent up Armstrong begins, approximately 0.5 mile from the summit of Upper Wolf Jaw.

Here the trail is not well marked and is very steep. The ascent begins with a fifteen- to twenty-foot ladder up the sheer face of the mountain. At the top of the log ladder, there is a shelf that provides footing to traverse the cliff. There are a large number of handholds if you look for them, and you will need them. There is also a small cable for support if it is needed. The rest of the way up is not quite as steep, but the climbing is still very rigorous because the trail winds back and forth over the ledges and outcrops. You will still need to use your hands for support. A second log ladder (in poor condition) helps you climb over a smaller cliff. The trail then moderates and passes through scrub conifers and comes out on the summit, after climbing 500 feet from the col. Turn right to the ledges with views.

ARMSTRONG TO GOTHICS

The distance from Armstrong to Gothics on the Range Trail is 0.9 mile, and is also described as a part of section 96. From Armstrong, it swings sharply left and drops quickly, levels off, and then follows a swampy ridge through a forest of small conifers. The trail passes up over a small knob and then drops down into the Armstrong-Gothics Col, 0.45 mile from the summit of Armstrong, after descending over 200 feet in the two drops. The ATIS trail from Beaver Meadows Falls joins the Range Trail in this col.

Leaving the col, the red-marked ADK trail heads southwest and crosses a long swampy area before beginning the steep ascent up Gothics. After about fifteen minutes of climbing, the trail crosses a small shoulder and then continues on upward through the scrub conifers and small paper birch. About ten minutes later, it breaks through onto the bare summit ridge of Gothics. The summit is 0.45 mile and 420 feet above the col between it and Armstrong.

The views from this 4733-foot (1220-meter) peak are spectacular. You can see Johns Brook Lodge, the boathouse on Lower Ausable Lake, the Dixes, Lake Champlain, and much of the High Peaks.

GOTHICS TO GOTHICS-SADDLEBACK COL

Before commencing the 730-foot, nearly 0.7-mile descent to the Gothics-Saddleback Col, the Range Trail winds south along Gothics' exposed ridgeline. It enters the scrub conifers and begins a moderate descent to a small col that separates Gothics from its lower, western summit. At 0.1 mile, barely into the conifers, the ATIS trail over Pyramid (section 95) forks left, south. Stay on the red trail along the conifer ridge and a moderate ascent brings you to the western summit, at 4640 feet (1415 meters).

Now the major descent from Gothics begins—you will drop 640 feet in 0.35 mile. The trail is precipitous. Yellow paint blazes on the rock face mark the route. Keep to the right as you descend, as this way seems to offer the better footing. After the first series of ledges, there is an opening between the rocks that contains a couple of small fault caves. Partway down the mountain there are two long, rubber-covered cables that lend a great deal of support.

After leaving the cables, the outcrop trail enters the scrub conifers, paper birch, and mountain ash. The grade moderates but it is still very steep. About twenty-five minutes after starting down the rock face, the trail reaches the intersection with the Ore Bed Brook Trail in the col.

119 Ore Bed Brook Trail

3 miles, 2¼ hours, 1780-foot ascent, blue markers

The route from the Ranger Station to the Gothics-Saddleback Col is variously called the ADK Range Trail and the Ore Bed Brook Trail. You will walk this route in the opposite direction to descend from the Range Trail after a climb over Upper Wolf Jaw and Gothics (section 118). A climb via this route is the beginning of a circuit over the Saddleback-Basin portion of the Range Trail (section 120), where you can choose one of several ways to descend from the Range Trail.

From the Ranger Station in Johns Brook Valley, the trail, unmarked at this point, traverses the clearing and crosses the suspension bridge over Johns Brook. Just beyond the bridge on the right there is a short connector trail that leads to the Ore Bed Brook Trail, which starts farther down, east, on the Southside Trail. This connector climbs moderately for approximately a hundred feet and joins the Ore Bed Brook Trail, which now has blue disks.

The beginning of the Ore Bed Brook Trail is wide, but covered with scattered boulders and wet spots, whose frequency diminishes after a few hundred yards. After five minutes the trail branches; keep left. (The road right, the more obvious route, leads to private property. Do not take it. Watch out, for hikers often lose the trail here.)

For the first mile, the ascent is moderate, with some ups and downs, as the trail passes through a mixed conifer and hardwood forest. At about 0.5 mile, fifteen minutes, you reach the trail junction sometimes called five corners. Two red ADK trails lead left. One goes to Short Job (section 110), the second is the Woodsfall Trail (section 109), which connects with the Wolf Jaws Trail. The red trail right is the portion of the Woodsfall Trail leading to Johns Brook Lodge and is used in low water by those staying at the lodge to reach the Ore Bed Brook Trail.

The Ore Bed Brook Trail continues straight ahead with blue markers. The gradient continues to steepen, beneath large maples and conifers with a ground cover of mosses and ferns. Approximately 1.2 miles, thirty-five minutes, from the clearing, the trail crosses a tributary of Ore Bed Brook. The Ore Bed Brook Lean-to sits high on the south bank of the tributary.

The trail stays to the right of the lean-to. About five minutes after passing the lean-to, there is a huge angular erratic that leans out over the trail. This erratic is partially buried, but looms at least twenty feet above the trail and has several trees growing on top, as well as mosses and lichens.

The trail steepens and, about ten minutes and 0.5 mile from the lean-to, at 1.7 miles, it crosses another tributary of Ore Bed Brook. The flat land around the brook looks like a good camping spot, but it is too close to the stream to be appropriate and so has been posted with conspicuous yellow No Camping disks.

Following along with Ore Bed Brook to your right, you have occasional views of the brook and some of its pretty pools and rapids.

Thirty minutes from the lean-to, the trail crosses a slide that occurred during the 1970s. Fifty minutes from the lean-to, at 2.5 miles, the trail crosses a split in Ore Bed Brook. It is poorly marked here, so you have to be careful to stay on the trail. After crossing the first branch of this split, go almost to the second branch (20 feet maximum) and look to the left—there should be a marker. If you do not spot it, stay in the center of the split and work upstream. You will come to the trail.

An hour from the lean-to, 2.6 miles from the Ranger Station, the trail reaches the base of a small slide. There is a much larger slide to the right, but stay in the woods on the small slide that has a tree-covering canopy. The real climbing begins at this point, and trail crews were busily installing several elaborate ladders here during the summer of 1988, so the following cautions may be superfluous: Follow the trail over the bedrock, up the very steep grade that leads to the col between Gothics and Saddleback. The distance is not great, but it may require nearly a half hour for the ascent from the slide. The trail is not well marked in this section but stay on the exposed water-worn rock, and when in doubt, keep right.

The trail levels off, crosses a small basalt dike that shows water scouring, and goes about 100 more yards to the col, where it intersects the Range Trail.

Saddleback Summit

120 Upper Range Trail to Haystack

3.4 miles, 2½ to 3 hours, 2404-foot ascent, 1446-foot descent, blue markers with yellow paint daubs

The Upper Range Trail from the intersection with the Ore Bed Brook Trail is a series of some of the sharpest climbs in the High Peaks. The first segment of the trail, the climb to Saddleback's summit, is 0.55 mile long with a 525-foot ascent that takes thirty-five minutes. The trail west, out of the Gothics-Saddleback Col from the intersection col, starts gradually, but the gradient increases sharply as the trail follows along a rock path that is interlaced with small dikes. The trail is very steep in places and secure footing and handholds are required to climb along the trail. The area has a windswept look, with lichen-covered balsams and spruce, small birches, and many dead stubs.

The first hump of the saddle is approximately 0.4 mile from the col, twenty-five minutes; the gradient and the fact that the hump represents most of the climb up Saddleback make it that slow. The trail descends slightly into the saddle and follows along this ridge for about 300 yards. Watch in this stretch for a path left that leads to a perch on an open cliff top, the best view on the mountain, and often out of the wind when you need better protection than the southwest face provides.

The trail then climbs to the second, higher summit at 4526 feet (1380 meters). The majority of the mountain is covered with small conifers, but just before the summit, the trees give way to a large outcrop with a steep face that offers excellent views of the surrounding mountains.

SADDLEBACK TO BASIN

The nearly 0.9-mile, forty-minute segment of the Range Trail between Saddleback and Basin is one of the most difficult in the High Peaks. Extreme care is required in the initial 380-foot descent from Saddleback. When you leave its summit, follow the yellow arrows. Caution is needed and when in doubt, keep right, away from the steep face to the left. You should spot yellow arrows on the right side of the open rock, just outside the brush which borders it. Always know where the next arrow is located. The first two are quite obvious, but the third may be difficult to find, so keep right, even climbing a little, to locate it. After a few feet, two sets of arrows appear. One set leads down through an opening between two rocks, the other goes straight ahead and then drops left. Both sets lead off the cliff and come together near the base. Regardless of which path you follow, use extreme care in selecting handholds. The paint blazes just give you the general direction. You will have to search about for the handholds on this route down the cliff face. Hikers have spent many unhappy moments on this rock face, which, like slide-climbing, is easier going up than down.

A yellow-paint-marked trail leads a little farther down the cliff and into the conifers. (If you are coming from Basin, a large yellow dot indicates the start of the ascent over the cliffs.) It requires about fifteen minutes to make the seemingly vertical 250-foot descent. Another five minutes brings you to the col between Saddleback and Basin, 0.2 mile and 380 feet below Saddleback. The col is a high, 4150-foot, wet meadow of mosses, ferns, and small birches and conifers with bluets in spring. It takes about five minutes to cross the col and begin the 676-foot ascent up Basin. That ascent starts gradually, but then quickly steepens, with occasional level spots and from these level spots there are magnificent views of Saddleback, the rest of the Range Trail, and Johns Brook Valley. Much of the trail is on bedrock, up through small cuts in the rock and over cliffs that require hand- and toeholds. At 0.5 mile, thirty minutes from Saddleback, the trail reaches the top of the first peak of Basin. It then drops down into a small notch and follows a relatively level course for about 0.2 mile until the ascent of the true summit begins. As you climb, notice the large perched boulder to the right and above the trail. You climb through a rock chimney that provides a route to the open summit of Basin, at 4824 feet (1471 meters). The distance between Basin's humps is 0.4 mile.

From Basin's summit at 1.45 miles, the views of Haystack, Marcy, the MacIntyre Range, the Ausable Lakes, and Johns Brook Valley are wonderful. Here too you will find an original triangulation bolt, set by Colvin in 1876.

BASIN TO HAYSTACK

The 0.8-mile, 987-foot descent from Basin to the intersection with the Shorey Short Cut Trail is precipitous, largely over bare rock, and takes forty minutes or more. This portion of the Range Trail begins by following a yellow arrow on Basin's summit that points to a cairn. The descent is very steep. Spruce and balsam grow only a few feet below the summit; but, nevertheless, openings in the trees offer spectacular views of Haystack, Skylight, and Marcy. The descent continues for about ten minutes, and then comes out on an open rock face at 0.2 mile. This is the site of an old log ladder that has been removed. A yellow arrow points down the cliff. Ignore it and walk across the top of the cliff to a newly cut trail to the right that descends to the base of the cliff before turning left and rejoining the original trail near the location of the old ladder. Because this trail loops through the woods, the descent is easier.

About five minutes later, you must traverse another cliff and you need much care to find hand- and toeholds. The trail continues downward and very soon comes to a large log ladder that is used to descend about 20 feet to the next level. The trail remains very steep and there are more rock faces to ease down until the trail levels off and reaches the junction of the Shorey Short Cut at 2.25 miles. This intersection, at the head of the cirque formed by Haystack Brook, has elevation about 3840 feet and is near the site of the old Snowbird Lean-to. Since the point is below 4000 feet and near water, a campsite has been designated across the trail. It is the only such site on the Range Trail west of Hedgehog. Note that unless you are going on to Haystack, this is a good place to head back to Johns Brook Valley via the Shorey Short Cut and the Phelps trails (section 122 and 124).

The Range Trail climbs fairly steeply from the intersection, past the camping site, to a second intersection, 0.2 mile away. Here the Snowbird Trail of section 55 forks left. The Range Trail crosses a small stream and starts to climb with the stream at first to the right of the trail. Erosion has left a series of boulders for foot tread—rough footing at best. The climb is consistently steep for just over 0.4 mile to an intersection at 2.85 miles. The Range Trail has gained 689 feet between the intersection with Shorey Short Cut and this intersection.

The right fork is the Blue Connector to the Phelps Trail described in section 121. Left leads to Haystack, a route marked mostly by cairns and yellow blazes painted on bedrock. This can be a treacherous ascent during times of poor visibility. Always be certain of the location of the next cairn before leaving your present, known position.

The trail ascends moderately 165 feet in elevation up the northern side of Little Haystack to this small summit, where you are overwhelmed by the mass of Haystack's rocky cone ahead. Continuing south over Little Haystack, the trail, all on exposed rock, descends on a diagonal to the left, then turns right and drops 80 feet or more into the col between Little Haystack and Haystack. (There is an alternate route down a small dike, but the beginning is relatively obscure and is only marked by a single cairn.)

The conifer-filled col is quite small. Beyond it, the trail leads moderately at first, and then quickly very much more steeply for the last 350 feet of climb up the north side of Haystack. The trail keeps off the ridge crest until just before it reaches the summit, 3.4 miles.

From the summit you look into one of the most concealed recesses of the High Peaks—Panther Gorge. Views are spectacular and unobstructed except those blocked by Marcy. More notes on the summit and the continuing route south are described in section 54.

121 Blue Connector Trail

0.5 mile, 20 minutes, 490-foot ascent, 100-foot descent, blue markers

This blue-marked connector leads from the turn to Haystack on the Range Trail to the Phelps Trail. If you are climbing from Johns Brook Valley via the Phelps Trail, you can reach Haystack via the Shorey Short Cut and a portion of the Range Trail, or via this connector.

Leaving the Range Trail below Haystack, the Blue Connector turns right, northwest, up a small knob, from which, at 0.1 mile, there are views in all directions. The descent from the knob through balsam and spruce is gentle at first, but becomes very sharp, dropping down over sheer rock faces, to the deep col on the narrow wall between Panther Gorge and Johns Brook Valley. In the col, at 0.5 mile, it intersects the Phelps Trail (section 124), with Marcy to the left and Johns Brook Valley to the right.

122 Shorey Short Cut

1.1 miles, 50 minutes, 340-foot ascent, 770-foot descent, yellow markers

Shorey Short Cut connects the Upper Range Trail (section 120) with the Phelps Trail (section 124), 0.2 mile above Slant Rock Lean-to. Use it as a link in a loop from the Range Trail to the Phelps Trail back to Johns Brook Lodge or use it in the opposite direction to climb to Haystack from the Phelps Trail. However, as a connector, it is little used, perhaps because it seems to climb unnecessarily over a shoulder of a nameless knob. It is a foul-weather escape route from the Range Trail, but there are those who think it should be abandoned and a new shortcut designed.

From the col below Basin, Shorey Short Cut heads northeast following a small brook that flows along a large rock face, ascending at a moderate grade. The ascent is broken with occasional level spots, but these levels are very wet and muddy. After fifteen minutes, 0.25 mile from the Range Trail, Shorey Short Cut becomes level and follows a level contour around the side of the knob. There are some huge erratics next to the trail and there are excellent views of Basin.

At 0.35 mile, the trail starts to drop off, very sharply at times, as it descends 770 feet in the next 0.75 mile. The descent oscillates between very steep and moderate, with the moderate areas being very muddy. After about fifty minutes, 1.1 miles, the trail crosses Johns Brook and joins the red-marked Phelps Trail about 0.2 mile above the Slant Rock Lean-to.

123 Hopkins Trail

3.7 miles, 2¹/₃ hours, 1640-foot elevation change, yellow markers

Two trails lead southwest from Bushnell Falls toward Marcy. The Phelps Trail, which climbs past Slant Rock to the head of Panther Gorge along the south side of Johns Brook, is described in section 124 in the descending direction, because it nicely finishes loops over Saddleback and Basin as well as one over Marcy. You need to reverse the lower yellow-marked part of the Phelps Trail to Bushnell Falls to begin the Hopkins Trail, which parallels the Phelps Trail (but on the north side of Johns Brook) and climbs to the Plateau area north of

Little Marcy. The distance to Marcy is about the same either way, so if that is your destination, you might want to go up one trail and return on the other. Substantially more traffic follows the Phelps Trail, just because it also provides access to the high southwestern summits of the Great Range.

If you are headed for Indian Falls, the Hopkins Trail will save you several puffs over following the Phelps Trail, but as you climb some 500 feet above the low point between Little Marcy and Tabletop, you may suspect that the trail was not cut out primarily to expedite the trip west out of Johns Brook. The trail ends at its junction with the blue-marked VanHoevenberg Trail (section 148), some 900 feet below the summit of Marcy, but already 800 feet above Indian Falls.

The trail begins in front of the Bushnell Falls Lean-to, 1.5 miles from Johns Brook Lodge, and angles to the left away from the left side of the lean-to. (The Phelps Trail, with red markers, drops straight down from the lean-to to cross Johns Brook.) You pass for several minutes through a fairly level area with many evident tent sites in open hardwoods. There are views out through the trees to the south, up Chicken Coop Brook toward Saddleback and Basin. Although you will be treated to no wide-open views of these peaks, they will follow you through the first half of your hike up to Plateau, as you watch your progress over your left shoulder.

You soon pass out of the hardwoods into fairly young spruce-fir forest, climbing gentle to briefly moderate grades as you cross several streams coming down from the ridge connecting Tabletop and Phelps peaks to the northwest. You will find the footing a pleasant respite from the heavily used trails that brought you to Bushnell Falls. Mud wallows are rare and there are few exposed roots or rocks for the first 1.5 miles, as lightly packed duff carries you through an area recovering well from the severe damage inflicted by the 1950 hurricane. The woods are mostly open, with the moss-covered trunks of old blowdown the predominant feature on the forest floor. Nearing the end of the easy grades, you pass through an unusually thick stand of scrub fir, arriving at a stream with a pool that is a sure midday delight for any July hiker.

Ten minutes beyond the pool, you may wonder why you left it. With 1700 feet to climb between Bushnell Falls and Plateau, you are here doing most of it. Staying on the north side of the stream, you climb steadily on trail that is in remarkably good condition considering the angle of ascent. When you finally cross the stream, now thoroughly moss-covered, and then soon recross it, you are some 800 feet above the pool. Another ten minutes at more moderate grades brings you over the crest at the edge of Plateau, to find the summit cone of Marcy looming dead ahead.

Marcy's close appearance is deceptive, however. You must tramp another quarter hour across Plateau to reach the VanHoevenberg Trail. And, if you are tempted to look up at the peak as it continually reappears ahead, you will sooner or later step into a puddle. The sphagnum that covers all of this part of Plateau is indicative of the underfoot conditions. You may improve your chances of arriving with dry feet if you watch for the mixing of red *russowii* with the always green, and most common, *girgensohnii* sphagnum. A sharp 40-foot pitch precedes your arrival at the trail junction.

From the intersection with the VanHoevenberg Trail, a right turn heads you down toward Adirondak Loj. A left turn begins the final 1.25-mile, 1243-foot climb to Marcy (see section 148).

If you are climbing Marcy from Johns Brook Lodge, allow three and a half to four hours via the Hopkins Trail.

124 Phelps Trail
From VanHoevenberg Intersection to Johns Brook Lodge

5.3 miles, 2½-hour descent, 2615-foot elevation change, red markers above Bushnell Falls, yellow below

The Phelps Trail is the most heavily used route out of Johns Brook Valley, the most direct route to Haystack, and one of the two most direct routes to Marcy from it. The trek to Marcy via the Phelps Trail is almost 6 miles long and the ascent takes four to four and a half hours. The other route, a bit longer, is a combination of part of the Phelps Trail and the Hopkins Trail of section 123. Both make the final ascent of Marcy along the VanHoevenberg Trail. Because this guide describes other routes climbing out of the valley, the Phelps trail is detailed as a descent, which completes one of several loops.

The Phelps Trail begins (or ends) at the intersection with the VanHoevenberg Trail, 0.6 mile below Marcy, and just over 0.6 mile above the intersection with the Hopkins Trail. Marked with red, the Phelps trail descends steeply along the ridge formed by the northern wall of Panther Gorge. There are occasional, excellent views of Haystack, Basin, and peaks to the east. Steep ascents alternate with gentle pitches as the trail drops down through a mostly small balsam fir and spruce forest.

The trail descends for under 0.7 mile to the junction with the Blue Connector to the Range Trail, in the col between Marcy and Haystack, on the narrow ridge that separates Panther Gorge to the south from Johns Brook Valley to the north.

The red Phelps Trail turns left, downslope, heading northeast, and very quickly reaches the small stream that becomes Johns Brook, following its right bank very steeply for 0.5 mile, where the trail crosses to the left bank. In another 0.4 mile, the trail has descended 655 feet from the col. In the past two summers, trail work has created staircases of massive rocks to protect the route.

At 1.8 miles, Shorey Short Cut forks right to cross Johns Brook. In 0.2 mile, the Phelps Trail reaches Slant Rock Lean-to, named for the huge slanted erratic that sits between the lean-to and Johns Brook. The area around Slant Rock contains several designated camping areas on both sides of the brook.

As soon as the trail leaves the Slant Rock area it fords Johns Brook, enters a forest of tall conifers, and swings away from the brook. The trail is quite wide and there are occasional muddy spots but again trail work in 1988 has hardened the route with many log walks and rocks. It continues a moderate descent, crossing several tributaries of Johns Brook. At 3.4 miles, about an hour and a half, the trail comes to the confluence of Chicken Coop Brook and Johns Brook. The two Bushnell Falls Lean-tos stand on either side of Chicken Coop Brook, though the falls are still way downstream.

During normal or low water, Johns Brook can be crossed next to the first lean-to you reach as you descend. During high water, you can cross a little over 100 yards upstream. After crossing the brook, the trail ascends at a moderate grade through mixed forest for about 200 yards and then levels off at the trail junction with the Hopkins Trail, which is marked with yellow disks (section 123). A third (or first, depending on your direction of travel) Bushnell Falls Lean-to is located at this junction.

The Phelps Trail, now on the north side of Johns Brook, continues from the junction near the Bushnell Falls Lean-to, with markings changed from red to yellow. This lower portion is sometimes called the Johns Brook Trail. Just beyond the lean-to, a side trail to the right, east, of the lean-to leads down to Bushnell Falls.

The trail rolls with an overall moderate descent for ten minutes, 0.5 mile, then descends steeply down an eroded moraine to cross Hogback Brook. The trail continues along the side of Johns Brook for 0.2 mile to the site of Hogback Lean-to, which was burned. That site is now posted against camping, but there is a designated site uphill to the left.

For the next 0.6 mile, the trail is a combination of hard and easy going. It then swings out onto rocks of the creek bed for a few yards and after that swings back up along the bank of Johns Brook.

The trail becomes almost level and easy walking as you approach a designated camping area, 1.5 miles from the Hopkins Trail junction, nearly forty minutes. Just beyond this designated camping area, you can see Johns Brook Lodge, with a huge guideboard marking the four-way intersection beside the lodge. The Ranger Station is 0.4 mile straight ahead on the Northside Trail.

If you use this route to complete a loop from Johns Brook Lodge over Saddleback and Basin, you will climb 3280 feet in just over 10 miles. If you use the reverse of this trail to climb to Marcy, trail hardening has made the route so obvious that you need no additional directions.

Cascade Lakes Trailheads

THE HIGHWAY WEST of Keene climbs to the plateau of the High Peaks through the deep cut of the Cascade Lakes. Two very different routes start from the highway: one, a path, is low in the valley and leads to a tiny mountain, Owls Head; the other is a well-traveled trail to the two most accessible High Peaks, Cascade and Porter. The latter mountains are sibling peaks with nearly equal elevation. Joined by a high saddle, they form the northeast corner of the High Peaks Wilderness Area. Though they are linked physically and geographically, they stand quite apart in the priorities of most hikers.

Cascade is a vastly more popular destination than is Porter. On an average summer day, you are likely to run into dozens of people on the summit of Cascade, while on the summit of Porter, less than a mile away, you will find few visitors, if any. There are several reasons for such unequal attention. First, Cascade is closer to the highway—indeed, looms over it—and the trail goes directly to the top; while, to reach Porter, you have to turn off the main route. Second, Cascade has a large, treeless summit, while Porter's summit is ringed with trees, and although open, it is quite small and nearly indistinguishable at the end of its long ridge. Cascade's summit is much photographed, Porter's less so; the summit of Cascade is bold—really quite stunning to behold—while that of Porter is much more subtle.

125 Owls Head of Keene
Path

To many people, this is the best of the little mountains. There is no question that, at least in the High Peaks, it is one of the smallest mountains with one of the biggest views. The path is not marked, but is so heavily traveled that markers are not necessary. It begins in the Owls Head Acres subdivision off the downhill lane of NY 73, 3.2 miles up from Keene Center.

Park in the small parking area to the left, a few yards down the unpaved Acres Road. There is another small parking area 0.2 mile farther, where the path begins. A sign there requesting that hikers not use it has been destroyed, and hikers continue to park there, but you should not because this is private property. Please respect the landowner's rights so that all may continue to have access to Owls Head.

The path starts climbing at a fairly steep grade as soon as it leaves the road. The grade eases to nearly level at the crest of the mountain's west ridge, where, at 200 yards in, the path makes a sharp left turn. From here it follows the ridge top all the way to the summit on alternating easy and steep grades. Along the way—and very soon, at that—views to the west and south begin to open up from the ledges atop the steep pitches. The last of these pitch-ledge combinations culminates in the summit itself. Here the path circles to the left to avoid a sixty-foot vertical cliff, which is a favored training site for novice rock climbers.

The path is only 0.55 mile long, rising 460 feet to the 2120-foot summit, a twenty-five-minute walk. From the summit, the panorama stretches from Hurricane Mountain in the east to Sentinel Peak in the north. North-facing ledges just below the summit give views over Brown Mountain, down the Ausable Valley toward Ebenezer Mountain and beyond, as well as east to Clements Mountain and the Jay Range. If you continue down the ridge east from the summit, dropping about 100 feet, you come to an east-facing ledge overlooking the village of Keene Center and encompassing everything from the Jay Range, clockwise to Porter and Cascade mountains. If you take a half day, you will be rewarded by the kind of scene that, on the higher mountain, is attainable only by those who can climb Owls Head in ten minutes.

126   Cascade

2.35 miles, 1½ to 2 hours, 1940-foot vertical rise, red markers

Cascade is not only the most accessible of all the Adirondack High Peaks, it is probably the easiest to climb. The easy ascent is due largely to the eminently sensible design of the trail. The older (though not the original) trail, which this one replaced in 1974, was notorious for long, very steep segments that had become badly eroded. The present trail has relatively few steep pitches, most of which are fairly short; and those that might be prone to erosion are paved with good-sized stones. Further, the grade is fairly mild.

The paper birch forests that cloak much of the mountain are a legacy of the 1903 fire, which destroyed the old spruce and fir cover. Now, a significant percentage of the young evergreens, raised in the shelter of the pioneering birch, are nearly as tall as the birch on Cascade's upper slopes. Twenty-five years ago they were half as tall. In another twenty-five years—provided acid rain and other unnatural disasters do not disrupt the natural pattern—the spruce and fir will be crowning out above the birches, depriving them of light, and thereby hastening the demise of the very trees that made their growth possible.

The Cascade Mountain trailhead is at a parking area off the Keene-bound lane of NY 73. This is 8.5 miles southeast of Lake Placid Village and 6.8 miles west-southwest of Keene Center. The trail begins by descending a series of

steps to cross a small brook, but soon begins an easy to moderate ascent to two more small streams at 0.35 mile, ten minutes. Except for one moderately steep pitch, the grade is then uniformly easy through mature hardwoods. At 0.7 mile, twenty-two minutes, the grade becomes moderately steep, with a ladder followed by a nicely designed stone section. The grade eases briefly, then becomes moderate again.

After forty minutes, at nearly 1.2 miles, the trail circumvents a low, wooded knob and gains the crest of the mountain's west ridge. On easy to moderate grades, it then heads off onto the north slope of the ridge, but soon turns and climbs steeply back to the crest, which it follows faithfully now up through a grassy patch and past a large boulder. Near the boulder, which you reach in just over an hour, a spur path breaks away to the right and peters out after a few dozen yards.

Beyond this, the trail ascends a quite steep pitch of bare rock which culminates at 1.8 miles, an hour and a quarter, on a small, open knob offering the first big view of the climb—an unbroken westward panorama from Dix Peak in the south to Whiteface in the north. Back into the woods, the route alternates between rock pitches and flat, muddy strips until a junction at 2.1 miles, an hour and twenty-five minutes. A right turn takes you to Porter.

Continuing straight ahead, the Cascade Trail ascends gently for a couple of minutes more among stunted conifers to timberline, where there is a stunning view of the bald summit dome rising abruptly from the flattened ridge-crest. Yellow paint blazes and rock cairns bring you in another five minutes or so to the top of that dome at 4098 feet. The vista is nothing short of magnificent.

127 Porter

0.7 mile from Cascade Trail, 20 to 30 minutes, 90-foot descent, 330-foot ascent, red markers

This mountain, much more a dominant part of the landscape from the Keene Valley side than Cascade, was named for Dr. Noah Porter, president of Yale from 1871–1886 and a very popular summer resident of the Valley. In 1875, he and Ed Phelps, son of "Old Mountain" Phelps and Verplanck Colvin's chief guide in the High Peaks region, made the first recorded ascent of what Valley people originally called West Mountain.

Phelps was paid by Dr. Porter to blaze the first trail, but it disappeared long ago. Many years later, two other trails were cut up the mountain from the valley (sections 106 and 107). The latter, the infamous trail over Blueberry, will give you 100 feet more ascent than the VanHoevenberg Trail up Marcy in a little more than half the distance.

The easiest way to Porter's summit is via the Cascade Trail and its spur, a 2.8-mile climb. Turning right (left, if you are descending Cascade) at the

Marcy, Colden, and MacIntyre from Porter

junction, follow the red disks down a fairly steep and somewhat eroded trail to the bottom of the saddle between the two mountains at 0.2 mile. Gently ascending, you reach the base of the north slope of Porter. Here there is a small open patch with a very good view back toward Cascade's crest.

Moderate to steep climbing brings you up onto the spine of Porter and then to a very large rock at 0.55 mile, only fifteen minutes from the intersection. From the top of this rock, you can look straight down into Railroad Notch and the westernmost pair of the four beaver ponds of the Little Meadows area. The trail takes a hard right at the rock, then drops to the left to circle around to its base where a path proceeds straight, north, while the trail turns sharply right. It continues at mostly easy grades along the ridge, arriving at the summit at 0.7 mile.

The view from Porter is not as spectacular as from Cascade, though from an open patch by two large rocks at the brink of Porter's extremely steep south slope, just past the summit, you can see the eastern part of John's Brook Valley and all of the valley of Slide Brook, including Little Meadows with its four ponds, and Railroad Notch. Big Slide and the Great Range are even more impressive from this perspective than from Cascade, where Porter blocks the view of the lower reaches. Now you can see the entire north side of the Big Slide structure, from top to bottom, including the Brothers; and you really get an idea of what a massive chunk of mountain it is.

Big Slide still interferes with a view of the lower slopes of the western Great Range, but the eastern part is visible from top to bottom, giving a truer sense of the height and ruggedness of that marvelous, serrated wall.

128   The Cascade on Cascade

Nature walk

Readily visible from NY 73 is the cascade that tumbles down toward the isthmus of land that separates the two Cascade Lakes from each other. Normally, the cascade is refreshingly picturesque, but at times it becomes a roaring torrent, best viewed from a distance. Climbers sometimes use this watery route through the erosion channel to head up Cascade, but this should not be done. The rare (for the Adirondacks) Grenville rocks, rich in limestone, are home to the most extraordinary array of plants, so this excursion is for nature lovers only—those who will carefully avoid the fragile plants.

There was once a hotel at this location and the 1902 USGS map shows a trail from there up the cascade to the summit. The little park between the lakes is accessible by car from NY 73, using a marked side road. The sharp turn onto that road makes it very difficult to enter or emerge from if you are traveling from the east and Keene.

Approach the cascade via the little bridge that crosses the connecting stream near its outlet into the Lower Lake. Across the bridge, follow the right-hand path southwest and then south, taking the left fork each time the trail branches. At a fork with a large, round, gray boulder on the left, take the right branch to the base of the cascade, where the remnants of old pipe denote the source of the hotel's water supply. Among the tumble of rocks are fragments of coarse-grained, sometimes colorful minerals.

On your way to the cascade, you may be surprised to hear the stream but not see it. This is because, not far from the base of the cascade, the stream disappears beneath the tumbled rocks of the talus slope.

You can scramble up the dry chutes east of the cascade, but use great care. *This can be a very dangerous place.* Near the base, the cascade is very precipitous. Higher up there are some relatively level areas below small waterfalls. These are the places to look for Braun's holly fern; slender cliff-brake, *Cryptogramma stellerai*; the berry bublet and fragile ferns, *Cystopteris bulberifa* and *fragilis*; and many wonderful bryophytes.

South Meadow

ADIRONDAK LOJ ROAD turns south from NY 73, 4 miles east of Lake Placid. Stop and enjoy the High Peaks panorama ahead, then continue 3.8 miles to a left, east, turn onto South Meadow Road, which has a wide, flat gravel bed and is currently drivable for 1 mile to a parking area. The ski trail to VanHoevenberg branches left, north, at 0.25 mile along this road and the Truck Trail to Marcy Dam branches right at 0.8 mile. Several places along the access road can accommodate a car and tent. The parking area is surrounded by many camping places, and this is an excellent place to camp if you plan to day-hike from the Adirondak Loj Trailhead. The route south along the Truck Trail is an alternate beginning for the trails south of Marcy Dam.

129 Marcy Dam Truck Trail

2.8 miles, 1¼ hours, slight grades, unmarked roadway

The Truck Trail from South Meadow to Marcy Dam is closed to all but emergency DEC vehicles. You can drive for the first 0.2 mile south to a gate, and there are a few parking places along this stretch of road. The 2.6-mile distance from the gate to Marcy Dam is only 0.5 mile longer than the trail to the dam from Adirondak Loj.

Many hikers use the Truck Trail to reach Marcy Dam; but several factors influence its desirability as an alternative: The gravel surface is rough underfoot, there are several hills to climb, and the extra twenty minutes or so in the morning as you start out may not seem like much, but wait until you return from a long day trip.

The road is so obvious, no further descriptions are needed, except to note the gate at 0.2 mile; the crossing of the Mr. Van Ski Trail (section 132) at 0.55 mile; and the several streams flowing from the slopes of Phelps that drain under the road. The large one at 1.8 miles now has the name Pelkey Brook. At about 2 miles, you cross another stream by dropping into and climbing out of a sharp gully. At 2.2 miles you cross Phelps Brook and shortly beyond reach the banks of Marcy Brook, which you follow to the Dam. See section 133 for more on Marcy Dam and the trails emanating from it.

130 Klondike Trail to Johns Brook Valley

5.2 miles, 2¼ hours, 450-foot elevation change, red markers

The Klondike Trail follows an old tote road and begins from the southeast corner of the parking area. You pass a trail register, cross a part of South

Meadow, cross South Meadow Brook, and walk through a red pine plantation. At just over 0.3 mile, the Mr. Van Ski Trail forks right (section 132). The Klondike Trail continues wide and flat. At 0.4 mile the Mr. Van Trail forks left toward the VanHoevenberg Ski Area.

The Klondike Trail continues relatively level (at elevation 2200 feet) until 0.8 mile, where it begins to climb gently through a stand of large aspens. At 1.6 miles, the trail narrows, follows a dry streambed, crosses a stream, and begins to climb moderately to the 2700-foot level. There, it continues almost level until, at 2.3 miles, it crosses a wide, shallow brook, which is flowing over a granite outcrop. After traversing a small ridge, the trail drops about 20 feet to the Klondike Lean-to, which sits close to Klondike Brook at 2.5 miles.

There is a flat area suitable for a tent in back of the lean-to. Several good campsites are located across Klondike Brook where the forest is open, relatively level, and free from blowdowns. (If you are heading north on this trail, note that it does not cross the brook by the lean-to to the opening with those campsites, but rather goes in front of the lean-to, turns right along the brook for a few feet, then sharply left, up a steep bank until it is about 20 feet above the level of the brook.)

South of the lean-to, the trail crosses Klondike Brook near where another tributary enters from the east. Climbing moderately, then at 2.6 miles more gently, the trail reaches a swampy area, elevation 2950 feet. More climbing brings you to the notch, elevation 3180 feet, at 3.3 miles. Log walks and corduroy carry the trail through a spruce swamp. The shoulder of Yard shows through the white birches and conifers as you descend at a gentle grade, reaching the intersection to Yard at 3.9 miles, only 150 feet below the notch.

The last 1.3 miles to Johns Brook Lodge, an 860-foot descent, is also described in section 115. This lovely wooded stretch draws close to Black Brook at 4.7 miles and follows that brook's left bank through a deepening valley to a bridge crossing less than 0.1 mile from Johns Brook Lodge. The 0.5 mile beside the brook is a handsome stretch, and if trail work currently being done is completed, it will become a pleasant stretch to walk as well.

131 Mount VanHoevenberg

3.8 miles, 2 hours, 740-foot ascent, 920-foot descent, blue markers

Mount VanHoevenberg is a homocline of moderate height. It was named in 1930 for the builder of the original Adirondack Lodge at the time the mountain was chosen as the site for the Olympic Bobsled Run.

A homocline is a landform, usually a ridge or mountain, that is quite steep on one side (the scarp slope) and relatively gentle on the other side (the dip slope). On Mount VanHoevenberg, the dip slope faces north, so it was a logical site for the bobrun as well as the Olympic luge and cross-country ski trails.

The precipitous scarp slope, rimmed with ledges and cliffs, faces south over the South Meadow Valley. By happy coincidence, south is where the main ranges of the High Peaks rise; so the views of Big Slide (another, larger homocline), Gothics, Marcy, Colden, and the MacIntyre Range are simply superb.

There is a signpost on the north side of South Meadow Road, 0.25 mile from the Loj Road. It marks the beginning of the trail, which starts out level in a pine plantation and remains level or descends gently through hardwoods to a wet spot and a small brook, which it crosses at 0.95 mile, twenty-five minutes. Now the trail ascends steadily, at first heading north as it has from the beginning, then veering more toward the east, recrossing the brook, and following it up through a ravine with fairly tall cliffs on the northwest side.

You reach a height-of-land at 1.8 miles, where a bushwhacking detour to the left can bring you back to the top of the cliffs you just passed. After going over a small hump and circling around a cliffy area, the trail now runs pretty close to the crest of VanHoevenberg's summit ridge, staying just below it on the north side and continuing to climb at moderate grades with some easier stretches. Before long, at 2.05 miles, you come out on a large, cliff-top ledge that gives a sweeping vista from the Gothics in the southeast to the McKenzie Range in the northwest. The Olympic ski jumps and the village of Lake Placid are visible below that range. Also in view, from left to right, are Saddleback, Basin, Phelps, Marcy, Gray, and Colden, all towering above the South Meadow Valley with its brook meandering though gardens of pale grasses and black swamp spruce. Farther to the right are Avalanche Pass and Avalanche Mountain, Wright and Algonquin Peaks, Indian Pass and Wallface, Mount Jo, Street and Nye mountains, Ampersand in the distance, and Scarface nearer above the farms along Bear Cub Road, which themselves seem to hang above the farms of the Plains of Abraham.

Above this first ledge is a second one giving a better view of Gothics. The slide on South Meadow Mountain is quite prominent.

Then there is a third ledge and, finally, a fourth—the summit ledge at 2.15 miles, 1 hour, with elevation 2860 feet, total ascent 740 feet. From these two ledges there are excellent views of Big Slide and Klondike Notch. The third ledge gives the best view of the South Meadow Valley—truly enchanting. From the fourth ledge you can see Porter with the upper part of Giant to its right.

If you park a second vehicle at the bobrun parking lot, you can add historical interest to the natural beauty of this walk by descending the north side of the mountain, first via trail to an old road, which marks the original start of the bobrun, 0.2 mile and five minutes; then down this to the present bobrun start, 0.65 mile and fifteen minutes from the summit; and then down beside the bobrun to the bottom of the mountain, 1.65 miles, forty minutes.

The Mount VanHoevenberg Bobrun was built in 148 days in 1930, completed on Christmas day of that year. The cost was $48,736.

132 Mr. Van Trail

5 miles, 2¹/₂ hours, 390-foot elevation change, red markers

The Mr. Van is a state-maintained cross-country ski trail that connects Adirondak Loj with the popular complex of cross-country trails operated by the Olympic Regional Development Authority (ORDA), on the north side of Mount VanHoevenberg.

The trail is fine for hiking, if you omit the first 1.3 miles (Adirondak Loj to the South Meadow-Marcy Truck Trail). It offers a pleasant, mostly lowland walk through fine hardwood forests and can be done at a very leisurely pace with lots of breaks in just a few hours. A vehicle must be located at both ends of this route if a one-way hike is intended. Alternatively, make a rewarding loop trip by climbing Mount VanHoevenberg, descending along the bobrun, then climbing back through the ORDA ski complex to the northern terminus of the Mr. Van Trail, and following that back to South Meadow.

The problem with the Loj end of the Mr. Van Trail as a hiking route is caused by extensive beaver-works, which exacerbate the crossing of a large alder swamp along Marcy Brook. This part of the trail, which starts as a sharp left turn from the blue Marcy Dam Trail, 175 yards from the Loj's Campers and Hikers Building, is fine for skiing when everything is well frozen. Otherwise, it presents a wet trudge indeed, and it can become impassable in spring or during rainy periods.

Because of this uncertainty, it is advisable to begin your journey at the South Meadow Parking area. Head south on the Marcy Dam Truck Trail for 0.2 mile to the gate, and continue for another 0.35 mile to the Mr. Van Trail and turn left.

The trail is now mostly level and not very interesting; but at 0.9 mile, just over twenty minutes, it comes close to the bottom of the 1979 slide on South Meadow Mountain (a shoulder of Phelps), and the upper part of the slide can be glimpsed through the treetops to your right. Three more minutes of walking brings you to the Klondike Notch Trail. Turn right and follow it for two minutes to a junction where the Mr. Van Trail turns left, 1.1 miles.

Now you enter a fine, second-growth hardwood forest and begin a truly lovely woods walk. Soon you cross Klondike Brook (this may be tricky in winter, as there is no bridge), after which the trail proceeds gently with a couple of moderate sections and one steep pitch.

As you go, notice that the proportion of large, old trees becomes higher. Also notice that the trail, in places, is actually an overgrown, graded road. This route parallels and occasionally coincides with the old "Tight Nippin'

South Meadow and Mount VanHoevenberg from the slide on South Meadow Mountain

Road," which began at the Garden above Keene Valley, skirted the base of the Brothers, followed the Slide Brook drainage up into Railroad Notch between Porter and Big Slide mountains, and descended along South Meadow Brook to connect with the South Meadow Road. This six-mile "shortcut" between the Valley and the high plateau of North Elba was built in the 1830s as a logging road; but it also served as a popular hiking route until the 1920s, when the section through the notch was flooded out by beavers.

After an hour, you cross a good-sized brook on a deteriorating log bridge; in five minutes more you begin to parallel another, smaller brook, descending slightly to the Mr. Van Lean-to at 2.65 miles, an hour and ten minutes. The lean-to faces South Meadow Brook; but is set back about 30 yards from it. South Meadow Brook is spanned by a long, plank-on-log bridge. This is a great place for lunch, enjoying the openness of the wide, stony streambed with its musical water.

After crossing the bridge, the trail goes through a fairly wide swamp broken by a couple of drier humps. Beyond the swamp, the trail begins its ascent of the low ridge that connects Porter Mountain to Mount VanHoevenberg. The grades are mostly easy to moderate with long, level stretches interspersed. Among the large hardwoods surrounding the trail is a particularly impressive clump of basswood at the south edge of the trail about twenty-five minutes from the bridge.

The crest of the ridge, at 3.7 miles and an hour and forty minutes total, is called High Notch, though it does not appear very notch-like. From here you descend via the ORDA ski system. If you are skiing, follow the one-way directional signs. If you are hiking, you can use a shorter route. Go straight ahead, round a hard left curve, and straight through a first trail junction, up a bit and down again, through a second junction (marked #35), then gently down with a couple of easy ups to a third junction (#36) at 4.3 miles. Here turn right, descend to junction #4 and go straight through it. Just beyond, you will see a large, double-trunked beech tree off to the left of the trail. The farther trunk is covered with marks of bear claws, while the nearer trunk is virtually untouched. At 4.75 miles, just over two hours, you come to a clearing where several trails converge. Bear left, and, at the far left of the clearing, exit by bearing right. You soon come to the cross-country ski stadium. Beyond it is the parking lot, at just short of 5 miles.

Adirondak Loj

IN THE 1920s, the Adirondack Mountain Club purchased the square mile surrounding Heart Lake and rebuilt the lodge that had stood on its shores. Gradually, lean-tos, tent sites, trails, and a nature center were added to the complex, which serves club members but is open to the public. In the late 1960s, the Club greatly extended its parking area and built a Campers and Hikers Building, which has a small shop, restrooms, showers, and laundry facilities for the hiking public. The camping area, for which there is a modest fee, is often full in summer, so advance reservations are important.

To reach the Loj, drive east from Lake Placid, and turn south on Heart Lake Road, which is marked with signs to Adirondak Loj. (See also the chapter "West of Adirondak Loj.") The view across the fields toward the MacIntyre Range, the cut of Indian Pass, and Wallface attracts photographers year round. The parking area is 4.8 miles south and the Loj is beyond the ticket booth. Note that there is no parking along the southern end of the road; you must either park at the lot or back at South Meadow. The Loj is the most popular entrance to the High Peaks and on weekends the lots may be full. In winter it is becoming a center for ski touring, with many trails on Loj property connecting with state trails nearby.

Public access to trails across Loj property was assured by covenant in 1964.

133 Marcy Dam

2.3 miles, 50 minutes, 187-foot elevation change, blue markers

The pond impounded by Marcy Dam is the hub of so many trails that you cannot avoid it. With seven lean-tos and fifteen designated campsites, it is almost always crowded. Its popularity with those who only want to climb Marcy is such that you will do well to plan your trips so that you fly through its intersections to more remote spots.

The hardened and rerouted trail leaves from the southeast corner of the Loj parking area. On its rolling course through a plantation it passes the red-marked Mr. Van Trail, crosses a small bridge over the outlet of Heart Lake, intersects several ski trails, and crosses the state land boundary before reaching an intersection just short of 1 mile and barely twenty minutes from the start. The yellow Algonquin Trail (section 134) is straight ahead.

Turn left through a wonderfully tall maple stand that is whitened with birches. A series of wide skiers' bridges carries the trail over small streams. Boardwalks and corduroy make you think you are on a paved sidewalk. You can hear then see Marcy Brook as you enter a beautiful ferny woods with big birch trees. About seventeen minutes from the intersection there is a path left to a hop-a-rock crossing of Marcy Brook, which leads quickly up to the Truck Trail (section 129). In low water it is a shortcut to Marcy Dam.

The trail assumes a winding course; Phelps is visible through the trees. After a slight upgrade, the trail descends over a series of log and stone-faced steps cut into the hillside to cross a tributary. Climbing away from it, the trail leads to a beautiful spruce forest with a lean-to and campsites off to the right on a knoll. At 2.3 miles you reach an enormously big dam. From the walkway across the top of it you can see the slopes of Wright and Avalanche mountains.

A combination of paths and trails leads around the pond in 0.5 mile, giving access to the lean-tos and campsites. There is a pipe in the hillside, below the dam between the truck trail and Marcy Brook, with good spring water. The Ranger Station is visible from the dam. Across the dam, there is a huge registration booth with all kinds of directions and trail signs.

To circle the pond, take the blue trail, which continues as the VanHoeven-berg Trail to Mount Marcy (section 147). Paths branch off in all directions and there are two lean-tos near the waterfront from which you can see Whales Tail to the north. In 50 yards, turn right on the yellow trail headed toward Lake Colden (section 140) and pass one more lean-to, before reaching, at 0.25 mile, a spur right. The spur bridges Marcy Brook, passes two lean-tos, crosses a branch of Marcy Brook and one more lean-to before heading north. The trail to Whales Tail Notch branches left from the spur at 0.4 mile. There is another lean-to here between the spur and the shore. The spur now swings back east to complete the loop at an intersection with the blue trail just north of Marcy Dam.

134 Algonquin Peak

4.15 miles, 3 hours, 2936-foot vertical rise, yellow markers

Algonquin is the most enticing of all the High Peaks. The second tallest peak in the Adirondacks, at 5114 feet (1559 meters), it is one of the most access-ible—a favorite for a century—with its well-hardened trail, superb views, and a broad, treeless summit ringed with alpine plants. The round trip of 8.3 miles challenges first time visitors. It is such an easy trail to follow that you need few directions, unless of course the summit is swirled in fog and clouds, and then the cairns and paint blazes across the open rock above tree-line are very important. Because this mountain is the best introduction to alpine flora, the trail description includes a natural history of the MacIntyre Range, of which

Mount Colden from Algonquin

Algonquin is the highest peak. This introduction applies equally to a half-dozen of the higher peaks.

While the MacIntyre Mountains were named in 1837, it was not until 1880 that Colvin named the highest peak Algonquin.

The well-marked trunk trail leaves the southeast corner of the Adirondak Loj parking area, headed toward Marcy Dam, and reaches an intersection at 1 mile. The MacIntyre trail is the yellow route, straight ahead. The trail winds across a hardwood hillside and through a wet, ferny area where, at 1.45 miles, the Whales Tail Notch Trail turns left. This is just before the main trail makes a sharp turn to the left and begins to climb more seriously.

Rising through tall birch and mixed hardwoods, the trail reaches stairs to aid the steepening ascent. Huge rocks in the trail keep it from becoming a muddy mire. An incredibly beautiful birch glade follows. You cross a ski trail that goes sharply up to your left near where the old MacIntyre Trail joins in from the right. As the trail makes a level traverse, a path branches up to your left to a designated camping spot. The level ends at 2.55 miles, elevation 3230 feet, below a chute of water over a moss-covered slide. This waterfall may be dry in midsummer.

The trail is distinctly less easy walking now, rocky, occasionally muddy, rooty, narrow for 0.45 mile more to the draw—at elevation 3770 feet—between the mountain proper and one of its many rock knobs. Paths lead toward the rock knob, from which there is a modest view. (Just beyond, you could commence a difficult trek, almost on contour, 0.4 mile and a little south of west to a draw below a bigger knob that is known as Little MacIntyre. It has good views. The botanically interesting and complex draw, which drains to the west, has many lovely slides and waterfalls. Logging roads and corduroy can be found high on the stream that drains toward Scotts Clearing.)

Beyond the knob, the forest, until now mostly birch with balsam coming through, changes to predominantly balsam and spruce. At just over 4000 feet elevation, 3.2 miles, the narrow trail to Wright Peak forks to the left.

From here to Algonquin's summit, the trail is mostly over smooth bedrock with some steep slides and a few scrambles. You climb 600 feet in under 0.5 mile as the trees grow distinctly smaller. Just short of 3.7 miles, elevation almost 4600 feet, you emerge above tree line. The summit appears close, but it is the first of several false summits you see on the steep 500-foot, 0.4 mile climb to the true summit. Cairns and arrows on the trail guide you upward over the open rock; be sure to stay on the marked route to avoid trampling the fragile alpine vegetation. Finding the route back down in clear weather is very easy, but in bad weather, the cairns become very important.

Walk a few feet south of the summit rock to a perch above the steep southern face and its dramatic view of Colden's slides. The rest of the magnificent panorama is described in section 141, which details the climb from the south and Lake Colden.

135 The MacIntyre Range—an Alpine Traverse

The higher the altitude, the shorter the trees grow. That gives a better vista, of course, and makes the trip more enjoyable; at the same time, it gives a visual signal to the shifting environment you are crossing. Shorter trees tell you that you are soon to reach the upper elevational limit of tree growth, the so-called timberline or tree line. At that point, the accumulative effect of deteriorating climate and infertile soils simply prevents the trees from producing enough food during the abbreviated summer to survive the long winters that are characteristic of these highlands.

From timberline to the summits, the open alpine zone, as it is called, is where smaller plants, covered all winter by a protective blanket of snow, can survive. It is that stressed world of arctic-like conditions that you can witness in an alpine traverse of the MacIntyre Range.

Only the hardiest, specialized species of plants can withstand these severe ecological conditions. The landscape is a rounded dome, here on Algonquin, dropping off quite abruptly on the east side, more gently on the other three sides. As you follow the trail up the north slope and then down the southwest side heading to Boundary and Iroquois, you soon notice there are three types of vegetation clothing the windswept rocks, each one adapted to the degree of exposure at the immediate location.

In the small depressions and ravines escaping the full blast of the wind, and to a lesser amount on the lee side of boulders and ledges, trees and a few taller shrubs find minimal conditions for their existence. They are enormously twisted, with intertwined branches such as you saw in the fir forest as you approached timberline. This is the *Krummholz zone*, where trees resemble shrubs. In these patches of dwarfed forest, only the balsam fir remains erect, perhaps six to eight feet tall at best, in the ravines; but they pay a price. Half the fir you see are killed back at their tops where they stick up above the snow cover in winter; it is the lateral growth of their side branches that produces the nearly impenetrable jungle of the *Krummholz*.

The two spruces—red and black—are more sensitive and responsive to the pressures of the wind and they shift their growth more readily into side branches, so you rarely see their tops killed back. Black spruce, with shorter and whiter needles, is elsewhere a bog species adopted to saturated soils, richly organic, but since those conditions repeat here above timberline, the species struggles along here against the wind; it, too, pays the price, for it reaches only two or three feet tall even though its branches may spread outward into a canopy ten feet across. Mixed in with these evergreens, you see occasional mountain paper birch and dwarfed mountain ash.

What is most interesting about these alpine forests—the patches found behind bluffs or as islands found in ravines—is how different the ground vegetation is under them. The ground, even in these isolated clumps of trees, seems to be more severely stressed ecologically and to consist almost entirely of mosses and a few lichens, whereas if you crawl around on your knees into the ravine islands where the canopy seems more open, you see the whole array of herbaceous species you thought you had left back at timberline: bunchberry, bluebead lily, snowberry, star flower, woodland aster, bottle gentian, twisted stalk, Canada mayflower, and a few others characteristic of the fir forest downslope. In effect, where plants can escape the wind, a microcosm of the balsam fir forest eventually develops.

At the other environmental extreme—the open rock surfaces—you find a *lichen-moss* community. The trail takes you over sections of this type, where the film of these lichen plants seems glued to the rock surface, though all you may notice is a faint color on the rocks. Actually, few lichens can long withstand the constant impact of boots, and only the pale greenish-yellow map lichen will be seen in the immediate trail area. Farther away, where traffic is only occasional, you may observe other crust-forming lichens, the *crustose* lichens that are mostly dark and inconspicuous. Where there is essentially no trampling, a trained botanist will see a second group of lichens that resemble small leaves attached on the underside to rocks; these are the *foliose* lichens.

Lichens are the toughest of all the alpine plants. They even grow on what otherwise would be bare rock, out in the full sun, dry as only a bare rock surface can be.

Meanwhile, in those more protected places where small amounts of water seep out over the surface, various species of mosses find a suitable home, many of them relics of the ice-age climate in the late glacial times. There are about sixty species of mosses up here, probably more than that of lichens. These life forms also occur at ground level under the third community type, the *alpine meadow*.

As you climb from timberline to the summit of Algonquin, most of the landscape to either side is covered with a mixture of plants mostly less than knee-high, and this might loosely look like a meadow, although the term is more descriptive than technical. In fact, it is a mixed community dominated in places by dwarf shrubs, barely two feet tall, occasionally interspersed with several species of grasses, and in only a few places by herbaceous plants like goldenrod—plants you would expect in a meadow below.

If you inspect the meadow carefully, you will discover the single most important fact of ecological life about the alpine summit zone: it appears as a bog surface blanketing the ground. Under such conditions, instead of grasses forming the sod in which everything else is rooted, here peat-forming mosses constitute the ground surface, as they have since the glaciers retreated. The peat mosses are members of the genus *Sphagnum*. They produce the organic soil that sustains the alpine ecosystem. Over the centuries, the two- or three-foot-deep banks of peat moss have been invaded by various heath-forming plants and a few grasses, which now cover and hide the peat below. Where the ground is flattest and thus wettest, the peat moss supports a population of grass-like plants, which we collectively call *graminoids*.

Beautiful as they may be, the graminoid plants are difficult to identify, yet the three most abundant species form big clumps that can be recognized by the hiking botanist. The tall one, with slender stems a foot or less long, in clumps of a hundred or more stalks and often covering many square feet of ground, is deer grass, the most important graminoid on the summits, one that binds the ground tight and prevents erosion. It does best and grows thickest on gentle slopes. Growing with it occasionally you see cotton grass (sometimes called bog wool), with its distinctive white cotton balls on tall waving stalks. The balls are nearly an inch across, blooming from late June into July, and without them, the leaves of these two species appear nearly identical. The third species is the *Bigelow* sedge, seen in the wet, flat area you pass at the very crown of Algonquin, the grass with only a few leaves, all attached near the base of the clump, and with three-sided stems. The less abundant species we leave to specialists to delight in.

The most conspicuous community type on all the traverse over the MacIntyre Range is the heath association, with both its familiar species from the lowlands and the rare plants from the Canadian Taiga. Old friends will be the bog laurel, with its paired, shiny green leaves, and its close relative the sheep laurel, with leaves in threes. Mixed with the laurels will be leatherleaf, elsewhere the most important and abundant low shrub of the Adirondack bog lands.

Most frequent of all are the blueberries. The alpine bilberry is the most abundant vascular plant on the summits, typically covering a third of the meadow. It is easily recognized by the distinctive blue- green leaves, more oval in shape than the other heath species. All across the Algonquin traverse you also see the tiny northern blueberry, hardly half a foot tall, with slender leaves barely an inch long.

Trailing over the sphagnum moss, you may glimpse the small-leaved cranberry, a hardy species from below. When looking for it in wet spots, also keep your eye out for the roundleaf sundew, a rare inhabitant of the summit wetlands.

Where large rocks interrupt the heath stands, you may see two true alpine species; the bearberry willow, with small shiny leaves and fruiting stalks persisting into summer, and crowberry, with trailing stems densely covered with leaves—it resembles a miniature hemlock, but with fruit just like a black blueberry.

You may see two strange birches as well, if you look carefully. Both are only shrubs. One, the glandular birch, with pale green leaves the size and shape of a fingernail, never gets higher than your knees, but the so-called dwarf birch, less common, may be head high and have leaves intermediate in size and shape between the glandular birch and the ordinary mountain paper birch, of which it may be a hybrid. Where you see one or the other of these birches, especially in sloping areas, you may also see a small shrub reminiscent of the speckled alder from the lowlands, but in this case the leaves are small and shiny green on both surfaces. The persistent cone-like fruit clearly identifies it as a mountain alder.

All along the trail, the most eye-catching species is the little mountain sandwort, which has the longest flowering season of all the alpines, mid-June to mid-August. Its white flowers appear too delicate to survive the hostile country and its leaves resemble a moss.

Where the alpine meadow gives way to open rock surfaces and water seeps outward on its way downslope, a rusty band of sphagnum moss marks the slow advance of the meadow out onto the rock, the very same process that over the last ten thousand years of post-glacial time has produced the organic soil necessary for the alpine community. Close up you will see how the wet mat, acting like a wick, maintains a soft, wet substrate in which various alpine graminoids and shrubs first take root, and in time expand and thicken into the typical meadow community. In your mind's eye, with a little imagination, you can almost see the process unfold as you look at it.

To see the Adirondacks' two most famous alpines, you should climb in early June when they are in spectacular flower. The Lapland rosebay is a dwarf rhododendron, only a foot high, with scarlet-purple blooms, making it the most conspicuous plant on the summits when in flower. Because it blends into the canopy of the larger heath plants, it is the least conspicuous the rest of the season.

The other flowering highlight, the Lapland diapensia, with its white flowers, is easily spotted all summer by the plant's distinctive shape—a giant pin-cushion of shiny green leaves so dense no stems are visible between matted leaves.

It takes more than a day to learn the alpine flora. They change as the season unfolds, and perhaps the best time to study them is September if you want to learn them by their vegetative features, for by then they are mature and each has a slightly different autumnal color.

136 Over Boundary and Iroquois to Iroquois Pass

Paths and bushwhacks

When you look southwest from Algonquin Peak, along the crest of the MacIntyre Range, the dominant feature is Iroquois Peak, imposingly placed between Indian Pass and Lake Colden and sloping steeply down to each of them. It appears highlighted because nothing rises high enough to form a backdrop to it; the main ridge and range drop away behind it over successively lower summits to the lowlands of Henderson and Sanford lakes.

Colvin gave both the name Iroquois and the name Clinton, for Governor Dewitt Clinton, to the peak in the MacIntyre Range that is only a mile southwest of Algonquin. The very worthwhile round trip between the peaks involves only some 800 feet of ascent. If you are on your way to or from Lake Colden (section 141), the side trip delivers a high return on a more modest investment.

There is no trail to Iroquois, but the path is easily followed. Head southwest on the yellow trail from Algonquin Peak, descending to the col. Here, at the foot of the open alpine slopes, the yellow trail turns southeast and descends into the woods toward Lake Colden. A large cairn marks the beginning of the path. You go straight ahead on the unmarked path, into a sub-alpine scrub forest of balsam-fir and mountain paper birch. You will stay pretty much in the center of the ridge as you follow it over the bare rock opening on Boundary Peak and then over the shoulder of the lesser height, Boundary II, which rises just above the low point on the ridge, immediately below the summit of Iroquois. Except in the driest conditions, you will find mud traps in the path in each of the sags you cross. Unless you are in a great hurry, you can avoid them.

The path climbs steeply from the low point, then divides about halfway up, giving you a choice of reaching the open summit ridge from either the north or west. The view back toward Algonquin from Iroquois is at least as imposing as that of Iroquois from Algonquin. To the southwest, with Marshall 500 feet below you and somewhat over a mile away, your view is essentially unobstructed.

If you are on your way to Marshall, you will of course scout the route from here. Strong parties of hikers do in fact make the traverse directly from Iroquois to Marshall, or vice versa, but few of them will recommend the trip except to their best friends or worst enemies. There is no path down to Iroquois Pass, although there is a good, though rather lightly used path from the pass on to Marshall (section 41). The real challenge comes in escaping the summit of Iroquois, which involves pushing through balsam thickets as dense as you are likely to find anywhere. You can minimize the duration of this experience by descending as far as possible down the open ledges, due south toward the 4500-foot Shepherd's Tooth, before wading through the cripplebush.

Shepherd's Tooth is one of the many bald, rocky knobs that lie along the slopes of the MacIntyre Range. It is an unexpectedly remarkable feature of the MacIntyre Range as viewed from the east side of Lake Colden, as well as from a variety of central High Peaks locations, including Gray Peak and Basin, and a particularly well-aligned section of Uphill Brook. The Marshalls called this knob Catamount's Rest, and more recently Paul Jamieson has referred to it as the "wart" of Iroquois. It was named Shepherd's Tooth in the course of an unplanned 1955 visit by members of the Zahniser and Schaefer families, both of whom have long associations with wilderness and Adirondack preservation.

If you pass to the right of Shepherd's Tooth you pick up a fault line descending directly toward Marshall, and keep this bearing all the way down into the pass. Below Shepherd's Tooth, the difficulties ease markedly, but by no means completely. Take care in selecting a descent route to the Iroquois Pass Trail through the considerable cliffs guarding the Iroquois side of the pass.

137 Wright Peak

3.65 miles, 2²/₃ hours, 2420-foot vertical rise, yellow and blue markers

Colvin named this peak for Governor Silas Wright in 1873. The Wright Peak Trail is a spur from the Algonquin Trail, leaving that yellow-marked trail at just over 3.2 miles. Here at elevation 4000 feet, the blue Wright Peak Trail turns left, east, and sharply up. The spur is just over 0.4 mile long, with two-thirds of its 585-foot climb to the summit on bare rock.

This trail was somewhat relocated in the early 1970s when the route was established as an alternate to the trail from the Whales Tail Notch. It was designed to protect Wright's fragile alpine summit, so please stay on the route marked by cairns and paint blazes. You need less than an hour to make the loop up Wright and back from the Algonquin Trail.

138 Whales Tail Notch

1.2 miles, 40 minutes, 375-foot elevation change, ski-trail markers

You can walk this route from Marcy Dam to the Algonquin Trail in order to climb Algonquin from a campsite near Marcy Dam, but the footing is rough and the route descends the same amount as it ascends into the notch. This route is one of the complex of ski trails south of Heart Lake and is best skied. The shortest loop from the Loj parking lot using this traverse is 4.5 miles with an elevation gain and descent of 590 feet. Most of the grades are moderate, except the portion immediately southeast of the Notch, a 0.15-mile stretch that is difficult for many skiers.

The trail leaves the Algonquin Trail 0.45 mile southwest of its intersection with the VanHoevenberg Trail and pulls gradually away from that trail before turning sharply east then southeast into the Notch. After the steep descent, the grade gradually decreases as the trail approaches the path circling Marcy Pond. Turn left on that route for 0.1 mile past a lean-to in order to intersect the VanHoevenberg Trail on a knoll within sight of Marcy Dam.

Note that a ski trail has been marked from the Notch to the summit of Wright Peak along a route that was eroded and abandoned. Do not hike it, because of potential damage to the trail environs.

139 Wright Slide

Bushwhack to a slide

This slide first occurred after a severe rain in September 1938 and was first observed by Alton C. (Clint) West, the long-time ranger at Lake Colden. He saw it first from Indian Falls, but it is obvious from many summits. He and Dr. Orra Phelps, Adirondack botanist, were the first to climb it two weeks later and both were impressed by the forces that created the wedge-shaped slide, which was 400 feet wide at its base, over 0.5 mile long, tapering to a very narrow point. Originally it was quite unstable, with much scree and loose rock. It is still somewhat unstable. Nevertheless, the Wright Slide is a relatively easy and rewarding one to climb, but it can be rather difficult to find.

Today, the open rock portion of the slide is no more than 400 yards long, while the bushwhack approach along Wright Brook, from the point it enters Marcy Brook less than 0.5 mile from Marcy Dam, is six or seven times that long. You will not travel the route very quickly and should not want to, but the total off-trail distance of less than 2 miles and the short distance from the trailhead make a reasonably short day trip feasible.

Your first problem is finding the mouth of Wright Brook, across Marcy Brook from the trail between Marcy Dam and Avalanche Camps (section 141). As you head south past Marcy Dam Pond, you find the trail repeatedly returning to the bank of Marcy Brook. When it finally pulls you away to the left, out of sight of the brook, return to the last place where you could see the brook and step down to its bank to look upstream. (If you have reached a lean-to on Avalanche Camp Trail, you have already gone too far.) Only 40 yards from this spot, you should see Wright Brook merging with Marcy Brook and curving slowly out of sight to the right, while Marcy Brook is curving left. This point is also just upstream from the second of two long islands that are visible in Marcy Brook as you hike along the trail. If you have trouble, persevere; this is a major tributary, you can find it, and it is the best route for the bushwhack.

Follow Wright Brook all the way to the base of the slide. It is easiest at first to keep it on your right; but after it turns due west, about 0.35 mile from Marcy Brook, it becomes narrower and steeper, and you may find the going easier on the other side, or even in the brook. Although this is a bushwhack, you will find more or less obvious traces of old tote roads—quite remarkably and impressively right up the brook to the base of the slide. This is the second potential problem area, for you cannot see the open rock of the slide from the brook. In fact, you must climb several minutes northwest from the brook to reach open rock, and they are likely to be minutes of uncertainty. Look for extensive rubble on your right to tell you where to start up, and do not be too early. You must climb over 1000 feet along the brook to the base of the slide area. On the other hand, if you overshoot, and find suddenly that you can look back and see the slide behind you, do not succumb to the temptation to leave it for another day. Algonquin's ferocious cripplebush does not treat lost bushwhackers gently; it *shreds* them. The slide is your escape route. Climb back down and use it!

You will find herd tracks leading the short distance from the top of the slide to the ridge, and easy going along the ridge to the left to the summit. Return to the Loj parking area down the Wright Spur Trail to the Algonquin Trail (sections 137 and 134).

140 Marcy Dam to Avalanche Lake and Lake Colden

3.05 miles to Colden intersection, 2 to 2½ hours, 635-foot vertical rise to Avalanche Pass, yellow markers

Do not just think of these three miles of trail as a way to get to the base of a mountain or to the numerous campsites around Lake Colden. This is the most spectacular trail in the High Peaks. The pass is awesome. The cliffs on Colden and Avalanche mountains rising from Avalanche Lake are astounding. Boulders torn from the walls above make a tortuous route for the trail along Avalanche Lake and wonderful frames for the unfolding tableau of mountains and reflecting water. Even if you want to use this trail to get to somewhere else, allow enough time to savor its striking views.

Follow the blue, then the yellow trail, which reaches Marcy Brook at 0.25 mile. A beautiful stretch of trail follows close by the brook. Two wide bridges cross small streams as you head uphill. An obscure path by the second bridge at 0.5 mile leads right to the Kagel Lean-to. The ascent continues and the rocks in the trail become larger and more numerous. At 0.8 mile, you can see the first of the Avalanche Camp Lean-tos to the right of the trail. A lovely upgrade through boulders follows. The stream and ledges beside it could not be more beautiful. Just past a wonderful boulder, turn right to cross Marcy Brook. One of the Avalanche Camp Lean-tos is up on the bank across the brook, the second is to the left. Here, at 1.1 miles, twenty-five minutes at most, the trail splits; left is the blue trail past Lake Arnold to Feldspar Brook (sections 146 and 147).

The yellow trail, a right fork at the intersection, leads around past the last lean-to and crosses a small stream. A boardwalk over a swampy area leads to a stairs, the beginning of "misery mile." After a stiff climb, a sharp left leads to a steep side-hill traverse. You cross a ski trail, walk on more boardwalks and stairs, cross another ski trail, and finally enter the beautiful valley of Avalanche Pass at not quite 1.7 miles. Misery mile is more like a half mile, but seems longer with a pack.

After another chain of logs and a ski trail crossing, you can see cliffs closing

Avalanche Lake

in on the left. More boardwalks bring you close to the stream that drains the pass and through a pretty, ferny glen. High up on the slopes to the left, water dripping from the cliffs to the left supports the rare fern *Dryopteris fragrans*.

The pass, a spruce swamp, is quite wet. It narrows as you walk under beetling cliffs to the right, then head downhill. Sheer walls above are encrusted with lichens. The trail is squeezed into a narrow place between boulders, then more boardwalks take you over boggy ground. You angle left to cross a tiny stream that drains west from the pass. The cliffs on Avalanche Mountain are close on your right. After a short rise you can see the first of the cliffs that thrust straight up from the lake, but before you can reach it you have to negotiate a series of little beaver dams that form a chain along the stream. A yellow arrow points you across a beaver dam and around the most serious flooding, down to the head of the lake at 2.25 miles, about forty-five minutes from the last of the Avalanche Camp Lean-tos. Avalanche Lake is long and thin, filling the fault valley that was blocked by the rubble from Colden's slides. Avalanche Lake was named by Redfield, who noted that immense slides and avalanches had raised the elevation of the lake. The lake, however, was first seen by Judge John Richards and Major Reuben Sanford, who surveyed the Gore Around Lake Colden in 1833. One of the biggest avalanches, which created a number of Colden's slides, occurred on August 20, 1869. In 1942, the hurricane of September 26 and 27 loosened a slide which raised the level of Avalanche Lake by ten feet.

The walls of both Colden and Avalanche mountains rise vertically from the lake at places along each shore, making travel around it very difficult. Log walkways, the Hitch-up-Matildas, were built in the 1920s and named after a comical scene described by guide William B. Nye in 1868. He had to carry a substantially built woman on his shoulders around the cliffs, while her family kept urging her to "Hitch up, Matilda" when she appeared to be slipping down into the water.

Those who remember the arduous trip around Avalanche Lake with no more than the Hitch-up-Matildas are in for a surprise—or a shock. The trip is still strenuous, especially with a pack; but the trail has been hardened to an extreme that is incongruous in this wilderness setting. Boardwalks, ladders, almost sidewalks take you up, over, and around the boulders that lie beneath the cliffs.

From the first Hitch-up-Matilda, now a substantial catwalk bolted to the cliffs, which here drop vertically into deep water, you can see the dike on Mount Colden. From the second, 250 yards farther, over 0.5 mile from the pass, you can look into the cleft formed by the dike. Colden's summit appears above the slides. Every step brings a changing perspective of the sheer walls that grasp the lake. Take at least a half hour to walk the 0.55 mile along it. At the foot of the lake you reach a boat ramp used by the interior ranger at Lake Colden. There is no camping near the shore, but if you turn right toward Colden, you pass paths leading up left to campsites. Less than ten minutes past the foot of the lake you reach the intersection with the blue trail. Both it and the continuation of the yellow trail are described in section 40, which also details all the camping possibilities near Lake Colden and Flowed Lands.

The blue trail leads right to the north shore of Lake Colden, with the intersection with the Algonquin Trail (section 141) 0.3 mile along it, and the Iroquois Pass Trail (section 45) 0.1 mile beyond. The yellow trail to the left leads around the south shore of Lake Colden, with trails to Mount Colden (section 142) and Marcy via the Opalescent (sections 46–48).

141 Lake Colden to Algonquin Peak

2.1 miles, 2½ hours, 2325-foot vertical rise, yellow markers

This trail to Algonquin's summit via the col between it and Boundary is not only the steeper of the two trails to Algonquin Peak in the MacIntyre Range, it is also the prettier. It is no place for a backpack, though, as it is one of the longest and steepest continuous climbs in the High Peaks. The grade means that descending along this trail is hard on the knees, so perhaps the best way to enjoy this trail is as part of a day-long, 11.75-mile circuit from Adirondak Loj

Colden Dike from Avalanche Lake

that climbs nearly 3000 feet. Section 140 and a descent via section 134 will help you plan this clockwise loop.

The trail begins from the blue Colden Lake Trail right beside the bridge over a brook—let's call it Algonquin Brook; it is far too pretty to remain nameless. From the intersection, elevation 2760 feet, 0 mile, the trail heads up on the east side of the brook. Algonquin Brook's ledges, little waterfalls, and pools will charm you while you are tackling the rooty, very steep trail. Within 100 feet of elevation gain, a wonderful series of waterfalls begins. Paths lead to the pools below each chute. After gaining 200 feet, the trail angles left and across the stream. On the west side, the trail is sheltered in a narrow gorge. Cliffs rise above on the left.

Just short of 3000 feet, the trail crosses to the east bank, where flooding from a beaver marsh adds mud to the route. In quick succession, the trail—a narrow path—crosses to the west, follows the stream bed, then crosses it again in 50 yards. At 3100 feet you reach a sign warning that higher elevations require adequate protective clothing. Next you pass a small waterfall—a slimy mass dripping over rock ledges. Just beyond, the trail joins Algonquin Brook and reaches a wide slide at 3200 feet. This smooth course does not last long and the trail is back in the woods to the east of the brook for a pitch to a level spot clearly marked to prohibit camping.

Algonquin Brook now splinters and some of its many channels disappear underground. A ladder, then a sharp pitch, and you are crisscrossing one channel. A real scramble over boulders at 3760 feet and more pitches leads to a great view of the slides on Colden at 3880 feet. More scrambling and at 4000 feet you see the slides on MacIntyre's flanks. The fierce scrambling persists, giving you an excuse to pause for the views. Above a stand of dead balsam, you see Gothics, Basin, and Saddleback. Armstrong and the Wolf Jaws appear, as does Marcy when you reach 4240 feet in elevation. Another scramble and you find yourself walking on a steep rock face as smooth as any slide. The view is wonderful. Finally, at 4560 feet, the trees are shorter, the trail narrower, and the grade easier. You can see Boundary to the west. Yellow arrows on rocks lead you north across the col to a cairn that marks a change in direction in the trail.

To the left of the cairn, west, is a path that leads up Boundary and Iroquois (section 136). Turning right, the yellow trail leads up Algonquin's treeless summit cone. Lichens color all the rocks green. You can see the narrow cut that marks the outlet of Flowed Lands, Calamity Mountain, Adams appearing over Calamity, Allen and Cheney Cobble, and the North River Mountains. Beyond Allen you see Boreas. As you approach the summit, you can see beyond Wallface to the Sawtooth Mountains and Ampersand. Iroquois rises above Boundary now. The Sewards are to the right of Wallface and the whole

Mount Colden from Lake Colden

Indian Pass Valley is spread out below. Lake Placid becomes visible, surrounded by McKenzie, Moose, and Whiteface. Skylight leads around to Redfield and Cliff. Northeast views from the summit include Pitchoff, Cascade and Porter, and the Sentinels. From the summit you see Giant, Dix (the Beckhorn is prominent), Hough (its slides are obvious), Nippletop and its slide, and the spectacle of Colden's slides below you. Yellow arrows point across the summit to the trail to Adirondak Loj.

To descend toward the Loj (section 134), head toward Little MacIntyre, the bump to the north which is west of Wright, then angle right following arrows and cairns. How small Wright appears. You can see Wallface and Scott ponds to the west as you start down, and Heart Lake and Mount Jo to the north, with Big Slide and Hurricane behind to the east.

142 Mount Colden from Lake Colden

1.6 miles, 2 hours, 1925-foot vertical rise, red markers

Colden's cone-shaped summit, 4731 feet (1437 meters), seems small, tucked as it is between the two giants, Marcy and MacIntyre, but it is still a substantial climb along this trail built around 1923 by Arthur Hopkins and Clint West. The trail branches from the yellow-marked one on the southeast shore of Lake Colden, about a third of the way along that shore, over 0.7 mile from the outlet of Avalanche Lake. It is a steep route, often avoided in favor of the gentler ascent from Lake Arnold (section 144), or the more exciting and even steeper climb up the dike (section 143).

You go sharply at first up large stone steps, then climb steeply along the bank of an unnamed stream that flows from the south shoulder of Colden. Continue to climb moderately for 0.5 mile until you reach elevation of 3250 feet, where the trail ascends a log ladder, turns northeast, and begins the very steep climb of Colden's cone. The trail has been eroded to bare rock, which is marked with occasional yellow paint blazes. There are no more red disks from here on to the summit.

The more precipitous rock faces have log railings and log ladders. At about 4400 feet, 1.3 miles, the trail passes between three huge boulders, climbs a log ladder, and finally moderates, emerging on the bare rock of the ridge that leads to the summit. Take care to keep the yellow blazes in sight, as there are several false herd paths leading onto the fragile alpine vegetation. Even more care is required during the descent, as it is more difficult to find the natural flow of the trail.

The open ridge offers almost a 360° panorama of the surrounding ranges. The ridge leads up a final log ladder to the summit.

143 The Dike on Mount Colden

Bushwhack and slide climb

Ebenezer Emmons first explored this dike in 1836, and it was the route of the first climb up Colden, made in 1850 by two young relatives of David Henderson, who worked at the MacIntyre mine.

To get to the dike from the outlet of Avalanche Lake, turn left from the trail, just past the outlet, on a herd path that leads around to the southeast shore. This is neither marked nor maintained and it quickly splits. One branch stays near the shore, another goes up and around a large outcrop. Both have their disadvantages: The upper is through thick brush; the lower goes through about 8 inches of water for about 6 feet. Logs in the water may keep you dry. Regardless of the path taken, keep below the cliff and work your way the 0.2 mile back to the dike, a trip of about ten minutes from the outlet.

In climbing the dike, try to keep out of the stream that runs down it as much as possible. In wet weather it carries a fair amount of water, in dry weather it almost dries up. At the start of the climb, stay a little to the right of the stream. As you climb the series of giant steps, natural levels appear. After reaching the first level you may have to use the stream bed for a short distance, and then, just before the second level, there is a small cut to the left leading to it.

The hardest portion of the ascent follows. It is quite steep, so you will need to look for good handholds. Do not use trees or vegetation for handholds. You may want to use a rope so that the strongest member of your party can assist the rest. The best route seems to be to the right of the stream. It takes about a half hour to climb from the start to the third level.

From the third level, an apparent opening in the dike appears. DO NOT LEAVE THE DIKE AT THIS POINT. The slide on the side of Mount Colden is too steep at this point and you could easily fall off the mountain.

Stay in the dike, where the climbing becomes easier, though it is still very steep. About one hour and forty minutes after entering the dike, it narrows and becomes filled with a great deal of scrub. On the right is a small pile of rocks and a small path. Carefully follow the path to a large rock; stay to the right of it. The path is hard to see. It bears right up over a rock wall and on to the scrub-covered face of Mount Colden. Follow the path through the sphagnum of the hanging bog across the mountain, and not up. If you lose the path, do not worry, just cut across the mountain. It is about 200 feet to the slide.

When you come out on the face, you should see a small cliff ahead and above you. Make your way toward the cliff as you ascend. The cliff is small and easily climbed. On top of it, look up toward the top and you should see a large boulder sitting near what looks like the top. Work your way toward the boulder. It is just off the trail and not far from the true summit.

Two hours and twenty minutes after starting up the trap dike, you reach the rock. The views are fantastic in all directions, although you must walk around to see everything as there are stretches of trees on the eastern side of the summit ridge. The true summit is about 200 feet northeast of the large erratic.

144 Mount Colden to Lake Arnold

1.4 miles, 1 hour, 940-foot descent, yellow markers

Of the two trails to reach the summit of Mount Colden, the yellow trail to Lake Arnold has the easiest grade. If you have climbed the dike you will probably want to descend via this route; you will find yellow blazes on rocks as you head northeast from the summit. Starting down from the summit ridge, the trail runs through scrub conifers and is very muddy in places. The descent begins gradually, with the trail going under a huge erratic that leans against a second huge erratic. The trail continues down at a moderate descent over some outcrops.

Views of Marcy and Gray are spectacular. You can look ahead and easily see where the trail leads.

The trail reaches a dip at 1.4 miles, and the yellow trail ends at an intersection with the blue trail to Avalanche Camp (section 145) or Feldspar Brook (section 147). There are many paths going to campsites from the trails near this intersection and also heading right toward the lake. You may need to look around for the continuing trail, but it is easy to find.

145 Lake Arnold to Avalanche Camp

1.55 miles, 1 hour descending, 1½ hours ascending, 1237-foot, elevation change, blue markers

This is a portion of the Lake Arnold Trail that also leads southwest around Lake Arnold toward the Feldspar Brook Trail of section 146. To return to Avalanche Camp along it, go north and a little east, away from Lake Arnold, a little downhill, and you will find blue markers leading to Avalanche Camp.

The trail leads away from the lake, over the outlet of Lake Arnold on rocks, as the bridge has fallen in. Continue downhill to the right of the brook. The trail is very rocky and the descent is slow at first, but the trail improves as it reaches sections that have been repaired by ADK trail crews.

After fifteen minutes of descent, the trail again crosses Lake Arnold Brook and curves left, northwest, arriving at a trail junction, which is 0.5 mile from Lake Arnold and 1.05 miles from Avalanche Camp. The yellow Crossover Trail (section 148) forks right toward Indian Falls here.

The Dike on Colden

The blue trail continues downward at a moderate descent, through a forest of mixed hardwoods and conifers. Much of the time, you can look down and see Marcy Brook.

Forty minutes after leaving Lake Arnold Brook, the trail crosses a wooden bridge over a stream. About a minute after crossing the bridge, there is a junction with the Avalanche Lake Ski Trail, and within 100 yards, the blue-marked Lake Arnold Trail joins the yellow trail at Avalanche Camp.

146 Feldspar Brook to Lake Arnold

1.6 miles, 1 hour, 570-foot ascent, slight descent, blue markers

The trail between Lake Arnold and Feldspar Brook is used principally by backpackers heading to the Uphill and Feldspar Brook lean-tos from Adirondak Loj or returning from them. The total length of the blue trail from Avalanche Camp to Feldspar Brook is 3.15 miles, and if you are climbing this way it will take over two and a half hours. It is an integral part of several long day-hike trips into the interior High Peaks when combined with section 46 through 51, providing routes to Marcy, Skylight, Gray, Cliff, and Redfield from the Loj.

This route is described as a descent. Beginning northeast along the Opalescent River from the Feldspar Brook trail junction, you drop down to cross Feldspar Brook on a log bridge, and then immediately pass a log bridge leading left over the Opalescent to Feldspar Brook Lean-to and camping area, on the west side of the river. Many planks and log-walks aid your passage as you continue across nearly level and largely boggy terrain for almost 0.35 mile to a bridge across the Opalescent. The river diverges to the east here, away from the trail, and is open, wide, and inviting as it starts its long curve past the north side of Marcy to its origin between Marcy and Little Marcy. The river was followed by those making the first ascent of Marcy in 1837 and today it is an unusual bushwhack route to Marcy.

Ahead along the trail, you soon outdistance the significant trail improvements as you climb increasingly steeply along sections wet enough to have exposed root systems. If you can look up from your feet, the woods are attractive and have never been logged.

Views ahead from the level area along the Opalescent definitely de-emphasize the rise and distance to the pass that holds Lake Arnold between Mount Colden and the high ridge extending northwest from the Plateau area north of Marcy. The signs and maps are correct, however. You climb 500 feet in the mile after crossing the Opalescent, and you will find yourself ascending long after it seems reasonable to expect to be at the height of the pass. The climb is along the left side of the drainage. Just before the height-of-land, you cross to the right, east, side in an attempt to minimize the wet underfoot conditions.

The trail stays right as it passes down past Lake Arnold to the junction with the Mount Colden Trail (section 144), a good hour from Feldspar Brook.

147 Marcy Dam to Mount Marcy
The VanHoevenberg Trail
5.1 miles, 3½ to 4 hours, 2978-foot elevation change, blue markers

In 1880, Henry VanHoevenberg had this trail built from his lodge to the summit of Mount Marcy, and the present trail follows the original route in all but a couple of sections. This is the shortest and easiest approach to Mount Marcy and even starting at Adirondak Loj, the round trip of 14.6 miles is considered a reasonable day trip. Just remember to start early enough! This route has the added advantage of having the most moderate grade—which means it also has immoderate crowds.

Starting from Marcy Dam, 0 miles, follow the blue-marked VanHoevenberg Trail. Fifty yards past the DEC registration booth, the yellow trail to Avalanche Lake (section 140) branches to the right. Continue straight on the blue trail, and about 200 yards beyond the junction there are two logs spanning Phelps Brook. This is the high-water crossing over the brook. There is a sign with an arrow that indicates the trail keeps to the right, away from the brook. However, coming downstream, signs indicate both the bridge and the fork. If you keep on the trail, about 100 yards above the logs, you will find the ford over Phelps Brook. The ascent is now moderate. Muddy spots are bridged with rock that the ADK Trail Crew has placed there to aid in hardening the trail. In addition to the rocks placed in the trail, boulders litter the route. Interspersed are occasional stretches of exposed bedrock or gravel.

The trail continues a moderate ascent, and about 0.6 mile from Marcy Dam, a path right leads to the site of the old Phelps Lean-to and a camping area. Someday, when you are not in a rush to get somewhere else, you should ford the creek to the designated camping area and find an abandoned portion of the VanHoevenberg Trail. It did not follow up Phelps Brook, although paths lead in that direction, but rather starts angling up the slopes of an unnamed hill immediately after the crossing. Away from the brook, the old blue markers were not removed and enough remain to reassure your progress along the old trail. It intersects the present route about ten minutes from Indian Falls and with some effort can still be followed. Even if you only walk a little way along it, you will experience something rare—a walk in an old-growth, undisturbed forest of spruce. Somehow, a patch of about two hundred acres on the slopes of an unnamed knob escaped the 1908 fire. Unfortunately, it is not escaping the ravages of old age and pollution, for many of the giants are dead or dying.

Continuing on the VanHoevenberg Trail, you come to the Phelps Mountain Trail intersection at approximately 1 mile from Marcy Dam. This red-marked route forks left (section 150).

The VanHoevenberg Trail continues straight, climbing moderately, and 0.2 mile beyond the junction, at 1.2 miles, the trail recrosses Phelps Brook over a wide ski bridge. Beyond the bridge, the grade steepens. There are two small wooden bridges over small intermittent streams that cross the trail. The ascent continues for about 200 yards, then the hiking trail makes a sharp turn to the right while the ski trail continues straight ahead. The ski trail rejoins the VanHoevenberg Trail near Indian Falls.

The hiking trail passes over a swampy area on split logs and continues upward, with the ascent alternating between steep and moderate. Wet spots are bridged with logs and log steps help prevent soil erosion over the steeper parts. The trail continues in this manner for 0.7 mile, until at 1.7 miles it ascends a final set of logs steps and enters a swampy area. Just after entering this swamp, there is a designated camping area on a knoll to the left of the trail. About 100 yards beyond the camping area, the trail crosses Marcy Brook, just above Indian Falls, 2.1 miles from Marcy Dam, after a 1260-foot climb.

Stop to see the falls, which are just to the right of the trail. There are excellent views of the MacIntyre Range from the top of the falls. Because of damage to the area, camping is restricted to a number of designated sites.

INDIAN FALLS TO PHELPS TRAIL INTERSECTION

After crossing Marcy Brook above Indian Falls, the VanHoevenberg Trail passes through an area where camping is prohibited, then reaches a junction with the yellow Crossover Trail (section 148). This yellow trail connects Indian Falls with Avalanche Camp-Lake Arnold Trail, and a short detour along it will take you to the base of Indian Falls.

Continuing on the blue trail, the ascent ranges from gentle to moderate, through dense conifers. The trail is muddy, but log corduroy helps make a dry passage. A steep, boulder-strewn ascent begins 0.8 mile from Indian Falls. After climbing for another 0.2 mile, there is a cliff to the right of the trail, marking the end of that pitch.

The trail now passes over a swampy area and continues at a gradual to moderate ascent. The Hopkins Trail that leads left to Bushnell Falls (section 123) intersects the VanHoevenberg Trail 3.9 miles from Marcy Dam.

The VanHoevenberg Trail to the right is relatively level as it dips and rises going past the site of the old Marcy Lean-to, which was located to the left of the trail. The trail now begins to ascend quite steeply as it passes over some rock outcrops, and at 4.5 miles reaches the junction with the Phelps Trail (section 124), after climbing 1214 feet from Indian Falls. Since the climb from Indian Falls takes an hour and a half, the trip from Marcy Dam to this point ranges from two hours and forty minutes to more than three hours.

PHELPS TRAIL INTERSECTION TO MARCY

The last stage of the climb to Marcy's gently rounded summit, elevation 5343 feet (1629 meters), is a more gradual finale to the 7.3-mile, 3165-foot (965-meter) climb from Adirondak Loj. This segment is 0.6 mile long and you can climb the 505 feet in a half hour. Above its junction with the Phelps Trail, the VanHoevenberg Trail is marked with occasional cairns and yellow paint blazes on the rocks. Note: When walking above tree line, always know the exact location of the next blaze or cairn before leaving the one you are on or near. This is critical during times of poor visibility.

The trail continues over bedrock as it ascends at a moderate grade in and out of the scrub conifers. Approximately 0.2 mile from the Phelps Trail Junction, there are nearly 100 yards of swamp that you will traverse on wide, treated planks. Just after leaving the swamp, the trail ascends a small shoulder of Marcy that offers a panorama of Marcy, the peaks of the western Range, and the northern summits.

After dipping into the conifers, the trail continues its moderate ascent. Less than 0.2 mile from the summit, the trail leaves the tree line and begins the final steep ascent up the northeast ridge of the mountain. There is a break in the climbing as the trail reaches a boulder-strewn, almost flat shelf just before the top of the mountain. At the southern end of this false summit is a rock face, about eight feet high, that is the true summit. A bronze plaque placed on the rock face in 1937 commemorates the members of the party that made the first recorded ascent a century before.

148 Crossover Trail
Between the Lake Arnold and VanHoevenberg Trails
0.8 mile, 30 minutes, 330-foot elevation change, yellow markers

This little-used crossover joins the major trail to Marcy with the trails to Lake Colden and Feldspar Brook, routes few hikers do in tandem. More than its location explains its lack of use, however; the trail is not in good shape and can be very wet.

A mile south of Avalanche Camp on the Lake Arnold Trail, this crossover forks left, down, and across the outlet of Lake Arnold, without benefit of bridge. The trail proceeds to descend—of all things—through a wet area, before turning back uphill toward Indian Falls, making an illogical loop to the north in the process. The 0.5-mile, wet, rubbly climb that follows leads to the base of the falls with the best view of them, then climbs steeply beside them to intersect the VanHoevenberg Trail, which has just crossed Marcy brook, 2.1 miles above Marcy Dam.

Colden from Phelps

149 Phelps

1.2 miles, 1 hour, 1360-feet vertical rise from the VanHoevenberg Trail, red markers

This mountain was named for Orson (Old Mountain) Phelps, Keene Valley's most famous guide. If you are planning to climb Phelps as a day hike, add the 2.2 miles to Marcy Dam plus 1 mile along the VanHoevenberg Trail, making this an 8.8-mile trip, a modest length in comparison with most High Peak climbs. And, at 4159 feet (1268 meters), Phelps is a modest mountain.

The trail to Phelps Mountain branches left, northeast, from the Van-Hoevenberg Trail approximately 1 mile from Marcy Dam. The trail begins a moderate ascent through a mixture of birch, maples, balsam, and spruce, with many cobbles and boulders littering the trail.

After 0.7 mile, at 3600 feet, about where the cover turns to all balsam and spruce, the gradient steepens and climbing becomes more difficult. Large erratics line the trail. Good views to the northeast start at 1 mile because the trail is now open. In another 200 yards, the trail becomes very steep as it heads up and over a rock face, guided by yellow paint blazes. The grade eases as the trail approaches the open rock summit with its many fine views toward the south and southwest and the MacIntyre Range.

150 Table Top Mountain
Paths

This is no one's favorite peak, but a fair exercise in path-finding, with lots of false starts and finishes. This short route is 0.7 mile long, climbs 700 feet, and requires about an hour from Indian Falls (section 147) to the 4412-foot (1345-meter) summit of Table Top. Before starting the climb consider the following:

1. Two major herd paths lead to the summit; both originate at Indian Falls. The first begins near the site of the old Indian Falls Lean-to near the falls; the other, not described, starts about 0.25 mile up the trail to Marcy. The area around Indian Falls is crisscrossed with herd paths and campsites. Most of the herd paths lead to one of the main paths or to a campsite.

2. If you are on a herd path and it peters out, retrace your steps to where it branches (they all seem to). This way you should be able to pick up a herd path that leads to the summit.

3. In a worst-case scenario, if you cannot find the path, a compass heading of 85° will head you toward it, but bushwhacking here is so miserable, you will probably then want to abort the trip.

When you reach Indian Falls, do not cross Marcy Brook, or if you cross the brook to admire the falls and the view of MacIntyre, go back across it to a herd path that runs along the northeast side of Marcy Brook. Follow this path upstream along the brook for about 25 yards. There will be a knoll with a clearing and campsites to the left. Follow any of the paths that lead to the knoll. Skirt the clearing, keeping it on your left.

At the rear of the clearing, almost due east and below the knoll, several herd paths converge into a more distinct and larger path that leads east up the mountain.

The path descends from the knoll, levels off, and begins to climb at a moderate rate. After ten minutes, the grade steepens and remains constant up the mountain. The path does an excellent job of skirting the many blowdowns on the ascent. However, when the path moderates near the top, there are several blowdowns. On the ridge that forms the top of the mountain, the path makes several turns—there are remnants of other herd paths on the summit—before reaching the register.

On the return trip, be careful not to lose the path on the blowdown-strewn ridge. There are many false herd paths that crisscross the ridge, including an especially treacherous one that will send you tumbling far off the mountain toward Phelps. It is quite easy to stray from the main one. On the trip down, enjoy the views of Marcy, the MacIntyre Range, and Phelps, which you no longer have from the summit.

References and Resources

References

Carson, Russell M. L. *Peaks and People of the Adirondacks*. Glens Falls, New York: The Adirondack Mountain Club, 1973.

Donaldson, Alfred L. *A History of the Adirondacks*. Volumes I and II. Harrison, New York: Harbor Hill Books, 1977, reprint of 1921 edition.

DeSormo, Maitland C. *Noah John Rondeau, Adirondack Hermit*. Saranac Lake, New York: North Country Books, 1969.

Forty-sixers. *The Adirondack High Peaks*, second printing, 1971.

Jamieson, Paul. *Adirondack Canoe Waters North Flow*. Glens Falls, New York: The Adirondack Mountain Club, Inc., 1981

Marshall, Robert. *The High Peaks of the Adirondacks*. Albany, New York: The Adirondack Mountain Club, Inc., 1922.

Masten, Arthur H. *The Story of Adirondac*. Syracuse, New York: Syracuse University Press/ Adirondack Museum, 1968, first edition privately printed in 1923.

Meigs, Ferris J. *The Santa Clara Lumber Company — 1888–1938*. Manuscript, two volumes, 1941, in the Adirondack Museum, Blue Mountain Lake, New York.

Pilcher, Edith. *Up the Lake Road*. Keene Valley, New York: The Adirondack Mountain Reserve, 1987.

Plum, Dorothy A. *Adirondack Bibliography*. Gabriels, New York: Adirondack Mountain Club, Inc., 1958.

Plum, Dorothy A. *Adirondack Bibliography Supplement 1956-1965*. Blue Mountain Lake, New York: The Adirondack Museum, 1973.

Redfield, John Howard. *Recollections*. Philadelphia, Pennsylvania: Morris Press, circa 1900, printed privately.

Redfield, William Charles. "Some account of two visits to the mountains in Essex County, in the years 1836 and 1837." *American Journal of Science*, April 1838.

Street, Alfred Billings. *The Indian Pass*. Harrison, New York: Harbor Hill Books, 1975, reprint of 1869 edition.

VanValkenburgh, Norman J. *Land Acquisition for New York State*. Arkville, New York: The Catskill Center, 1985.

Other Resources

Magazines: If you are interested in more information on when trails were built, who built them, who made some of the first ascents and the first winter ascents, and descriptions of unusual climbs and adventures, consult the back issues of Adirondack Mountain Club's magazines, *High Spots* and *Adirondac*, the Forty-sixer's *Peaks* and *Yearbooks*, and ADK Albany Chapter's *Cloudsplitter*. Back issues of *Adirondack Life* and *Conservationist* contain much history of the High Peaks. Collections of these publications are available at the Adirondack Museum and other libraries in the region.

New York State Department of Environmental Conservation, Region 5 Headquarters, Ray Brook, New York, 12977, 518-891-1370.

Trail maintenance: If you want to volunteer to help maintain trails and lean-tos, contact the Adirondack Mountain Club, 518-793-7737. For reservations at ADK's Adirondak Loj or Johns Brook Lodge, 518-523-3441.

Index

Guidebooks from Backcountry Publications

State Parks and Campgrounds
State Parks and Campgrounds in Northern New York, $9.95

Walks and Rambles Series
Walks and Rambles on the Delmarva Peninsula, $8.95
Walks and Rambles in Rhode Island, $8.95
Walks and Rambles in Westchester (NY) and Fairfield (CT) Counties, $7.95

Biking Series
25 Mountain Bike Tours in Vermont, $9.95
25 Bicycle Tours on Delmarva, $8.95
25 Bicycle Tours in Eastern Pennsylvania, $8.95
25 Bicycle Tours in the Finger Lakes, $7.95
25 Bicycle Tours in the Hudson Valley, $9.95
25 Bicycle Tours in Maine, $8.95
25 Bicycle Tours in New Hampshire, $7.95
25 Bicycle Tours in New Jersey, $8.95
20 Bicycle Tours in and around New York City, $7.95
25 Bicycle Tours in Vermont, $8.95

Canoeing Series
Canoe Camping Vermont and New Hampshire Rivers, $7.95
Canoeing Central New York, $10.95
Canoeing Massachusetts, Rhode Island and Connecticut, $7.95

Hiking Series
50 Hikes in the Adirondacks, $10.95
50 Hikes in Central New York, $9.95
50 Hikes in Central Pennsylvania, $9.95
50 Hikes in Connecticut, $9.95
50 Hikes in Eastern Pennsylvania, $10.95
50 Hikes in the Hudson Valley, $9.95
50 Hikes in Massachusetts, $9.95
50 More Hikes in New Hampshire, $9.95
50 Hikes in New Jersey, $10.95
50 Hikes in Northern Maine, $10.95
50 Hikes in Southern Maine, $10.95
50 Hikes in Vermont, $9.95
50 Hikes in West Virginia, $9.95
50 Hikes in Western Pennsylvania, $9.95
50 Hikes in the White Mountains, $9.95

Ski-Touring Series
25 Ski Tours in Central New York, $7.95
25 Ski Tours in New Hampshire, $8.95

The above titles are available at bookstores and at certain sporting goods stores or may be ordered directly from the publisher. For complete descriptions of these and other guides, write: Backcountry Publications, P.O. Box 175, Woodstock, VT 05091.

Lee M. Brenning is an engineering technician at General Electric in Utica, New York, and he lives in Nobelboro on the banks of the West Canada Creek. Using his backpacking and bushwhacking skills, Lee researched and wrote the chapter on the Raquette River and the Seward Range for this guide. He also contributed to two other Discover guides, Southwestern and West Central, for which he covered the Black River Wild Forest and the land north of Old Forge. With his wife, Georgie, at his side, he is hard at work on the final guide in the series — the Northwestern Adirondacks. Lee is also active in conservation and recreation organizations.

Photo by Georgie Brenning

Phil Gallos has worked in positions as diverse as reporter/photographer for the *Adirondack Daily Enterprise* and Black Fly Control Field Technician for the Town of Franklin. He has also been the chief researcher and writer for Historic Saranac Lake, a historic preservation organization. Phil contributed some of his excellent photographs to the Northern Adirondack guide, and for the High Peaks guide he wrote about and photographed part of the northeast boundary region. Phil is also the author of *By Foot in the Adirondacks* and *Cure Cottages of Saranac Lake.*

Photo by E.H. Ketchledge

Don Greene retired as a computer programmer to live and hike in the Adirondacks. He thinks that hiking is what life is all about. During the summer months, Don spends three or more days a week in the High Peaks. He knows almost every corner of that region, including secrets not even revealed in this guide. Don described the slides on Dix and Wright and the climbs to Shepard's Tooth, Cliff, Redfield, the upper Opalescent, and the Santanonis for this book.

Photo by Barbara McMartin

E.H. Ketchledge has studied the Alpine flora of the MacIntyre Range since 1949, and he directed a program to stabilize fragile summits. Retired as Distinguished Professor of Botany at the State University of New York at Syracuse, he has written the section describing the Alpine flora of the MacIntyre Range, which is applicable to all of the Adirondacks' Alpine summits. Ketch continues to hike and study threats to Adirondack forests. He is active with both the Forty-sixers and ADK. As of September 1989, Ketch will have climbed the MacIntyre Range 160 times.

Photo by Phil Gallos

Gary W. Koch divides his time between managing a retail business in New Jersey and pursuing his love of outdoor recreation from his base camp on Big Tupper Lake. Hiking, fishing, and camping were his first loves, but in recent years he has explored the Adirondacks on skis and snowshoes and by canoe. He is a long-time member of several Adirondack organizations. Gary researched and photographed the wonderful new slide on Santanoni for this guide.

Photo by Barbara McMartin

Willard Reed teaches earth science and biology at Northville High School as well as a course in mountaineering. A member of the Board of Directors of the Adirondack Forty-sixers, Bill co-chairs their Leadership Workshop program. For this guide he revisited many of the Forty-six peaks with his son Kris, who is well on his way to becoming a Forty-sixer himself. Bill is an avid bushwhacker and hiker and has worked on several guides in the Discover Series.

Photo by Kris Reed